EAST PRUSSIAN DIARY

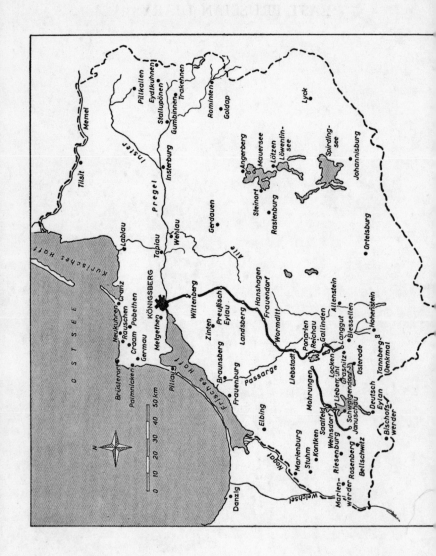

EAST PRUSSIAN DIARY

A Journal of Faith
1945-1947

by

COUNT HANS von LEHNDORFF

With an Introduction

by

CONSTANTINE FITZGIBBON

OSWALD WOLFF (PUBLISHERS) LIMITED
London
1963

First published in Germany by Biederstein Verlag Muenchen
Second Impression

© 1963 FOR ENGLISH TRANSLATION BY
OSWALD WOLFF (PUBLISHERS) LTD., LONDON

Translated by
VIOLET M. MACDONALD

MADE AND PRINTED IN GREAT BRITAIN BY
THE GARDEN CITY PRESS LIMITED
LETCHWORTH, HERTFORDSHIRE

CONTENTS

v

INTRODUCTION

AUTOBIOGRAPHICAL works are of many sorts, and Germans describing the part that they played in the dreadful shipwreck of their country —a catastrophe for which they or at least other Germans were so largely responsible—have adopted every tone, from justification to defiance. For it is and will remain for many years, perhaps forever, too painful a subject for those who were directly concerned. Can an individual describe an atrocious illness through which he has passed followed, if he were an East German, by an even more atrocious amputation of his native province?

The illness was this: the Germans, appointed by geography to convert the East while continuing to defend European civilisation so long as that East remained savage, misunderstood their rôle, attempted to become the masters of the Christian world, and when their bid for hegemony failed in 1914 turned increasingly to the methods of the barbarous East. The destruction of Germany began in 1933, not in 1942 or 1945. The disease that produced the first concentration camps led inevitably, one way or the other, to the putrefaction, the physical putrefaction as well as the spiritual nihilism, of Auschwitz and of Russian-occupied East Prussia. And when some Germans smashed the Jewish shops and burned the synagogues and beat or murdered their Jewish fellow-citizens in November of 1938, it was only a matter of time—and not much time at that, six and a half years to be precise—before they, or more usually other Germans, must be treated likewise by the even more barbarous enemy to whom they had thus opened their doors.

In the pages of Dr Lehndorff's diary we are given an awful and vivid picture of the Nazi tide at its ultimate ebb: his mother arrested by the Gestapo for the crime of enquiring after a Lutheran pastor arrested because he had listened to the B.B.C. news: boys of sixteen and old men of seventy driven out by the SS to fight

Red Army tanks with rifles, amidst a welter of lies about secret weapons : civilians in flight in mid-winter beneath the ceaseless rain of bombs. Then the terrible moment of stillness as the eye of the hurricane passes overhead, a moment when many committed suicide for fear of the wrath to come. And finally the flood tide of barbarism, the raping, the burning, the shooting, the desecrations, the venereal disease, the filth and the drunkenness, the starvation, the insane smashing of people and of things, and all this repeated again and again and again, as wave after wave of troops followed by the inevitable secret police came ravening across an already ruined countryside.

If that were all, this book would be a monumental warning and a terrible indictment. But it is more.

Count Lehndorff symbolises in himself, and in his activities during the period of which he writes, two of the supreme values of our civilisation. He is a Christian with a profound, an almost unshakable love of God. If in the torments which he had to undergo, and the perhaps worse horrors that he was forced to witness, he sometimes may have wondered why his God had forsaken him, he never forgot that Another had asked the same question and that the question had been answered. If at times his attitude towards his persecutors seems almost contemptuous, it is not in fact the contempt of the aristocrat for the brute nor even that of the educated man for the deliberate idiot—though both emotions are on occasion visible—but rather is it the pity of the man who knows divine beauty for him who will comprehend nothing beyond animal satisfaction. Whenever he could, whenever there were two or three gathered together, Count Lehndorff would hold a divine service. When alone he read the gospels. His own sanity was thus preserved against the encircling madness of lust and fear and greed, and enabled him undoubtedly also to save the sanity of many with whom he came into contact.

There is another powerful strand to our Christian civilisation. Mysticism, magnificent as it may be, is for us something of an alien flower. Our faith is justified by works, and Dr. Lehndorff was and is a surgeon. It is not hard to imagine how invaluable his training, his talents and his unquestioning answer to any call were during the three years of which his diary tells. Only once does his doctor's courage seem to have deserted him. Trying to run a hospital in Koenigsberg amidst looting Russians who raped nurses and dying patients alike, who fired into the wards and tossed hand grenades

into the blaze when the hospital caught fire, who smashed irreplaceable bottles of medicines and stole his surgical implements, his heart
almost broke, and he was glad when he was arrested and the
responsibility taken away. But as soon as he had escaped he was a
doctor once again, no matter how discouraging the circumstances,
and he has remained a doctor ever since. It is in such a story as his
that the alleged antithesis of Christianity versus humanism is
revealed for the nonsense that it has evidently become and presumably always was.

It is not perhaps as paradoxical as it sounds to say that this book
contains superlative descriptions of natural beauty and some joyous
writing such as is seldom encountered. The author was himself an
East Prussian, and he had known and loved his countryside with
the eyes of a child and later with those of a sportsman. Though the
country houses in which he had stayed might be gaunt ruins or
nests of drunken enemy with their women, and the fields were
untilled expanses of weed dotted with rusting, ruined tanks, the
forests and the lakes remained. He had ridden and hunted through
these forests. In some of them he knew every path and every glade
and many a tree was a personal memory. Now, as the hunted and
not the huntsman, he learned to know them again and perhaps
more intimately even than before. And his realisation of the un-
failing beauty of nature and of wild life can only have been
increased by the daily spectacle of that foulness of which man and
man alone is capable. His descriptions of the days and nights that
he passed in the forests are as memorable for their poignant love
and gratitude as is the rest of this book for other reasons.

Most of the women, and above all the nurses, behaved as usual
better than most of the men. One, who died in Koenigsberg, said
to him as he was leaving that doomed city :

'You must go now, Doctor. I wished only to accompany you to
the edge of the city. Greet the people, and tell them that they
must reflect, so that what has happened to us shall not happen
to them.'

CONSTANTINE FITZGIBBON

AUTHOR'S FOREWORD

'We beheld His glory'

THIS account was written twelve years ago, partly from notes in a rescued diary, partly from memories still only too vivid. The author has withheld it from publication until now because he felt he had not yet gained sufficient distance from it. But the events of that period have become history meanwhile, and the personal aspect of them has broken the bounds of the individual. So an attempt may now be made to communicate this experience, even at the risk of reviving past suffering.

May these pages help to make a fragment of the past comprehensible, and of service to this life of ours, with its daily demands upon us.

1961   H. L.

INSTERBURG

Summer 1944 to January 1945

ONCE again, before the bulldozer of the war drove over it, my East Prussian homeland unfolded all its mysterious splendour. Whoever lived through those last months with receptive senses must have felt that never before had the light been so intense, the sky so lofty, the distance so vast. And all that impalpable essence distilled by the landscape, lending wings to the spirit, took shape with an intensity that only the hour of farewell could have given it.

The first harbingers of the catastrophe made themselves felt at the end of June—faint shocks, hardly perceptible to the senses, which set the sun-drenched land quivering as if from some distant earthquake. And then all at once the roads were thronged with fugitives from Lithuania, and ownerless cattle went straggling across the harvest fields, following the irresistible urge towards the west.

It was difficult to grasp what had happened, no one dared give open expression to his fears. But by the time the storks were getting ready to leave a clearer notion of what lay before us could no longer be blinked. Everywhere in the villages one saw people standing, staring at the sky where the big, familiar birds were circling, as though this time it was to be the last goodbye. And all those watching them must have had the same feeling : 'Yes, *you're* flying away ! But what of *us*? What is to become of us, and our country?'

Soon after this, enormous herds of cattle came down along the watercourses and gathered in the flat valley that the Pregel meanders through. They had been driven out of the eastern part of the province, and stood now, an overwhelming sight, by the thousand in the wide meadows. For the moment there was food enough for them there; but if you went nearer and looked at the animals, one by one, your heart was wrung. With no tie between them, looking on human beings as enemies, they went blundering through the countryside, treading down the hedges, forcing their way into paddocks and gardens and eating trees and bushes bare. They seemed to have come from a country where no order reigned. You could still see that many of them were of outstanding breed, but the instinct for mutual protection that had made them into a herd had died.

In the night, at this time, we saw the eastern frontier towns arrayed before us as if on a map. Memel, Tilsit, Schirwindt, Eydtkuhnen—those were the brightest points, flaring up again and again under the bombing attacks, on a line of fire that ran in a curve from north to south. And one day we heard that the frontier had been surrendered. The enemy had crossed it to a depth of twelve miles—eighteen miles; then the front came to a standstill again. What things looked like behind it, nobody knew. One could only hope that nobody had survived, for what was reported of a few advanced points which the enemy had abandoned after a brief occupation froze one's blood.

Another few days of immeasurable fugitive misery on all the roads—then a sudden quiet, an almost inconceivable quiet. The rumbling of the front died down, the fires went out, even the nightly disturbance flights had ceased. The deserted land, with its farms and villages, lay as if under a spell in the splendour of an incomparable autumn, offering an indefinable experience to the few who came back from places further west, to fetch something from their house or see to the livestock they had left behind.

It was uncannily quiet still after the November gales had swept the land bare and the frost had withered the last blades of grass in the meadows. Scattered for miles over the fields, along the roads and the railway lines, we saw the neglected cows standing, singly or in little groups, hardly able to move, with dried-up udders and prominent backbones, threatening and complaining. And when the first snow fell they collapsed, silently, one after another.

Christmas came, and could be celebrated almost as in peace-time by all those who had remained in their own homes. Shooting parties were actually organised, and people gathered to see the Old Year out in traditional fashion.

A fortnight later it was all over. The Russians had allowed themselves three months to prepare the final assault—now they broke in in full force.

13th January

Towards seven in the morning I was awakened by a monotonous

roaring and rumbling. The window-panes were rattling. It sounded as if a lot of heavy lorries were standing round the building with their engines running uninterruptedly. In the dim light I could as yet distinguish nothing. I stood in the window, collecting my thoughts. This could only mean the end.

Towards midday the roaring became as loud as the fall of an avalanche. Gusts of air met one that made one hold one's breath. People looked meaningly at one another, and tried to trick themselves into believing that all this was merely the effect of our new Wonder Weapon.

Later on there was a sudden, complete silence. At dusk aircraft made their appearance. Three, four fighters dived down out of the grey winter clouds and began firing on the railway station and the airfield. Others dived after them. Dog-fights developed. In a few minutes the uproar was over.

17th January

The Russians have broken through in several places and are advancing. Gumbinnen is on fire. At night the whole of the east is a sea of flame. Single aircraft come out to us and drop flares. We have brought all the patients left in the hospital down to the ground floor.

18th January

We can still telephone. I've talked to my mother and my eldest brother, who has just come home on leave from the southern sector of the east front. They are in the midst of preparing a trek. It has to be done secretly, because no official permission has yet been issued. My father is toying with the idea of giving one more shooting party. There are more red deer in the forest than ever before. Only he doesn't see how he can get the guns together.

19th January

Our hospital is being evacuated. All the patients and most of the nurses are going to Pomerania, where they are to be given shelter in a private house. We are left without work. I packed a few things I value in one of the many thousand cases they've been turning out for months for transporting the whole inventory of the town to the west, and took it to the goods station on the toboggan. There it vanished among hundreds of others like it.

On the way back I noticed a lady standing by the roadside, surrounded by packages. As I passed her, hesitating, she said to me, 'Oh, could you please tell me of a furniture remover? I want to send away the antique furniture from my flat. I've just got it out of Gumbinnen with the greatest difficulty, but the soldiers who helped me with it couldn't take it with them any further. They are all valuable pieces that I took from Wuppertal to some friends in Gumbinnen two years ago on account of the bombs. These things here are only the little ones, the big ones are over there in a courtyard.' We went across the road to look at them. There were eight enormous pieces, including an oak dresser weighing at least half a ton. I can't think how she managed to get all that out of the burning town, surrounded on three sides by the enemy. We went back to the road again, and stood there to try and hold up one of the military vehicles that were rushing past at break-neck speed, for we were hardly likely to find a removal firm still working. Meanwhile I made a timid attempt to persuade the lady to leave without her furniture; but she wouldn't hear of it. Her husband had fallen in the war, she had no children, her house had been destroyed. These were the only things left to her and that she cared for.

While we were talking, heavy aircraft appeared at low altitude over the town. I couldn't believe my eyes when I saw every soldier within sight dive as quick as thought into the houses round. Only the civilians were left. But then a flashing and rattling started up overhead. Oh, so that was the explanation! It was the Russians! So near as that! We'd never yet seen them so near by day. They circled, and began firing on the station. Then at last our flak went into action. Like ships in a rough sea the heavy machines rose and fell, followed by our fighters, and turned away to the east. As though he had burnt them, the giant withdrew his fingers again. But he had broken open the door. I felt the icy draught as I returned to the hospital.

All was quiet in the afternoon. Only high up in the sky invisible aircraft went on tracing their bold condensation curves. I walked over the Tilting Square once more, and along the Angerapp, in sunshine and deep snow. The waxwings were there, pecking red berries off the bushes. Not a soul left on that side. They've all cleared out.

And in the evening, after dark, I went once again into our church. Ever since the bombing attack last summer we have gathered there daily for evensong. The doors are all smashed in, and through the main entrance the snow has drifted between the pews. I sat down under the pulpit and sang the hymn 'Mein schönste Zier' by way of farewell.

20th January

On my way to the station to enquire about trains I found all the furniture belonging to the lady from the west where she had left it. She herself was busy making a few moderate-sized parcels out of the smaller things, which she intended despatching by express train. I went with her to the station. It was swarming with people wanting to send off more and more cases and trunks. As we were standing there in a long queue beside the counter, there was a sudden bang, and broken glass flew about our ears. Everybody rushed to the exit, glanced upwards, ducked their heads and took to their heels. I seized my companion's hand and dashed off with her. Ten or twelve bombers were hovering like dragons in the air above us. We raced across the station yard and dashed into the underground shelter, which was already overcrowded. At that very moment the load of bombs came crashing down. A brief, ear-splitting shattering and rending, then the human stream welled up out of the ground again and scattered at lightning speed in all directions. Beside us lay two dead horses, steaming, on the road-way. The hotel behind us was riddled like a bit of theatrical scenery. Fire was spreading everywhere. Memories flashed through my mind of happy childhood days that had so often led me past this spot, when we came to Insterburg from Trakehnen to see the Tilting Show. Now Judgement has overtaken the world.

The station has not been hit, so far. There are hospital trains standing there with a lot of wounded. Our flak took no notice this time. They say the aerodrome has been evacuated too.

Going along the Danzig road, I saw some more bombers coming, dashed into the cellar of an empty house and waited till they had released their bombs—this time obviously more in the centre of the town. And then all at once I saw a whole lot of them flying to and fro to the north-east of the town. So that's where the front must be. Another formation was making for the town when three German fighters appeared suddenly from the west and hurled themselves straight at the enemy. Like a skein of wild geese attacked by falcons, the unwieldy machines went blundering about, and then dog-fights started up just above the housetops. With only a few yards between them, two fighters raced over our heads, the hinder-most pouring continuous fire into the other, which disintegrated before our eyes. Just as he reached the power station we saw the pilot bale out and fall heavily to the ground before his parachute opened, while his pursuer turned away in a steep climb.

When I looked round I found Doktora, our young assistant doctor, standing beside me. She had just come back from Königs-berg, where we had sent her to her parents, to recover from a severe attack of diphtheria. But she couldn't stand it for long; tor-mented with anxiety, she had travelled through the night in one military vehicle after another, by a roundabout way, as far as the outskirts of the town. Here she met the stream of fugitives pouring out of it, and nearly turned back because they assured her that the Russians were already in the town. We were mutually delighted at her having got through, though there is really nothing left for her to do here.

About three in the afternoon bugle calls were sounded—the sirens are no longer working—for the last inhabitants to leave the town for good. We took the nurses who had remained behind to the station, where the last train was standing with steam up, and waved to them with a feeling of relief as it drew slowly out of that threatened place in the gathering darkness towards the west. Left behind with us on the platform was the lady from the west, who had looked us up earlier at the hospital and helped to push the wheeled stretchers, loaded with the nurses' trunks, to the station. She had meanwhile freed herself, inwardly and outwardly, from her furniture, and promised us laughingly to seek the open as soon as she could get a lift in a car.

Back at the hospital, we sat down to a really good meal for the last time. The cupboards were all standing open, and there was something of everything left in them. As we had been taking leave of the place for months in imagination, it was impossible to feel sad about it now. The last hours of an age must be lived with clear and happy senses. God is demanding the return of the talent he lent us and asking what we have made of it.

Late in the evening the head of our hospital came along in his car to fetch us. He was followed by a Red Cross lorry, which we loaded with all the most valuable things from our operating theatre. While we were at it, a few isolated aircraft came back again to drop flares and incendiary bombs. Men of the Volkssturm armed with sporting rifles stood around in the street, watching us. At the last minute I threw my bicycle on the lorry, and then we drove slowly, avoiding the ruins of walls and the dangling overhead wires, out of the burning, firelit town. We reached Gerdauen about midnight. We had wanted to avoid the stream of fugitives, and the military vehicles coming the other way, but we hadn't expected to find the roads on this detour so completely empty. Not a cart, nowhere even the slightest sign of any lingering intention of defending East Prussia on this side. It was like driving through No Man's Land already.

Towards four in the morning we drove into Königsberg in bitter cold. The snow-covered ruins of Sackheim glided past us like ghosts. Then our ways parted. I am to lodge with Doktora's parents in Juditten, a suburb of Königsberg, for the time being.

2

FORT KÖNIGSBERG

21st January to 8th April 1945

Sunday, 21st January

A RADIANT winter day! Gardens snowed under, tall snow caps on the fence-posts, all the children out with toboggans. I went to the Central Office of the Red Cross in the Kastanienallee and met my chief there. Somebody gave us a lecture on the military situation with the aid of a big map. Judging by this, there is no reason for the slightest apprehension. The Führer has ordered East Prussia to be held; and in the event of the Russians advancing to the Weichsel and cutting off the province—an idea that hadn't yet occurred to me—the sea route would still be open. We listened attentively, and refrained from asking what this route would be like, for several million people, in the middle of winter.

From the Medical Committee, where I went to ask for work, I was sent to the railway station, where a transport with wounded civilians had just come in. Somewhere near Tapiau a train had been hit by bombs or had run over a land mine. It had happened so suddenly that nobody could say what it really was. A doctor and several assistant nurses were already on the spot, dressing the wounded and arranging for their removal to the various hospitals. One of the nurses with whom I got into conversation told me in a whisper that Russian tanks had advanced from the south as far as Elbing, and trains to the west could no longer get through. I held my breath. That meant the end of all the places that mattered to me. 'There go all the V.I.P.s with their luggage,' said the nurse, as a couple of transport planes roared over our heads. Thank God we're free of *them*! We can breathe freely at last!

Doktora turned up to lend me a hand. More and more fugitives from the eastern part of the province were gathering inside and outside the station, often in fantastic parties. I was suddenly surrounded by fifteen Polish women, all of them close upon their time.

One or two had actually started. We lodged them in the station bookstall to begin with, and later on some tolerable quarters were found for them in the aliens' hutments behind the station.

It was getting dark when we cycled back to Juditten. We passed the Nerve Clinic on the way, and called on the Director, who as Senior Health Officer was more or less in the know as to the military situation. According to his information the Russians are already advancing on the Deime Line. The Deime Line! How grand it sounds! I wonder if the enemy colossus, if he has reached this little river valley by now, will even notice that it is meant to be a line of defence. Last autumn the men building the East Wall were there, felling the trees in the parks on the west bank, cutting away the slopes to make a vertical wall, and surrounding each village with a circular trench, to make so-called hedgehogs of them. By now the whole place is probably garrisoned with Volkssturm men with sporting rifles and artificial legs.

22nd January

This morning I went to the suburb of Ponarth. In the 'Südpark' restaurant there, a great glass box alongside the brewery, emergency quarters are to be prepared for patients that may be coming in from the country. At the present time 3,000 workmen are being fed there daily. The restaurant keeper had heard nothing of the intended alteration, but sounded very glad, as the crowd of diners had obviously given him a lot of trouble. No patients have arrived as yet, only a few men who are to fetch the emergency beds stacked up in the neighbouring school.

As I still had the afternoon free, I took advantage of it to go and look up my relations in Preyl. The road there was completely deserted; I rode my bicycle in utter solitude over the untrodden snow. Even the new airfield, which I had to pass, looked as if it was no longer used. In the fields, to right and left, a few communication trenches had been dug. My relations are still there; after a long search I found my aunt in a corner of their house, which is occupied by the military. My uncle came back later from a ride on his white horse Jaromir. They have made no fixed plans so far, and don't know either what their daughter intends to do, who lives some sixty miles away and can no longer get in touch with them by telephone.

We spent the evening sitting quietly together, not worrying about what is to come. It no longer matters so much what becomes of us, now that they have fallen, one after another, the sons of this house, the brothers, the hope of the country we love. I stayed the night, and dreamed of all the loveliest days we had known in that house.

23rd January

Next morning I found the big square in front of Königsberg Main Station crowded with refugees. Farm wagons piled up with baggage were drawn up in serried rows, and more and more of them were coming out of the side streets, mostly driven by women. One dare not think where this is going to end. The trains are coming back from the west already, because the line is blocked. There is only the road to Pillau left. But that doesn't seem to be worrying people for the moment. They drive complacently along the street, eyes glued to the car in front, trying to find somewhere to put up. Pastor Müller of Haberberg, whom I called on on my way back, took me into a big room in which a number of these refugees had spent the night. There were a few sick people among them that he wanted me to have a look at. Everything was quiet and orderly here too, as at military manœuvres. I got the impression that nobody there had any clear idea of the situation. A woman stretched out a leg towards me, with a big varicose ulcer on it. It was a couple of years old, she said, but up to now she'd never had time to get it treated. Now I must do it. I tried to make it clear to her that in my opinion it was more important to get away from Königsberg first. She could then have it treated somewhere else, where she would have a better chance to rest. 'Where are you supposed to be going?' I asked her. She didn't know; only that they were all to get into the Reich. And then she added astoundingly : 'The Führer would never let us fall into the hands of the Russ; he'd gas us first.' I stole a glance at the people round us, but nobody seemed to think there was anything extraordinary about this declaration. Dear God! I thought, if only we had as much faith in *You* !

Sick people have arrived in Ponarth, hospital patients from various towns in the east, and with them a couple of dishevelled nurses who had had to evacuate a hospital thirty miles away at a moment's notice. The doctor and the matron had decamped earlier, taking with them, so the excited nurses assured me, two hundredweights of butter. A young woman doctor had remained behind with the seriously sick.

My new patients are already in their beds. Hardly one of them has the slightest idea why they have been brought here. Their food has been provided for, and I myself was given such a feast as I hadn't enjoyed for a long while. I've taken a room close to the Südpark and left my rucksack there.

In the afternoon I went to Maraunenhof, to say goodbye to my chief. He is going to try and get through to the west in his car, via Elbing and Marienburg. The Russians are said to have advanced to Elbing with only a few tanks so far. Later on I went to the Red Cross again, to try and recover some of the operational material we brought with us from Insterburg. It's lying among a great pile of the same kind of stuff from other hospitals that have been evacuated since then. The ambulance drivers, sitting idle in front of the hutments, had evidently been left to their own devices, and seemed inclined to assume a threatening attitude towards me; but with the help of my elbows I managed to haul out as much as I could carry away on my bicycle.

In the evening I met Doktora at the Nerve Clinic as we had arranged. There they had heard that the Russians had crossed the Deime Line and their spearheads were outside Königsberg. The town has so far taken no notice of the fact. The trams are running as usual, people are getting their hair cut and going to the cinema.

On the 24th January the main mass of the refugees who had come into the town from the country began slowly to get under way again. One car after another drove out of the rank and steered along the old Pillau highway, on which an endless chain of vehicles is rolling westwards. From what we hear, there are a number of overcrowded ships lying in Pillau harbour already, unable to leave on account of mine danger. The patients from several evacuated Königsberg clinics are among those aboard them.

I met Doktora at her parents' house in Juditten. She has turned down several opportunities of leaving the town as doctor in charge of refugee transports, and has taken over the practice of a doctor who has been called to service elsewhere. We were just having a discussion with her parents as to whether and how they should get away, when we were called to the Children's Clinic by telephone. A big children's transport was expected there. We found the Clinic empty; only a few members of the staff were still about. The house was heated. We seized brooms and floor-cloths and put a couple of wards in order, but waited in vain for the children we had been told to expect.

Towards midnight a rumour spread that one of the ships had

left Pillau and been sunk. On the ground floor the head physician of the Clinic walked past us, unseeing. He had just come back from Pillau, where he had put his wife and their seven children aboard that ship.

25th January

Everything was still quiet in the morning. I stayed in the Ponarth Südpark, where a lot of old, frail people had gathered meanwhile. They are in need of care, but not of any special treatment. In the evening Doktora came to have a look at my new field of activity. As she was mounting her bicycle late at night to return to Juditten, we heard aircraft approaching. I tried to keep her back, for—apart from the danger of the long ride—it had grown very cold and she had lost her gloves. But after dithering a bit she rode off after all. She had hardly turned the first corner when the whole place was lighted up, sulphur-yellow. Close overhead hung the flares, like hanging lamps in the workshop of a giant. I ran after Doktora and stopped her. We stood and stared. Beyond a wide yellow expanse of snow the town of Königsberg stood out to view, with its roofs and towers, more clearly than by day. As we walked slowly towards it, single bombs fell here and there, showing the immediate nearness of the enemy.

26th January

Russian artillery has begun firing into the town. As I hadn't much to do in Ponarth, I went to the Auxiliary Hospital at Maraunenhof to offer my services as a surgeon in case of need. But the hospital had just suffered two direct hits, and while I was talking to an acquaintance working there as theatre sister the order came to evacuate. Some of the wounded are to be taken to Pillau, although the news from there is not very hopeful. People are stowing away in the dunes. Russian aircraft appear from time to time and circle over the harbour. The ships that are lying there, crammed full of people, are in perpetual danger of being sunk by bombs.

I called on the Army Surgeon-in-Chief of East Prussia and asked if he could make use of me in one of the other hospitals, as my time was not fully occupied. I'm no stranger to him, he's been trying for years to lure me into the Defence Service. But even today we were both unlucky. A telephone call to the Medical Committee elicited the fact that I'm not yet to be released.

I found the Haberberg pastor alone this evening. He had taken his wife and daughter to the harbour, where there was still room for them on board a little steam launch belonging to someone they know. There are quite a lot of his parishioners still in the town, because most of the houses on the Haberberg escaped the bombing attacks in the summer. He is planning a church service at his house for next Sunday, and has invited me to it.

Later on I met Doktora again at the Nerve Clinic. Several professors of the Medical Faculty are assembled there: as holders of superior military ranks they have received orders to leave the town. There is obviously no intention, on the part of the Supreme Command, to treat Königsberg differently from any town in the enemy's country that we had had to surrender. One will just have to make up one's mind to it. But it rather annoys me to see these gentlemen obeying the order so willingly. I can't help thinking of the seven new professorial chairs we had the audacity to found only six months ago, on the occasion of the four-hundredth anniversary of the University, among them several for the Medical Faculty. Now, to a thousand wounded, it seems, there is to be only one doctor left behind to hand them over to the enemy. Nothing definite is known, but anyway one big clinic, now an auxiliary hospital, has already been left without medical supervision, and when it was suggested to me that I should take it over I accepted the job gladly as a gift of God. Doktora got one of the professors to give her the key of his duty room, which is said to be still very comfortable. A certain cupboard with food in it was specially recommended to us.

It was dark by the time we left. Along the Old Pillau highway cartwheels went creaking past in endless succession. In among them, people of all ages and conditions were dragging their toboggans along, or pushing perambulators in front of them, piled high with their belongings. None of them looked back. One couldn't but think of the words of Holy Scripture: 'Pray ye that your flight be not in winter.' It's a blessing to have the Brotherhood's[1] 'watchwords' at hand—the only thing left to find one's bearings by.

The Surgical Clinic is more or less intact, although it is almost on the edge of the town centre, which has been destroyed by bombs. The upper storeys have been evacuated; all the wounded, some

[1] The Moravian Brethren, a Protestant body founded 250 years ago, which publishes a selection of biblical texts every year—one from the Old Testament and one from the New for each day—regarded by many Protestants as 'watchwords' for their daily conduct.

180 in number, are lying on mattresses in the basement, and in the wing of the building on two-tier camp beds. You go down a few steps from the yard and you're in the midst of them. Exactly opposite the entrance is the room in which operations are performed. There, to our surprise, we found a gynæcologist from Insterburg we used to know, who had dropped in by chance and been begged by the nurses to carry out the operations that had fallen due in the meantime. We worked together for a few hours, and then he left the field to us.

27th January

At daybreak work began again, after a few hours' interruption. Gunfire has become somewhat heavier, and as there is no indication that the town is to be defended, we take it that the Russians will make their appearance here in the course of the day.

The watchwords had a special surprise for me today: 'Give me thine heart, My Son, and let my ways be pleasant in thy sight.' That is my baptismal text, and can only signify the final alert: Stay here! Keep your eyes open! Stop thinking 'How am I to get away?' See how all those that ask themselves that question lose their heads. Stay here, quite close to Me, and you shall behold My Glory!

In the afternoon the shelling suddenly stopped. Fighter aircraft arrived and began firing on the street from a low altitude. The harsh rattle of machine-guns alternated with the rough 'toff, toff, toff' of aircraft guns. Now for the first time people realised what was up. Not far from us we saw everybody crowding into the air-raid shelter under the big square by the church. It seemed odd that the aliens, far outnumbering the other men, hadn't taken things into their own hands long ago. People came pouring into our cellars too, from the street, every time an aircraft appeared. When the attack was over, casualties were brought to us, accompanied by their relations, who refused to be parted from them again. Our place got fuller and fuller, like a lifeboat. I took no notice. Nurses and orderlies remained magnificently calm. We carried on as though we had been working as a practised team for years.

In the evening we had a call from the Army Matron—by some extraordinary chance the telephone still works—all female assistants were to be discharged at once and leave the town during the night on their own responsibility. Our nurses talked it over for a moment, then the staff sister came to me and asked if I would allow them not to obey the order. I told them how glad I was they had come to this decision. The domestic staff were formally dismissed, with a warning of the danger threatening them from the Russians. But as they refuse to be parted from the nurses everything remains as it was, and work can go on unabated.

Meanwhile the former head physician of the Clinic, Dr. Hetzar, had turned up again in the operating theatre. He had been detained for a few days at some military post or other, and then set free again when the post was disbanded. The seat in a car that had been promised him had been taken by somebody else, and as he didn't feel like walking all the way to Pillau on account of his lame leg, he had come back to the Clinic. He gives one the impression of a broken man, and alone of us all he keeps talking of his imminent death.

28th January

We have had a quiet night. Early in the morning snow began falling in big flakes. It was so quiet, we could only conclude that the town was already in enemy hands. But towards ten o'clock shelling began again. It suddenly occurred to me that the Haberberg pastor might just be holding his service, and as there was nothing more important to be done at that moment we thought we might allow ourselves this little outing. It didn't take us long to get there on our bicycles. To our great joy, the first person we met at the parsonage was 'Brother Martin'. He too had come from Insterburg with his detachment, landed up in Königsberg, and been quartered in the Trommelplatz Barracks. About forty people attended the service and heard a sermon on the Epistle for the day, from the First Epistle to the Corinthians: 'Know ye not, that they which run in a race run all, but one receiveth the prize? So run that ye may obtain.' During the Communion Service that followed, fighter aircraft were roaring over the town once more.

When we got back to the Clinic we found some more wounded there. The Trommelplatz Barracks had been hit by heavy artillery, and several women assistants in the Intelligence Service had been so badly injured that nothing could be done for them in the way of medical aid. They were left lying on stretchers in the entrance hall, because there was no room for them anywhere else. Other wounded had come on foot, and were waiting patiently till it was their turn. Some of these, too, were badly injured, though they hadn't yet realised it. For instance, a woman held out her left arm to me, with a splinter of wood as thick as a broomstick right through the elbow, sticking out on both sides like a cross. She begged me to pull it out. She herself and other people had tried to do it but hadn't been able to.

Late in the afternoon we went to Juditten for a moment, to see how Doktora's parents were. They haven't been able to decide on flight, and are thinking of putting an end to their lives. The idea of being perhaps forcibly separated after thirty years of happy married life is more than they can bear. We could do nothing to dissuade them, beyond pointing to the eternal truth, that it is not we ourselves that determine our lives.

They are not the only ones facing this decision. Wherever you listen, you hear people talking of cyanide, which the chemists are distributing liberally in any quantity asked for. The question as to whether one ought to have recourse to it is not debated; only the necessary amount is discussed, and this in a casual, nonchalant way, as if it was a matter of food.

We went back to Juditten again at night, and found the dead couple in their beds, carefully laid out by the elder daughter, who had already left the house. The window was open, the room was icy cold. We stood for a moment in silence. On the stairs outside we said the Lord's Prayer. As we came out of the front door a woman rushed towards us from the other side of the road, screaming 'Frau Doktor, is that you? Come quick, my husband has poisoned himself with gas!' Doktora went with her. I followed after a while, and found a fat man lying on the floor. Doktora, who had been kneeling beside him to examine him, stood up, and told the agitated woman to leave him in peace. Then she gave me a long, straight look and said we could go.

Doktora's sister was waiting for us at the Clinic. She had come by a roundabout way, and wants to work with us as Nurse Ina.

29th January

Nothing happened last night, either, to alter our situation.

In the morning there was a sudden commotion among the patients, when a Czech orderly started taking away their arms. I had been struck earlier by his oily, furtive manner. When I took him to task he explained that we simply must prevent the Russians being shot at. I gave him to understand that this was no business of his, and begged a wounded major, who had been in the hospital for a long while and could walk about, to take what preventive measures he thought necessary. He suggested discussing the matter with the head physician, and that we should meet towards one o'clock in the latter's room.

When the time arrived I was busy with an operation, and Dr. Hetzar was on his way up to the first floor, so as not to keep the major waiting, when suddenly there was a roar overhead, followed by a couple of deafening bangs. The walls rocked, and we were smothered in a cloud of whitewash. The orderly standing opposite me was bleeding from the forehead; in the background a woman was yelling at the top of her voice. Then through the fog came the soothing voice of theatre sister Ida : 'Be quiet, no harm has been done.' As the cloud subsided we saw she was right. The people round us had only been slightly injured by fragments of brick. The orderly in front of me was the first to recover his senses : he beckoned to me and ran out of the room. I followed him upstairs to the first floor. Everything was in an awful mess. All the doors and most of the partitions had been blown out; in the head physician's room, which we were making for, the entire outer wall was missing. On the floor lay a heap of splintered wood, covered with a reddish layer of brick and mortar dust. Under this we found Dr. Hetzar, dead, with a big, gaping wound in his head; then, after a moment's search, the major, who was still alive. We dragged him out. His face was pierced by a thousand tiny fragments of brick, and looked like sandpaper. Both eyes were destroyed, otherwise he was uninjured. We carried him downstairs, and his wife, who is working at a Red Cross station near by, was sent for to stay by him.

I ran through the building to ascertain the damage. In the basement only the store-rooms had been blown open, the wounded had not been touched. On the yard side an enormous bomb crater fills the whole of the space between the operation wing and the side wings. The wall of the house, close up against which the wounded are lying, is still standing. Outside there the grey winter air smelt of gunpowder, iron and snow. Trees lay uprooted, fire was raging in the neighbouring houses. One dead man, one blind one ... and myself, totally unhurt. Doktora came quietly up to me. We stared for a while into the grey mist.

Meanwhile the operating theatre had been tidied up. The attack had brought us some more wounded, and for the next few hours that wonderful sense of perfect co-operation of all one's powers held us absorbed. Even the kitchen, overworked as it is, was in great form, and actually posted sentinels to make sure of serving the food at the right moment. All secondary considerations were pushed aside.

Late in the evening, to our surprise, three officers of the active forces turned up to inspect the condition of the hospital. I was made to account for my being on the job there. Then they went to assess the damage, and told us to look out for a sanitary column that might possibly arrive during the night to take the wounded to the railway station. A train was standing there under steam, which was to attempt to get out of the town before daybreak. They took the blinded major with them there and then, to be examined by an eye doctor at his own request.

Meanwhile a change had come over the place for some reason that I couldn't fathom. The orderly staff, who had behaved in exemplary fashion up to now, were in a state of increasing agitation. The men were rushing hither and thither, and suddenly I saw one of them coming towards me with a lot of bottles under his arm. I barred his way; he fell down and began rolling about in a pool of red wine. Alcohol was taking a hand in the game. Strangers from the street had found their way through the holes in the walls and were plundering our stores. Some of our people had engaged in a hand-to-hand fight with the intruders, and had then started looting themselves. There was no consideration now for the wounded, the chase went on over their heads; it was enough to drive one to despair. Then, fortunately, the ambulances arrived. One after another drove up. Our people came to their senses, the strangers ran away, and the wounded could be transferred in peace. Only the dying were left behind. Towards eleven at night the long train of ambulances moved off, each carrying nine patients, and there followed a ghostly drive through the snow-covered Old Town, now reduced to a field of ruins by a single night of bombing. There was not a soul to be seen in the streets. The moon stood cold and clear above the rows of roofless houses. Isolated shells whistled through the air, to fall somewhere with a crash.

The drivers were very nervous; we took a roundabout way to the goods station. On the furthest line of all stood a long train, in which a lot of wounded from other hospitals had already been accommodated. Most of them had their arms and legs in splints, and lay two to a berth. The goods platform sloped so steeply that the ambulances threatened to overturn. It took an endless time to get the wounded on board. The ambulance men were cursing; the man in charge of the transport was hardly approachable. Dok-

tora spent the whole night going to and fro among these over-
wrought men, trying to pacify them. Judging by the fiery glow,
the town was already completely surrounded, and there seemed
little hope of the train getting out of it. From over the heights of
Ponarth, on which a few houses were already on fire, isolated
shells came plunging between the rails. The night was bitterly cold.

Towards four in the morning Doktora succeeded in persuading
one of the drivers to return to the town. We wanted to pick up the
nurses, who, on my advice, were holding themselves in readiness
for any emergency. A second ambulance followed us. As soon as
we stopped at the Clinic a horde of aliens, with their luggage,
flung themselves upon the ambulances before the nurses could get
in. I told the drivers to proceed slowly in the wrong direction until
one passenger after another had dropped off again; then they
drove back by a detour to where the nurses were waiting. The
nurses got in quickly and were driven off; there was still room for
them in the hospital train, and they were needed there.

It was very quiet in the Clinic. The Czech had remained there,
and now received us more or less as our host. Two ladies had
joined him, one fair and one dark. They had arranged the operating theatre very snugly, and offered us coffee to warm us up. Then
we went to visit the dying, the care of whom had been taken over
by the Czech. Between two of them, on their mattress, lay a newborn child. A Polish woman had come in to bring it into the world,
and then disappeared again, promising, however, to fetch it later
on. It was nearly day when we went to bed.

30th January

During the afternoon two young men came to take leave of us,
who for the last few days had rendered us valuable service as
assistants. I now discovered that they were medical students, who
for want of anything better had spent their three days' army leave
with us. Luckily there was still a bottle of champagne—red, moreover—in the aforementioned cupboard, and we drank it up
between us. I wrote out a chit for each of them, saying where they
had been in the interval. Then they started off to look for their
unit, though they had no idea whether it still existed.

A change had now come over the street. Officers were going
about, singly, with pistols drawn, searching shelters and cellars for
hidden soldiers. At my request one of them came with me into the
cellar of the Clinic, where the looters were at work again. He fired

off a few shots, upon which they all vanished like rats through the exits.

We said goodbye to the Czech and took our luggage to the Children's Clinic. Fifty civilian patients are lying there in a bunker built into the side of a hill. Most of them are in plaster and therefore almost immovable. An iron door leads into the hill, and behind it runs a narrow passage between two-tiered beds, round several corners to a second door leading into the open again. The five nurses working there still have room for us, and received us very kindly. Alongside, in the Children's Clinic, there is still hot water for baths—an opportunity we availed ourselves of with enthusiasm. When my turn came the bombers were on their way again, and I was twice forced to leave the bath for a time, as it is on the second floor.

By the afternoon there was thick snow on the ground and the sun was out. Not a soul in the street, which only a few days ago was filled with a stream of fugitives. Isolated enemy aircraft sweep like hawks over the town. I set out for Ponarth, on foot this time, for the snow was too deep for cycling. Doktora and her sister were going to reconnoitre the Inner Town, to see if there is work for us anywhere.

I tramped through the powdery snow in a curiously exalted mood, as if the whole town and its fate belonged to me alone. As I went, I sang a hymn in praise of God, and my voice moved me to tears of joy. The greatest moments of a man's life arise when the Last Judgement is near at hand; the world rolls round like a ball beneath his feet.

As I was going past the station I saw to my horror that the train with my wounded was still standing there. It hadn't started till daybreak, and couldn't get through. Now it was back again, waiting for tonight. One dare not think what will become of those thousand young creatures in their helpless condition if they are unable to get away. They are all still full of hope that next time they will be lucky.

Ponarth has suffered from shell-fire already; on the south side there are great holes in the houses. The house where I took lodgings has been hit, and an old couple on the second floor have lost their lives as a result. Some women came hurrying towards me: they were going to try and escape to Pillau.

German tanks drove past, and the crews threw bars of chocolate to the children playing in the road. Perhaps that is to raise the morale. The children grabbed them delightedly.

The Südpark has lost most of its roof, and all the glass lies strewn around. The patients have retreated into the cellar. A young woman was standing by the fire in the kitchen, cooking dinner for the entire personnel, and surrounded by nothing but debris. Beside her stood a young subaltern peeling his baked potatoes with a pen-knife. I sat down at the kitchen table and had the situation explained to me, with an ear-splitting roar going on meanwhile. A tank battle was in progress at that moment. The Russians were aiming at the cross-roads where the Südpark stands, but they were firing too high, and only hit the roof all the time in consequence. Our tanks, which were returning their fire, were stationed about a hundred yards away. I asked if one could see the Russian tanks from there. No, they were standing on a lower level, about 1,500 yards away, in the direction of Wundlacken.

While we both ate his baked potatoes I heard some more about our tanks. They had come from Tilsit a short time ago, and driven twice through the Russian lines on the way; they would do that again when the Russians arrived here, perhaps in an hour's time. I looked at the girl calmly going on with her cooking as though the affair had nothing to do with her, and I heard the rest of the story with only half an ear. At the end of it the subaltern suggested that I should accompany him. His captain was a splendid fellow, and would be delighted. I hesitated for a moment. The thought of a drive almost at the eleventh hour, with people who could at least defend themselves, was very tempting. But just then the clatter suddenly stopped. I came to my senses again, and we parted with mutual best wishes. He had come from somewhere near Berlin, and for him Königsberg was only one of the many stages of his adventurous journey.

On my way back to the town I saw that the railway lines at the station were empty, so it looks as if the train had left again after all. Over the wide fields I saw soldiers coming towards me at the double, throwing themselves down on their stomachs in the snow, getting up again and running on. I asked one of them, who had thrown himself down beside me, what this meant. 'Infantry fire!' he shouted, and ran off again in haste. My ears were still drumming so that I hadn't noticed the little dull thuds on the field. As I went past the houses I saw women sweeping in front of their doors, and children building snowmen in the gardens.

Near the Haberberg parsonage some soldiers were hurriedly erecting a barrier of branches and twigs across the road. This was meant for a tank barricade, but it looked more like a racecourse hurdle.

The Pastor was at home, and asked me in to coffee. We sat by the window, keeping watch in the direction from which the tanks must come. While we waited he told me of the heavy task now laid on him. Every morning he finds unknown corpses lying in front of the church door, many of them completely naked. They have to be buried, which is almost impossible with the ground frozen so hard.

A little later, as I was walking towards the town along the Altstädtische Langgasse, people came running towards me again, soldiers and civilians together, scattering right and left down the side streets. The cause of their headlong flight appeared to be a tank barring the Pregel Bridge. Was this a Russian one already? If so, it was too late to run away. I walked quietly towards it, but as I came nearer I discovered that it was a German tank, and that the man standing on it was delivering a fiery speech. Every passer-by was being held up, apparently. And when something about 'our beloved Führer Adolf Hitler' reached my ears, I too chose to vanish with all haste down a side street.

It was nearly dark when I returned to our bunker. Doktora, who had been to the Samaritan Hospital with her sister, had already come in, bringing with her a placard they had found stuck on a lot of tree-trunks and street corners that afternoon. It was headed 'Hate and Revenge', and this was followed by a long-winded defamation of the Russians, full of obscene expressions, and finally a summons to use all possible means of getting rid of the enemy. This appeal aroused our indignation, and not being prepared to sail under this flag, we resolved to go and see the Fortress Commandant and call him to account about this poster. It was possible that he knew nothing about it; his name appeared at the bottom, it's true, but only on the second line, below that of the District Governor, who has obviously seized the last shreds of power for himself.

After a useless journey to Corps Headquarters, which took me right through the town, I found the man I wanted at last, at the General Post Office, where he has taken up his quarters. To give myself a more military appearance I had buckled on my Russian Kommissar's pistol, given me by a friend. The guard let me pass without difficulty, but I was held up at the General's door by a major who simply barred my way. The General would not see anybody, under any circumstances. If it had anything to do with defence, he himself was the man I must speak to, authority for this rested with him. I asked him what else people had assumed authority for in this place, and we got into a somewhat heated altercation, in the course of which I discovered that nobody here has yet thought of acting on their own responsibility; everything is still subject to Adolf Hitler's orders. Even the Hate-and-Revenge appeal seems to have met with complete acceptance. 'Can you think of any other way?' asked the major in a quite friendly, rather helpless tone. I said I could, and begged him again urgently to let me see the Commandant, because I could only say this to him. But it was no use, he stopped me by force. I asked him his name, and in the end he promised to pass on a letter to the General. So on the back of a temperature chart I wrote something to this effect: 'Herr General, what do you hope to obtain by the appeal we have found posted up everywhere, with your signature appended? Königsberg is not just any sort of town, it has a great history. Wouldn't it be better to honour the truth, which as far as one can see, we shall all soon have to acknowledge before the throne of God? You are not going to bamboozle anybody with "Heil Hitler" any more, let alone the wretched Home Defence men, who are all creeping into holes. "Kyrie Eleison" seems to me the only war-cry left to us. Many a desperate situation has been saved by it before now. I am at your disposal.'

It has done me good to get all this down on paper, even though I very much doubt its reaching the addressee. I came back to the bunker late at night, quite exhausted. There's a clattering and crackling going on all round the town, and coloured Very lights soar up on all sides out of the ring of fire. Mortars rattle like the wheel of fortune at the annual fair. And yet the harsh reality is still difficult to grasp.

31st January

After many hours of dreamless sleep we are in daylight again, astonished to find nothing altered so far. Aircraft fly to and fro, artillery fire from near the old railway station comes at intervals flat over our heads. Now and then a shot is fired in return.

I met the head physician in the Children's Clinic; he was on board ship when they hauled him off again by force; as he's not in uniform he's got to stay here. He has unfavourable comments to make on the subject of Hitler and Gauleiter Koch—a form of criticism that seems to us a bit belated.

Doktora has been to Juditten with her sister, to see to their house and their dead parents; but near the front they were held up by soldiers and had to turn back without accomplishing their object. On the way back they discovered that a field hospital was just moving into the Nerve Clinic, and as we foresaw the possibility of being wanted we made our way there at once. We hung about the entrance at first, to see what was happening. One ambulance after another drove hurriedly through the narrow gateway and was unloaded by the front door. Everything had to be done at great speed, since another field hospital was known to be on its way from Ballieth, at the edge of the town, where it had been fired upon and had to be evacuated in a hurry. Many of the wounded were lying naked on the ambulance cars, covered over as best they might be.

We pushed our way inside the Clinic and saw that it was crammed with people up to the roof already. They were lying higgledy-piggledy in the passages, on the floor and on tables. In the lecture-room they were clinging to the tip-up seats. Many were obviously no longer alive. Faced with this excess of suffering suddenly thrust upon us, I felt everything inside me defending itself against sympathy with any of it.

Stepping over arms and legs, we reached a door at the end of the corridor on the ground floor, behind which there seemed to be a lot going on. Wounded were being carried in and out; we let ourselves be pushed with them through the doorway and found ourselves in a small room swarming with medical personnel. In the adjoining room we saw a tall, stout man with bare arms, wearing a rubber apron. On the operating table in front of him lay a stark naked casualty that he was busy with. He looked like one of the Caesars. Above his enormous, protuberant forehead a strip of gauze held back his sweaty hair. In a voice hoarse with shouting he was hurling outrageous curses at the orderlies to make them hurry. 'What a butcher!' I thought to myself, and I threw a meaning glance at Doktora. 'There may be more behind this,' her expression seemed to reply.

Suddenly he looked up, noticed us, and asked roughly what we wanted. 'Adam!' thought I, 'a man equal to everything.' I explained that I was a surgeon, and asked if he could make use of me and the two women. To our astonishment he laid down his knife, and almost embracing me, pushed me out before him into the corridor, where he croaked out, 'Look at this swinish mess! I've been coping with it all alone for days. It can't go on like this. Do try and clean things up a bit. Begin anywhere you like. And if any of those medical students get in your way . . .' Here followed some more than drastic instructions as to the manner in which I was to treat them on his behalf.

We went to work. On the first floor, where there was most light, some of the wounded had already been laid in rows. Two junior surgeons and a number of orderlies helped us to renew the dressings, which were hanging in rags round the shattered arms and legs. We knelt on the floor, trying to immobilise the limbs to some extent with the help of splints. The wounds were running with pus. It would have needed at least an hour to fix one of them properly, but it had to be done in five minutes, because hundreds were waiting. Many of the men were still in uniform, just as they had come out of the trenches, and nobody had yet seen their wounds. While the work was going on our helpers provided us most kindly with coffee and the best of tinned foods. Doktora and her sister were the first women, we three the first civilians, to be allowed to work in this field hospital.

Some time during the night I was called down by Dr. Bode, the portly staff surgeon, to help him with an operation. Much to my relief; for after kneeling for six hours, the task of dressing wounds had become a form of torture. The women, on the other hand, were still quite fresh. Downstairs I had a rubber apron tied round me, and we started off. Our schedule of operations was indescribable, and the next hours went by like a grotesque dream.

Towards morning I was operating alone. The staff surgeon was sitting in a corner, grunting to himself, dozing, sleeping a bit, getting up again, settling the order of the interventions, and alternately holding a cutlet, a cigar, a glass of champagne or a sandwich under my nose. Later on, Doktora was fetched down to lend a hand as well, and fed personally in the same way by the staff surgeon. Heavy firing was going on outside all the time, and the not very stable building shook ominously. Suddenly the rumour spread that six Russian tanks had driven past on the Old Pillau Road and penetrated to the Inner Town.

At some time or other a halt was called. I lay on the floor among the orderlies and slept for an hour. Then we went on again—for at least a whole day, for when we finally broke off and walked, half stupefied, out of the front door, it was getting dark again. The wintry air and bluish snow did one's eyes good. The soft glimmer in the trees of the cemetery across the pond was a sign of thaw. With a sense of deep satisfaction we groped our way back silently, in single file, to our bunker.

At midnight we set out again—four of us this time, for I took Sister Minna from the bunker along with us; she has done four years' work as theatre sister. It was thawing. There was only a faint glow coming from the front, and it was so dark and slippery between the cemeteries that we were half an hour on the way. As soon as we reached the Clinic we were engulfed again in the work of the hospital. On the left beside the main entrance is where the lab used to be. The new arrivals were lying there on the floor round the big lab table. They all had head or abdominal injuries or both. All other injuries are sent straight from the front to the five main dressing-stations inside the fortress.

There could still be no question of working systematically. The man lying next one's feet was taken to the operating table, though among the newly admitted we tried to sort out those whose pulse could still be felt to some extent. We can't do anything to help the others, as there is no possibility of treating them for shock. After-treatment is out of the question too; one can hardly even keep account of those that survive operation, or know where to find them again. We can only take thought for the present.

In the upper storeys more sorting out had been going on mean-while. The patients were laid in rows, and the dead carried out and piled up against the rear wall of the building like wood. This gave us more room indoors, so that mattresses could be laid down and two-tier beds set up. Another surgeon has joined us; he belongs to the second field hospital, which, with its staff, has taken over one half of the house.

The house surgeons of both hospitals dislike coming into the operating theatre, because Bode always showers the coarsest impre-cations on them. Sister Minna was fully employed at once. The orderly that had been carrying on up to then yielded his place to her with relief. And if it had ever occurred to me that she might feel a bit shy among all these men, I should soon have learnt better. Hissing, rolling her eyes, she sent the tired warriors to and fro, and saw to it that nobody should stand about doing nothing. Even Bode contemplated her at times with a certain respect, and reduced his style of expression to a minimum of distinctness, visibly glad to be able for once to save his utterly overstrained voice.

An eye ward had been opened too. There, lying on a stretcher, I found the blind major again. His wife is still with him and is helping to look after the other wounded. Other women are being roped in as nurses; a couple of deaconesses are already at work. Order is appearing here and there in the confusion, enabling one to make personal contact with some of the wounded. And out of the grey mass of humanity that one's sympathy seemed incapable of reaching, because too much misery had flowed over it, here and there an isolated being stands out, longing for a friendly word.

As we busy ourselves with the wounded the days and nights melt into one another, and we are always surprised to see that it has grown light or dark again outside. The Russians are evidently allowing themselves and us time. Defences are now being erected in the streets; barricades of bricks, planks, brushwood and old vehicles left lying on the roads by the fugitives. The dead piled up against the wall of the house are being buried in one enormous grave in the cemetery on the other side of the pond, with the two hospital chaplains, one Evangelical and the other Catholic, officiating.

One day we had a visitor. The M.O. of the Corps District flew back to the town in a Fieseler-Storch and resumed his office. Bode and I, both the same height but of very different girth, received him in the operating theatre, standing side by side. The M.O., formerly famous for his corpulence, and still very portly, noticed the Staff Surgeon first, looked him up and down with disapproval and started rebuking him for the disorder in the hospital. As I was afraid Bode might go for him I seized his right wrist and held him fast. Fortunately, however, the General had now recognised me, and turned to me in a far more friendly manner, wanting to know the date of my enlistment. I told him I was still a civilian and hoped to remain one.

A few hours later the first of the two field hospitals, to which our Staff Surgeon belongs, received orders to move into the East Prussian Power Station, near the Northern Railway Station, which is to be cleared for the purpose. The removal took place as follows : before we knew what was happening, everything in one half of the Clinic that was not actually fixed to the walls was taken to pieces, dragged out and loaded on to the ambulances. Only the wounded were left behind and had to be taken over by the second hospital.

Three hundred patients were thus left, all at once, without medical personnel, table utensils, basins or means of washing, all of which had so far been available, if only in meagre supply. We parted regretfully from the Staff Surgeon, who had endeared himself to us by his ferocious humanity. By way of farewell he gave me a few more drastic pieces of advice as to how to treat soldiers, especially Staff Surgeons.

My group now consists of Doktora, her sister, an assistant doctor, four medical orderlies to lend a hand and Sister Minna as theatre sister. The wounded are to be brought in by Russian prisoner volunteers. I have made up the instrument supply from the stocks lying about unused in the town. I've even hauled out a plastering table from among the ruins of the Surgical Clinic. Our new admissions consist solely of people with abdominal wounds, though they have usually been hit by shell splinters in other parts of the body besides the abdominal cavity. All those with head injuries are henceforth to be taken to the power station.

We have given up our quarters in the bunker at the Children's Clinic and moved into the house of the Director of the Nerve Clinic, where all the other doctors—house surgeons, eye and ear doctors belonging to the field hospital—have been quartered. We know the rooms well from more peaceful times. I have been given the children's bedroom on the first floor, overlooking the pond. I reach it through a room in which the Evangelical hospital chaplain lives. We have come to know him better through his constant visits to the operating theatre.

The two operating groups have now divided their duty time so that each of them is at work for twelve hours. Mine works at night and gets to sleep about eight in the morning. At that precise moment, across the pond, the Volkssturm starts anti-tank practice. The resulting double detonation makes the tiles above me flap up and down like hen's feathers in the wind, and the holes in the roof are getting bigger and bigger.

In the wooded cemeteries on either side of the Pillau Road lie mountains of ammunition. Two riflemen posted there fire at random from time to time from behind the palisade. Now and then there is a return shot. In general, however, things have become much quieter. Fighting takes place only on the outskirts. We are kept aware of it by the rattle of 'Stalin-organs', the movement of aircraft back and forth, and the fact that fresh wounded keep coming in.

Once during her time off Nurse Ina succeeded in getting as far as Juditten and persuading two old men to help her bury her parents. The front is only a few hundred yards away, and the houses are occupied by the military. Next day, the 7th February, Doktora and I went to the Juditten churchyard. There, in the deep, melting snow, in the middle of the open field, a grave had been dug. Nurse Ina had gone on ahead to help the men. We met them at the graveside, and when the men had gone we recited the 139th Psalm together.

The town was entirely surrounded for some days; then the road to Pillau was freed for a time by force of arms. Fresh troops came in, the wounded could be evacuated. Transport is only possible at night, however, and is not always successful even then, because the road is shelled, and the vehicles are often obliged to turn back.

Further transport from Pillau itself is even more difficult. Homeless people are huddled together in the dunes, and casualties from Heiligenbeil are arriving there by way of the Haff. The Haff itself is the scene of immeasurable misery today. Thousands of refugees are trying to cross the ice in their carts to the Nehrung sandhills, with the Russian bombers circling overhead. At night the whole region is lighted up by flares.

Meanwhile the Russians are advancing through Pomerania towards the sea. Some of them have reached the Oder already, so the radio informs us. Very few people realise what this means; they hardly think about it at all. The Führer has planned everything up to now, and must have had some definite reason for allowing the Russians to penetrate so far into the country. They put their faith, too, in the new weapons of which rumours have been circulating, although nobody knows how they can be employed without annihilating friend and foe alike.

The suburb of Metgethen has been in Russian hands for some days, and is now retaken. What happened there, what state the inhabitants, especially the women, were found in, is reported in all the ghastly details by fly-sheets. This is probably done to spur us to desperate resistance. But there is little appearance of any deeper reaction to news of this kind. People are still incapable of realising that such things exist and are happening in their immediate neighbourhood.

With the return of the active medical officers to the fortress, ritual warfare has broken out again and demands its victims, of which I am one. I have been sent for by the Surgeon-General, to

clear up my relations with the military, for it is considered in-
admissible that I should be working as a civilian among soldiers.
With my pistol buckled on I made my way to the office in question
alongside the theatre. An officer received me and tried, tactfully, to
convince me that I must now become a soldier. I asked him if that
was worth while for so short a time, and whether I couldn't do
without a uniform. As far as I was concerned it wouldn't make me
feel any stronger than before, and it would only entail tiresome
complications in the hospital. They always addressed me as Staff
Surgeon as it was, and so far nobody seemed to have noticed that
I was in civilian dress. But to turn me out of my job in the operating theatre would be very inexpedient, because in any case we had
never yet been able to get through our daily task. That was not at
all the intention, I was then told. In recognition of the voluntary
work I had put in up to now, I was to be appointed Junior Surgeon, with three weeks' back pay, and my basic military training
postponed, by way of exception, to a later date. From the point of
view of maintenance I should be better off too, if I belonged to the
Forces. I assured him that I was satisfied to remain in the hospital
without any pay, and had plenty to eat; I also reminded him that
we shouldn't be able to demand any maintenance from the Russians. But this made no impression on him; we were obviously talking at cross-purposes. So I finally submitted to my fate, and
enquired as to the formalities to be carried out on my return to the
hospital. The first step, he told me, would be to report to the
company sergeant-major; all the rest would be easy.

As I was taking leave of him, someone came in with news of the
hospital train with my wounded from the Surgical Clinic. It had
never left the town in spite of repeated attempts, and was still
standing in the goods station. Those of the occupants that are still
alive are now to be distributed among the hospitals and main
dressing-stations of the town. Several of the accompanying nurses
will also have to be admitted as patients. My imagination fails me
when I try to picture to myself what they have had to go through
in the past fortnight.

On my return to the hospital I dutifully reported to the company sergeant-major, who agreed at once with marked affability
to regulate what remained to be done. What this represented remained a mystery for the time, as I was at once engulfed in
surgical work again. I learnt only incidentally that misgivings had
arisen as to the propriety of my continuing to share the doctors'

midday mess. This was good news, for we had never much cared for the arrangement, and would rather have slept at the usual dinner hour than join in conversation. To the general relief, however, the situation was cleared up sooner than expected owing to a sudden exchange at headquarters. The Surgeon-General's successor came in person to inform me that everything could go on as before. To conform to the demands of the ritual warfare I was to be officially listed as a consulting surgeon.

In the middle of February two new surgeons were sent us via Pillau, which considerably lightened our work. Only two groups out of four are now ever at work at the same time, and this gives us a chance to visit the patients, which was impossible hitherto. Each group now has a trained theatre sister, and there are proper nurses working in the wards. The ground floor is being reserved, as far as possible, for new admissions. This means a perpetual to and fro, for many of them have to be carried out again as corpses in a few hours' time. Unforgettable people are at work there, foremost among them frail old Sister Ursula from Coblenz, almost floating over the ground from sleeplessness, and Galla, the medical orderly, a man of unexampled loyalty.

The hospital chaplain has succeeded in fetching our 'Brother Martin', whom he has known from his student days, out of the Trommelplatz Barracks and quartering him with us as a hospital orderly. He was allotted to my group and had to go straight into the operating theatre, of which he had never had any practical experience. He was given no time to get used to things, but had to take hold of arms and legs as they were amputated, and carry them away. We are thankful to have him with us, and not a day goes by without our meeting at some time to read the 'watchwords' together and discuss the Scripture text for the day. This gives a meaning to our work—often so desperate in appearance—and a special tone to each day.

Our very cramped operating theatre has now been enlarged. The bigger room adjoining it has been cleared out and added to it, and we operate there now, while in the anteroom the wounded are sorted out, undressed, examined and X-rayed. Besides which, bandaging and plastering for transport are carried out there. We have made a valuable acquisition in the person of the old male nurse Didszus, who worked for thirty years in the Surgical Clinic. I engaged him off the street, at his urgent request, and as he can turn his hand to anything he saves the work of two men and a lot of talk.

At midnight we usually have a 'luncheon' break, squatting in a circle on anything available in the way of seats, both operating groups together, and have coffee and sandwiches. Brother Martin fetches the stuff from the kitchen. We all look forward to this, because it's an opportunity for a good talk; and many a secret dilemma can be discussed. But the extra meal has come to have an importance of its own for us too, for our official rations are becoming daily shorter. The only meat is horsemeat—in plenty, incidentally, owing to the number of horses constantly killed by bombing.

Among the wounded sent us, an increasing number can no longer be termed regular soldiers. Many of them are over service age, but they are shoved into Defence Corps uniform and let loose at the enemy straight away. One of these was sent us along with six other men and a chit from the District Commander demanding special treatment for him. In spite of his severe injuries he was almost crazy with self-admiration because he had succeeded in shooting down four Russian tanks, one after another, with his anti-tank gun.

Alongside of these we get boys of fifteen and sixteen, who have often been taken from the street and sent to the front only a few hours earlier. As they are local youths, of course their mothers soon make their appearance. We let them stay beside their children, for as we only get those with abdominal injuries, most of them haven't long to live.

I have had several surprise visits from my relations. B. Finckenstein, who is in command of a battalion in Metgethen, has come twice. The second time he brought me brandy and cigarettes—things we have been kept short of in the hospital since our stout staff surgeon left, though there is reason to suspect that our stocks are not as depleted as the authorities maintain.

Another day my cousin Knyphausen came to see me. He is on the staff of the 5th Panzer Division, which is divided between Königsberg and Pillau. He is quartered in Vierbrüderkrug. Nobody in the Division believes in the possibility of effective defence once the enemy begins the last assault. I'm glad to have had such an honest opinion.

As against this we have been pestered by a so-called NSFO[1] with a shameless lecture on the military situation, which he delivered to the wounded during a visit to the hospital towards the end of February. Hundreds of German tanks, so he declared, had

---

[1] = National-Socialist Public Relations Officer.

just arrived in Pillau. These were about to advance, with the help of the new weapons, and join a second lot of tanks, now on their way from Breslau in the rear of the Russians, somewhere near Warsaw. This was the Führer's long-cherished plan—to let the Russians in, the more surely to destroy them. If the population of East Prussia were now to flee to the west, every man of them could be sure of returning in peace in a few months' time. They would all be back in good time for the spring sowing. Those who chose to stay at home were defeatists, and would suffer the fate they deserved.

It was no use saying anything to him; he knew himself what frightful lies he was telling. But it gave me pleasure to stare him in the face, from a few yards' distance, the whole time he was speaking. I gladly declined an invitation to the 'informal gathering' arranged for the evening with the lecturer, but next day I was reprimanded by my apprehensive colleagues for my challenging behaviour to such an important personage.

We are treated to all sorts of other things. A capering café violinist in uniform, along with ten other unmilitary musicians, played the latest sentimental popular tunes to the wounded for a whole afternoon. And then we were urged to go and see the film *Kolberg*, which is being shown at the theatre. As it was bound to consist of the grossest mass propaganda, we declined the pleasure on the score of our heavy duties.

At the beginning of March a thaw set in, with sunshine. Now and then one felt a quite unseasonable breath of spring. Swans came flying in orderly formation over the town, keeping us continually on tenterhooks lest they should be shot down by the flak.

Work at the hospital had shrunk to such an extent that we began to wonder what things looked like outside. The first time I went out I met a red deer coming towards me unexpectedly between the two cemeteries; it crossed the Pillau Road and disappeared in the Park. I was on my way to No. 5 post office at the Central Railway Station, where there is a main dressing-station. Wounded are sent to us from there, now and then, who have already been given proper treatment. But the most remarkable thing about them is the carefully written hospital report they bring with them, for that sort of thing went out of fashion a long while ago in the general confusion. I was curious to meet the man signing these reports, Head Surgeon Bothmer.

The walk there proved more hazardous than I had bargained for. As I was about to turn off to the right from the Pillau Road

I saw some people at the cross-roads suddenly throw themselves on the ground. I did the same, automatically, and heard aircraft roaring overhead. Lying on my back, I saw them appearing between the clouds at a moderate height, and then down crashed the bombs with a noise as deafening as the roar of a powerful waterfall. The hits followed; then everybody jumped up again and went on their way.

A few minutes later I passed the spot where the bombs had fallen, near the Holländerbaum Station. The houses on both sides of the road were riddled through and through—they had obviously been empty to start with. But the bridge the attack must have been intended for was undamaged. I ran over it as fast as I could, for more aircraft were coming. One bomb fell in the water, the rest further away among the ruins. A third formation came streaking above the railway line just as I reached my destination. I slid down the nearest cellar opening and found myself in a large, half-darkened room, leading to further big rooms in which the wounded were lying. People in white jackets were moving about in the background. I looked at them one by one, trying to guess which was the man I wanted. None of them stood out in any way. Then I saw him coming towards me, almost like an old acquaintance. I let him go past, and followed him unobtrusively to the X-ray apparatus, where he asked to be shown two radiographs. As he was holding one of them against the light, I asked him a question from behind. He answered first, and then looked slowly round for the questioner. He looked me up and down with a tinge of curiosity. 'Are you a soldier?' 'No, anyway not a proper one. I'm merely working at a field hospital, and wanted to see who it is that sends us such beautiful hospital reports.' He laid down the radiographs and took me into the next room. There we seated ourselves on a table, and were soon far away from that dark hole of a cellar. He comes from Kiel, where his wife and two small children are living. We managed to say a lot in a few words. We mean to keep in touch as long as we can, if only by telephone, which is working again between the hospitals.

On the way back I called on the Haberberg pastor. Once again he and his house have remained untouched, but the houses behind the church, which had withstood the attack in the summer, have been hit this time. Dead people were being brought out from under the heaps of splintered wood lying on the road. More and more one feels one's own existence to be a miracle.

After walking through the ruined town, whose immensity always grips me in the same spell, I ended up at the power station. Our portly staff surgeon received me in a silk robe reaching almost to the ground, which he had found in an abandoned medical store belonging to the SS. He looked like a maharajah. He still had some very good brandy, and showed me a beautiful spaniel he intends training as soon as he gets a chance. He really seemed to think this was possible.

When I left him it was nearly dark. The Public Prosecutor's Office, which I passed, looked exactly as it did last autumn : the house at the front torn open by an air mine, the prison behind it undamaged. My mother had been inside it at that time as a prisoner of the Gestapo, having been arrested in June.

Without saying a word as to the object of her journey, she had gone to Königsberg to discover the whereabouts of a pastor who was a friend of ours. He had been taken to this very prison a short time before. For four days my mother could not be found; then information seeped through as to where she should be looked for. But it was four weeks before I could get permission to speak to her under observation. I shall never forget the moment when, after waiting for an hour in the anteroom while all the close-cropped, famished men and distressed women in their prison dress were driven past me, I heard her at last coming down a long stone passage, and her escort unlocked the iron door that separated us from each other. In what state should I find her? I was immediately reassured. She was still wearing her own clothes, and was treated with obvious respect by the wardress superintending our conversation. Brimming with energy, full of indignation at being deprived of her liberty, she laid a whole list of commissions for me on the table, which we went through one by one. They consisted mostly of instructions concerning my brother's household, which she had been running in his absence. The actual danger in which she stood had not yet entered her mind.

My subsequent interview with the public prosecutor in charge of her case was far more disturbing. He wanted to persuade me that she had committed high treason by not denouncing the pastor. She must have known that he was listening to foreign broadcasts. Two years' penal servitude was the least she deserved. He would doubtless have liked me to beg mercy of him, on the score of my brothers who had fallen in the war, and the grief their death had caused us; but I could not give him this satisfaction, and when we parted the gulf between us was wider than before.

At that very time Königsberg was celebrating the four hundred years' existence of its University. The Rectors of all the German universities turned up in full fig; for days together there were festival recitals, torchlight processions and concerts, and seats of honour were fought for as in times of profoundest peace, while the dull thudding of the Russian guns was beginning to make itself heard in the east. I had just returned, laden with poignant impressions, from Berlin, where I had been trying to visit a friend in the Moabit prison, already seriously damaged by bombs, who had been condemned to death by the People's Court. No wonder the Königsberg proceedings seemed doubly fantastic to me.

Three weeks later the situation had entirely changed. The attempt of the 20th July[1] had taken place, and many of my friends and relations were in custody, awaiting an entirely uncertain fate. It now seemed almost a piece of luck that my mother should have been arrested earlier, so that she could not be implicated in this fresh affair.

When I was allowed to see her for the second time I realised at once fom her demeanour that she knew all about the events of that day. She had already picked up some of the prisoners' tapping language and was quite self-controlled—obviously aware into whose hands she had fallen. Knowing her passionate temperament, I was struck with admiration to see her as vigilant as an animal in peril, every word, every movement under control. I felt ashamed of being still at large myself.

The trial began soon afterwards, and I was allowed to attend it. The pastor, who had been singled out as a test case, had died, and this considerably reduced the interest in my mother and the other persons arrested on the same charges. She was condemned to nine months' imprisonment, and I reckoned that the Russians would have arrived long before their completion.

In that very same month Königsberg was destroyed by bombing. From the roof of our Insterburg Hospital, fifty miles away, we could see the fiery glow rising into the night sky. The prisoners, meanwhile, were raving in their cells, till at last a couple of compassionate warders came running down the corridors, drawing back the bolts on their own responsibility.

Three days later it was possible to travel to the town. Everything

[1] On Hitler's life.

was still smoking and charring under a radiant September sky. A road had been cleared for traffic through the unimaginable sea of ruins, and on either side of it lay the iron skeletons that had come down as whirling firebrands. The prison was still standing; destruction had halted just in front of it. The roof alone had caught fire, and had been extinguished with the help of the prisoners. The building in front had been torn open by an air mine, so that one could enter unhindered and rummage in the Public Prosecutor's documents lying knee-deep on the floor.

On the score of the destruction, and the obvious temptation to the enemy to make a further attack on the outskirts of the town, I asked one of the prosecuting authorities whether he couldn't let me take my mother away, and found him sufficiently shattered by events at least to give me a hearing. But he demanded to see the documents, without which, he said, he could do nothing. I asked where they might be found, and was shown into a big room on the first floor.

After searching aimlessly through an enormous heap of paper for at least an hour, I spoke to an old office clerk sitting at a table in the next room. I explained the situation to him and found him a most sympathetic ally. He was acquainted with my mother's case, and told me in a whisper what he thought of our present rulers. It was incredible, the way they treated people, he said. Then he advised me to give up my hopeless efforts, and betook himself to the public prosecutor I had spoken to. Half an hour later he came back to fetch me, and worked on the already half softened prosecutor, in my presence, until he promised to give my mother a month's leave on a properly founded appeal. This did not take long, either. My helper called in a secretary, and told her to type out on the spot the appeal we had drawn up together. I was then sent round to the prison, and after barely five minutes' waiting my mother came downstairs, escorted by several wardresses, who took leave of her in the most friendly fashion and expressed a hope that she would now be free for good. She had received official instructions to report to the women's prison at Stulm in West Prussia in a month's time. Fortunately even this could be prevented when the time came.

I met Doktora outside the hospital; she had been to Vierbrüderkrug on her bicycle, and gave me an enthusiastic account of this rather daring exploit.

One evening soon after this my new friend at the main dressing-station rang up to say he was coming to see us. As he didn't know the way I went to fetch him. When I left our hospital at about eight o'clock it was raining in torrents; you couldn't see your hand before your face. I had only gone a few paces when I was held up by a sentry and asked for the password. 'Theatre?' he said. 'Curtain,' I replied, and was allowed to proceed.

Immediately afterwards I heard aircraft approaching again. A few bombs fell, and the nearby harbour district flared up a dull red. The clattering enemy machines circled slowly, at low altitude, over the town. Now and then one of them would be caught in a searchlight, only to disappear again at once in the thick cloud ceiling, followed by the trail of light from the anti-aircraft guns. Heavy return fire came from the aircraft. The whole place was growing lighter from fresh fires. I hesitated for a moment, then summoned up my courage and ran along the deserted streets till I reached the main railway station, where we were to meet, quite out of breath. We waited there till the attack was over and then walked back the way I had come, which was lighted up by the red glow.

In the course of the evening Bothmer told us of his adventures in Africa. He had spent two years there, deputising for a very busy doctor, and had occasion to take part in some very exciting lion hunts. When the war broke out his fiancée was on her way to join him, while he, unaware of this, was trying to get back to Germany overland. Her ship was torpedoed off the coast of Kapstadt, and she had to swim ashore and remain there for a year, till she too managed to return to Germany.

When I took our guest home the night was nearly over. We talked of the only things that were still of any importance; he is one of the few that have no illusions on the score of what is to come. As we parted at the Holländerbaum Bridge a flock of heavy birds came rustling overhead through the early spring night.

Most people are still convinced that the Führer's present conduct of war is in accordance with a predetermined plan. And the fact that the Russians have already reached the Oder, and we are now living, so to speak, on a little remote island, is hardly realised. This is borne in on one every day, in half alarming, half comical ways. The reopening of the banks, for instance, has spread a great wave of reassurance. The possibility of paying money in again, and drawing it out, shows clearly enough that things can't be so bad after all.

I came across much the same thing talking to one of our nurses. She had been a parish nurse for years in L., and I said I wondered what it looked like over there now, under the Russians. She stared at me, speechless. The Russians in L.? It simply wasn't possible. And I have the impression that this nurse has been considerably more reserved towards me ever since.

The following is significant too. On my way to the Children's Clinic, where a lot of patients are still lying in plaster in the bunker, I met a number of horse-drawn vehicles, laden with people, driving westwards—a sight one hadn't encountered for weeks. I asked one of the deaconesses in the bunker what could have induced people to leave their homes just now, when things had quietened down a bit, to attempt the dangerous journey to Pillau. She explained it in this way. 'At first they refused to leave. But I believe they've been told the English may come and bomb everything flat; so now they're going.'

General von Thadden, who as O.C. of the so-called 1st Division —which may no longer exist—has come to Königsberg viâ Berlin, told me a similar story when I called on him at the General Post Office. A Königsberg artist sought him out, and began raving about the stimulating material offered him as a painter by Königsberg today. Much impressed, the General expressed his appreciation, and enquired incidentally where he had sent his family. Oh, they were still at home, and all quite well. 'But isn't there too much shelling going on? The Russians are no more than a thousand yards away from you.' 'That's true. The top storeys have had one or two hits; but we live on the ground floor.' And when the General asked discreetly whether it wouldn't be better to take his wife and children out of the town while it was still possible, he got the naïve answer, 'D'you think that's necessary, Herr General?' 'Necessary? That depends on . . . your feelings towards your family.' How was he to convey the truth to him, unobtrusively, without being cried down as a defeatist? In the end his guest thanked him for the suggestion and promised to talk it over with his wife.

The radio is imperturbable. We are told of the frightful bombing attacks on Dresden, and hear Goebbels's brazen speech, in which he admits that we could now say like the Romans *Hannibal ante portas!* But we must remember there was not only one, but three Punic Wars, and in the end the Romans came off victorious.

With the house physicians in the hospital, who feel rather out of it because of the almost exclusively surgical character of the work, I have the reputation of attracting enemy aircraft. And it is a fact that whenever I go out, whether by day or by night, hardly ten minutes go by before they arrive. I have been asked quite seriously to let everybody know before I go out, so that they can take shelter in time.

These aircraft do really wear you down. They go buzzing singly over the town for hours, dropping a bomb from time to time. Moreover our hospital is the only large building, over a wide area, that can be considered a worthwhile target. Those that have nothing to do go down to the cellar whenever they can; only Doktora and her sister show an almost offensive indifference to the bombs. During attacks they are always to be found in the topmost storey, cheering up the wounded.

Only once did we witness a counter-attack, equally surprising to both sides. I saw an approaching formation suddenly scatter as though a hawk had flown into their midst. A single fighter swept repeatedly, three times as fast as the Russians, across my field of vision. One of the bombers caught fire, eight men baled out and hung on parachutes over the harbour installations, the rest of the aircraft made off. We were told later that the pursuer had shot them all down one after another. Even if that is much to be doubted, this effective defence did at least provide a moment of excitement in our fortress existence.

What a lot of different people go through our hands here! And what frightful injuries! The 'right to health' has become a special grace. We have made room for a few isolated cases, in which we happen to be specially interested, immediately alongside the operating theatre, so as to be able to take a quick look at them from time to time. Foremost among them is nineteen-year-old Seppl, a huge lad from Innsbruck. He has lost an eye, and one of his legs has had to be amputated high up in the thigh. His other leg is still in danger. We often hear him screaming with pain. But as soon as I go to him he leaves off, and his expression seems to say, 'Dear Doctor, I know you have no time, and I'm only one of many, but stay with me for a moment; I'll be quite good.' Then he tells me all the plans he's making, supposing he's never able to ski again. And one goes away feeling comforted.

A stud groom from Trakehnen is here too, whom as children we used to admire as a daring rider. While serving in the militia he stumbled on a mine near Lauth, and I have had to amputate his right hand and foot. He has reminded me that many years ago

I sat by his bed for a whole night after he had had a bad fall, and tells me how happy he is to have landed up again in my care.

In the matter of surgical treatment as a whole, one has daily and hourly occasion to tremble at the weight of responsibility laid upon one, and still more at the rapidity with which one has learnt to take the gravest decisions. What is it in oneself that decides? Is it merely practical considerations, or does one's mood of the moment play a part? I have sometimes amputated ten legs in succession, which I had hoped up to then to be able to save.

In decisions of this sort the question always arises, too, as to what will become of these people if the Russians suddenly arrive. Won't the amputation cases be the worst off? I try to eliminate this point of view as far as possible, because it lies outside my responsibility. But it keeps thrusting itself upon me, and if I didn't believe in forgiveness I don't know how I should stand up to it at all. The men are dying like flies in any case, from exhaustion and because one can't give them the necessary after-treatment. Used dressings are piling up, yards deep, in front of the house, and beginning to slide down into the pond; while over in the cemetery the line of fresh graves lengthens unceasingly. Lately we have even had wounded coming to us viâ Pillau, because all accommodation there is full to overflowing, and ships can hardly ever get away on account of mine and aircraft danger. We hear of desperate fighting round Heiligenbeil, where a whole army has been surrounded by the Russians and driven towards the Haff. Thousands of wounded are being transported over the ice under impossible conditions. A few pockets of resistance are still holding out in the cliffs round the Haff, with the Russians only a few yards above them. Aircraft fly to and fro over the beach, firing into the cliffs. When that is over it will be our turn.

Pastor Müller has been transferred to Pillau, and Brother Martin has taken his place as hospital chaplain. We are glad not to have to misuse him in the operating theatre any longer, but to be able to leave him entirely to the wounded.

On the 20th March I was asked by the Chairman of the Medical Committee to take charge of the surgical department of the Municipal Hospital, which has not been properly staffed for some time. I am now free to take up this new task, because another surgeon has come to this hospital who can take over my section. So I shall become a civilian again. Doktora and her sister will remain here for the time, as they cannot be spared.

That evening I succeeded in bringing Bothmer and Staff Surgeon Bode together. We met in Bode's room at the power station, and the two of them were soon deep in a professional discussion on head surgery, assisted by a neurologist from the erstwhile Nerve Clinic, who is now working at the power station. Our host treated us to the positively last drop of his Martell, which we drank out of little red-rimmed glasses.

I'm finding the organisation of the Municipal Hospital difficult to sort out for the moment. The separate blocks have been badly damaged in parts, and the wards that can still be used lie far apart on different floors. It's like being in a labyrinth and never knowing where one is. The operating theatre in the basement of the second block, which belonged originally to the gynæcological department, is really splendid. One feels at home there. It is as well equipped as in peace-time, with instruments, linen and lighting, besides two perfect theatre sisters, Martha and Ruth, who are both longing to be at work, and glad that operating is to start again.

The out-patients' department, which is in the front building on the street, is also run by two very capable young nurses. They live in a room alongside, behind a curtain. Left without any medical support for weeks, they have been extracting shell splinters themselves and doing all the necessary plaster dressings. Anything that is beyond their capacity they send to the Samaritan Hospital across the road. The basement they are working in is not quite below ground level, but is well protected on the road side by a screen of masonry. Here, as on the other side near the operating theatre, a lot of patients have been accommodated, at very close quarters, it's true, but pretty well in safety. There are about 150 altogether, half of them foreigners, French, Polish and Russian, including a certain number of women. Fifteen Frenchmen and one Russian medical student are functioning as stretcher-bearers and assistants, in addition to Stantus, a male nurse with years of experience in surgical work. There are a few Russian women among the domestic servants. The nursing staff is very mixed; some of them belong to the Brown Sisterhood.[1] Many nurses are said to have left the hospital already. The House Governor, Professor Boettner, has stayed on with one intern and two women assistant doctors. I myself have been given a young Ukrainian doctor as assistant. I'm to have the former head physician's room on the second floor.

[1] A National-Socialist non-religious organisation, habited in the Nazi brown.

On the 22nd March I cycled to the Field Hospital to take my leave. As I was passing the Treasury a single, huge black aircraft passed over the town like a demon in the twilight. Points of light shot up from innumerable guns on the ground, followed by a thousand pairs of eyes, up and up, only to ricochet ineffectually from the armoured fuselage. The demon pursued its way imperturbably. And then a thick black column of smoke arose from the immediate neighbourhood of the main station, followed by the dull boom of the impact. A single bomb on a whole town—but how profoundly it can disquiet one! It must have fallen quite near Bothmer's place. I hadn't time to go there and find out what had happened, and my anxiety was not relieved till I returned to the hospital and found a letter from him there. He has sent me a wounded Frenchman, and is keeping four German soldiers who were hit by the dreaded bomb just outside his door.

Next day I called on my colleagues in the Samaritan Hospital. On the table in the mess stood a photograph of Churchill, and people were busy learning Russian forms of greeting. I was advised to do the same, and they thought me very unenterprising because I considered it waste of effort.

Their cellars are overflowing with patients, and they intend sending fresh arrivals over to me in future. They have lost some of their staff already, including their Sister in charge of X-ray, who was killed by a shell while at work. The X-ray department at the Municipal Hospital is run by a big, blonde woman assistant, who takes excellent photographs and is glad to have something to do once more.

I have been given a pass allowing me to circulate freely inside the fortifications. In recent weeks a number of barricades and barriers have been built up out of the ruins. At one time the whole place could have ranked as fortifications. The area between the Castle pond and the University has now become quite unrecognisable. The debris have now been mostly removed; one winds one's way up and down, along narrow beaten tracks between great piles of bricks. Every now and then the place comes under heavier gunfire; one has a definite feeling that one is approaching the finale. At night we hear the Russian radio blaring from the outskirts of the town; between intervals of music it appeals to the population to surrender unconditionally.

I shall use this opportunity of operating on peace-time lines as long as time allows. I have even had a soldier brought over to me from the Field Hospital, with the consent of the Medical Committee, for an operation for cancer of the stomach. Doktora is coming to assist me with it, and will stay on afterwards, having been released from over there.

23rd March, Palm Sunday

Brother Martin held a parish service at the Ratshöfer church, and we attended it. What a spring-like March! There has been no snow on the ground for a long while. Swans and geese fly over the town; the cemeteries are dripping wet. There are still mountains of ammunition between the black tree-trunks, with the guns it was intended for standing in more open spaces. There was a large attendance at the church. In default of wine, strawberry syrup was administered at Holy Communion. At the conclusion a small child was baptised.

Maundy Thursday

I have been ordered to report to the Chief Burgomaster, to have my new appointment to the Municipal Hospital confirmed, and the question of my pay settled. The Burgomaster is supposed to be found at the Town Hall beside the North Station, but my search for him in the badly damaged building was unsuccessful, and as my pay doesn't interest me particularly at the present time I gave up the attempt, and paid a visit instead to the Medical Institute behind the police office. There I found the chairman of the Medical Committee, with a few younger colleagues and Chief Medical Councillor Dembowski, a man who is entirely alive to the situation, as one can see at once. With him one can risk an outspoken word.

While I was there two general practitioners from the Insterburg district, with whom I was acquainted, put in appearance. Together with an older colleague they have taken over the deserted Red Cross headquarters. One of the young doctors is planning to break out of the fortifications, and I was able to give him a letter to take with him. A short time ago I received a field postcard with the immensely comforting news that my sister and her husband had got through, and that my father, too, was in the west. My mother's and brother's fate, on the other hand, is still uncertain. They have not yet turned up with their trek on the other side of the Oder.

I also paid a short visit to the Girls' Industrial School near by, which now houses a main dressing-station. It had suffered several direct hits, that morning, in the upper storey. To my joy I found the two students there who had given me such loyal assistance at the Surgical Clinic at the end of January. They are in charge of the X-ray department and are in thoroughly good spirits.

Then I went with my two Insterburg colleagues to their duty room, which is now in an underground shelter at the Medical Clinic in the Drummstrasse. They still have astonishingly good food there. I was invited to dinner. They brought me back afterwards to the Municipal Hospital in their service car, after filling my pockets with provisions. As I got out I asked where they were going. On duty to Juditten, they said, to a Women's League tea party. One of them was to make a speech there. 'My God!' I exclaimed, 'is the Nazi ghost not yet laid?' They shrugged their shoulders.

30th March, Good Friday

Brother Martin was to have come and held a prayer meeting here, but we waited for him in vain. In the evening I went through the building and invited all the nurses and personnel I came across to a meeting I would hold myself. I read the Gospel of the two crucified thieves : 'Verily I say unto thee, this day shalt thou be with me in Paradise.' The text was not inapposite : we know now more or less how we stand. The Russians have dropped leaflets telling us that we may celebrate Easter, but after that it's all up with us. We've heard that Danzig was destroyed a fortnight ago, but Breslau is still holding out. The towns in the west are still being plagued by bombing attacks, Dresden has been burnt down, with ten thousand refugees besides its own inhabitants. Where are people to go?

Late in the evening Bothmer came to see me, having found his way on his bicycle, although he could hardly see three paces in front of him in the fog and drizzle. Over a bottle of bad wine, which we managed to ferret out, we spent the night in our beautiful yellow-tiled underground labour ward, discussing the events of Good Friday and all their significance for us. Towards morning I went with him through the rows of ruins in the Rossgarten, which were momentarily lighted up by the moon, as far as the Rossgärter Markt. As we said goodbye I asked him his Christian name. 'Unfortunately I'm called Adolf,' he replied, 'but my friends call me Alf.' And I remained silent, forebearing to tell him that the man on whose account he had said 'unfortunately' was also called Alf by his friends, as long as he had any left.

1st April, Easter Sunday

The account of Christ's resurrection according to St. John formed the central point of a private service we held in the operating theatre. We even managed a little singing, though only very few of the congregation appeared to be familiar with church hymns. Doktora went to the Field Hospital and saw her sister and Brother Martin, both of them well. A corner of Brother Martin's room had been blown out in his absence. An artillery shell crashed through a window of the house and was found lying, a dud, on the bed of one of the interns.

Tuesday, 3rd April

Quite early in the morning I began to feel uncomfortable in my room on the second floor, on account of the heavier shelling that was going on, although I had figured out that nothing could actually reach it by way of a direct hit. I took nearly all my goods and chattels downstairs and stowed them in the room alongside the operating theatre. An hour later, just as we were operating, a load of little bombs rattled down on top of us. Parts of the house wall detached themselves from the upper storeys of our old, tall box of bricks and crashed to the ground. We were well protected in the theatre and hardly felt the hits. Soon afterwards somebody came in and advised me to go and have a look, some time, at the house wall opposite. I ran out of doors and saw a big hole in the second storey. The only bomb to hit the house from the side had gone in at my window and torn a big hole in the wall. There was nothing but ruins above it, the inside walls had been torn out, and my bed, with the rest of my possessions, was in fragments.

Wednesday, 4th April

The night was quiet again, but in the morning drumfire started up. All day the ground trembled and the sky reverberated. We could only distinguish details when stones came rattling down in our immediate neighbourhood. We were like a ship tossing on the ocean. All the patients were taken down to the cellars; new arrivals were left lying on the floor of the operating theatre and the adjoining rooms. Doktora and I operated on two tables; one was not enough for the number of wounded arriving. Women and children with serious shell wounds were brought in, and soldiers as well. We have become a sort of field hospital.

Thursday, 5th April

Today it was the turn of the aircraft. From early morning till late afternoon of this lovely sunny day they circled, first at 1,500 feet, then much lower, over every quarter of the town. More than a hundred were always in the air at a time, dropping heavy bombs and firing with all their guns on the streets. There was no sign of any defence. The fighter-bombers pursued their way calmly and evenly. A prodigious spectacle met our eyes every time we passed the exits facing the Castle pond. In the steely blue sky a tearing gale, blowing towards the middle of the town, sent the mounting smoke-clouds swirling in all directions. Over the inner town lay a black mountain range, out of which flames were shooting, and above this circled the aircraft, pressing in from every side, plunging into the witches' cauldron and climbing up again unharmed on the other side. The stone stairs in front of our door were strewn with shell splinters, but only when there were aircraft immediately above us did we run back a few steps into the basement. Otherwise we stood outside, staring spellbound at the infernal racket. We couldn't make each other hear, but there was no need. We knew we were both thinking of the same thing—our Saviour's promise for days of terror and destruction such as these: 'Then look up, and lift up your heads, for your redemption draweth nigh.'

I noticed that Doktora was singing; and then we sang out together into the tumult: 'Praise the Lord, O my soul; while I live will I praise the Lord. Yea, as long as I have any being, I will sing praises unto my God.' We are living an ardent life these days; all our thoughts revolve round the one imperishable focal point, and believing has almost become seeing.

As for our fellow-workers, no better functioning of the whole staff can be imagined. The Frenchmen, who accomplish wonders in the way of transporting the patients, and go fearlessly from one block to another with their stretchers, across the yards, I assembled for a moment to thank them for their magnanimous service, which nobody could now force them to render. One of them answered for them all, saying they were here as conscious representatives of their country, and would render us the service demanded of them to the end.

When the engine-house between us and the Castle pond started burning, we organised a fire-fighting squad with the help of the Frenchmen, to prevent the fire from spreading to the hospital. We ran down with buckets, in single file, to the Castle pond, and succeeded in extinguishing the flames without suffering any injury ourselves.

The nurses, too, are beyond praise in their sublime fearlessness and zeal. One of them, our devoted, totally self-sacrificing Sister Maria, I remember particularly because of the unexpected answer she gave me when I asked her how she had come to join the Brown Sisterhood. 'Well, Herr Doktor,' she said, 'at first we belonged to the Christian Community; but then the Englishman came with his bombs and destroyed our trombones. Then what had we left to attract people with? So we went over to the Brown Sisters.'

When towards evening things grew quieter, we found to our joy that we were all still there.

Friday, 6th April

After another, somewhat quieter night, the day began with renewed drumfire. One's nerves are already so greatly overstrained that one lives in a strange state of divided consciousness. While I was doing my work with more or less outward calm, trying to take the hits on the thick walls of our block and the crumbling down of the brickwork as part of the natural order of things, I became increasingly invaded by a dream world. I saw us sitting in a thatched cottage at the foot of a wooded slope under deep snow. It was night, and swarms of Russians with torches in their hands were gliding down upon us through the trees. They hadn't quite reached us yet, but we were staring into their strange, wild faces.

In between-whiles I caught remarks that brought me back completely to reality, so unique were they in their simplicity. I shall never forget this one, out of the mouth of one of the wounded soldiers lying in rows on the floor of the operating theatre. Just as a fresh hail of shell came rattling down alongside of us, I heard a loud, clear voice declare in the purest East Prussian, 'Well, now they'll conquer us all right, but never in *spirit*!'

During the night we too lay down for an hour at a time on the floor. The town was a sea of flame.

Saturday, 7th April

I was wakened by the sudden fall of four lamps from the ceiling of the operating theatre, one of them on my body, accompanied by the reverberation of a terrific shock throughout the building. A moment later, heavy hits resounded a little further off. It was daylight. Stantus the male nurse came staggering towards me in the hall. He had just been to the upper storey to fetch something from the evacuated ward when the bombs fell. He was flung with tremendous force against the wall, together with the Russian girl Wally, who was accompanying him and was now lying there unconscious. We hastened to bring her down, because aircraft were coming close over the houses again. Up there everything had been torn out in the way of remaining doors and partitions. The east entry was blocked by a crater forty-five feet wide. A rack-wagon carrying beds, which must have been standing there, had vanished into space. Another crater of much the same size was separated from the operating theatre only by the outer wall. The third bomb was a dud as big as a man, which had come to rest in the first storey, just overhead.

In the course of the afternoon we found ourselves between the two fronts. Armed troops were retreating between our block buildings, emptying their rifles skywards over the roofs and then running round the Castle pond towards the town. On the opposite bank of the pond a new defence line appeared to have been formed. Shots from that direction came flying uninterruptedly flat overhead, splitting off bits of our roof. There was hardly a hundred yards distance between us and this line, but their defence sounded like small-calibre firing beside the vicious 'toff toff' of the aircraft guns when the fighters were approaching.

The further side of the pond looks like a cabbage-field destroyed by hail. One is involuntarily reminded of pictures of Douaumont and other shattered fortifications of the First World War, except that those had been erected specially for war, whereas the Königsberg pond seemed to have taken a perpetual lease of civilian quietude. Now it is being completely ravaged.

Nerves are beginning to give way among us here and there. I've found people lying in a deep sleep, obviously as a result of taking too many tablets. Lest the idea of suicide should become infectious I gave a little address in the operating theatre on the text 'Fear not those which kill only the body, but cannot kill the soul. But fear that which can destroy both body and soul.'

In the course of Sunday (8th April) firing became gradually less frequent, like machinery slowly running down. The uniform roaring and booming had dwindled to a rattle at isolated points. Rumours sprang up that the town had been summoned by parley to surrender. The Commandant had wanted to consent, and had been shot by the SS, who had now entrenched themselves in the Castle and were determined to fight to the last man.

Peculiar individuals keep turning up here, trying to make contact, storm-driven, no longer quite in their right mind. They talk like wandering Fates, and one wonders what they used to say and do when they were still normal. One listens to them, nodding agreement, and discovering the significance of war in the fact that it makes people like this.

Late in the night the firing stopped altogether. After the hammering and shaking of the last few days one can no longer feel the ground under one's feet. One feels oneself falling, sinking into an eternity. We look at one another with doleful smiles, almost disappointed to be still extant, so that the whole thing must go on somehow or other. We hadn't expected to emerge any more from the fiery sea. Now we are floating on the surface again, aware of only one thing—that we shall no longer be equal to any fresh demands. After reading a little more of the scriptures, and praying, we lay down on the floor to sleep.

3

KÖNIGSBERG UNDER THE RUSSIANS

9th to 24th April 1945

I ONCE saw a cat playing with a mouse. The mouse was very lively and appeared to amuse the cat. It kept trying to escape, and I thought more than once that it had really got away. But when I went closer to the bored-looking cat I discovered that it had long ago seized the little creature in its teeth. Many hours later the mouse was still alive. The little mangled animal no longer wanted to run away, it rolled aimlessly to and fro at the cat's instigation. The cat was trying hard to find some amusement in this unequal game; its excitement seemed greatly overdone, considering the condition of the mouse.

I could have run up and killed the little creature for my own peace of mind. But what use would that be, I thought, to all the thousands of mice threatened with the same fate, with nobody there to help them? Shouldn't one harden oneself to a problem that is always recurring in the same form? And can I find the solution otherwise than by realising that I myself am in the same situation as the mouse?

9th April 1945

Towards five in the morning I was wakened by a babel of voices and hurrying footsteps outside my door. I woke Doktora and told her to get dressed. 'What's up?' she asked, drunk with sleep. 'I think the Russians are here,' I said, 'I'm just going to see.' 'The Russians? Oh, have they actually come? I'd quite forgotten them.' 'Well, there you are,' I said, 'it was your own choice.' She nodded. I put on my white jacket and went out into the passage.

Czernecki, my Ukrainian assistant, ran up to fetch me to receive the Russians. The patients I went past poked up their heads. 'Two of them have been through here already and taken our watches, and Wally's had a knock-out.' Wally, our plucky little Russian nurse, was lying among the patients with blood streaming over her face, not stirring. The Russians she had tried to intercept had seized her by the hair and dashed her to the floor, face downwards. Her upper jaw was broken and several of her teeth had been knocked out. She was conscious, but made no sound.

Outside the main building two Russians were rummaging in a trunk. There was something frightening in the sight. I felt like someone who'd gone bear-hunting, and forgotten his gun. As we approached them they left the trunk alone and transferred their interest to us. With tommy-guns pressed to our bodies we were honoured by a thoroughgoing examination. An attempt by my companion to address them had no result. They made short, growling noises and carried on methodically with the work. Other Russians, meanwhile, came out of the main block, hung round like sleigh-horses with the most fantastic objects. They too ran their hands over us; my fountain pen vanished, money and papers flew all over the place. My shoes were too bad for them. They hurried away with a short-legged gait over ruins and through bomb craters to the other blocks and disappeared in the doorways. Their mode of locomotion left us gaping : when the situation suggested it they dropped on their hands and ran on all fours.

In the main building they were already hard at work. As I was forever having to stop and let myself be felt all over, I advanced along our basement passages as if through dense undergrowth. Stifled sounds of protest came from all the wards. Patients were being rolled out of bed and their bandages removed; here and there masses of paper were being burnt to improve the lighting, and our people were desperately trying to extinguish the fires. We kept looking in vain for an officer, for if this sort of thing went on, there soon wouldn't be much of us left.

In the out-patients' department the young nurses were fending off some importunate fellows. I dare not think what it will be like when they've become more assured. For the moment they seem determinedly bent on looting, as we discovered when we reached the provision stores. I was struck dumb by the sight of the multitude of foodstuffs there, which we had been denied in the fortress days; it infuriated me to think I had let myself be hoodwinked into allowing both ourselves and our patients to go hungry all that time. Now a wild, howling mob was fighting over the finest tinned foods, and provisions that hundreds could have lived on for a whole year were being destroyed in a few hours.

In the middle of the main store-room lay a pile of broken glass jars and empty tins. Sack after sack of flour, sugar and coffee were being emptied out over it. Alongside, half covered over, lay a dead man. On top of it all the Russians, soldiers and civilians, were rampaging, raking down more and more piles of valuable stores from the shelves. I tried to fish out a couple of unbroken jars, but a Russian knocked them out of my arm.

In the operating theatre Doktora was busy dressing patients' wounds. A crowd of nurses had taken refuge there and were pretending to be hard at work. In the background the Russians were prowling round the patients, searching for watches and wearable boots. One of them, a mere lad, suddenly burst into tears because he hadn't yet found a watch. He held up three fingers : he would shoot three men if he didn't get a watch at once. His despair brought about the first personal contact. Czernecki entered into a long palaver with him, and finally, somewhere or other, a watch was found for him, with which he ran off, beaming with joy.

The arrival of the first officers destroyed my last hopes of coming to endurable terms. None of my attempts to address them was any use; even for them I am only a hall stand with pockets, they see me only from the shoulders downwards. A couple of nurses who got in their way were seized and outraged from behind, and then released again, thoroughly dishevelled, before they realised what was happening. The older ones could hardly believe their senses; they went wandering aimlessly about the corridors. There was nowhere to hide, and fresh tormentors kept falling upon them.

I crept through our basement as if in a dream, trying to puzzle out what God demanded of me here. Czernecki had found out from a Russian who proved approachable that we couldn't reckon on any sort of order for the next six or eight days. The town has been delivered up to the troops. I then realised that this was the first time during their campaign that women had fallen into their hands in any number, a fact that had escaped me and now recalled me to the naked truth. The responsibility we were allowed to shoulder during the siege, hadn't we thereafter laid in God's hand, commending ourselves and those entrusted to us to his mercy? Now it is being flung back at our feet in an unbearable form. We had expected a savage horde, seeking a justified vengeance, to break in upon us and destroy so much at the very first moment that no single individual would have time for reflection. For anyone coming through alive the situation would be so novel that his behaviour in it would result automatically. He would then be able to begin life more or less afresh. We had relied all too rashly on the first of these assumptions.

What, actually, is our situation now? Nothing has really changed, except that the process of attrition that began with the houses is now spreading to the people. The final decision concerning us has not yet been taken. I'm so exhausted that I can't even pray.

At the same time, to my horror, I feel a new sense awakening in me, a sort of cold curiosity. What is it really, I ask myself, that we are witnessing here? Is it simply an expression of natural savagery, or of revenge? Of revenge perhaps, but in a different sense. Isn't the animal revenging itself upon the human, in one and the same person—the flesh upon the spirit it has had forced upon it? Where do these types come from, human beings like ourselves, in the thrall of impulses in horrific contrast with their outward appearance? What a struggle to bring chaos to light! This dull, growling speech, from which words seem to have withdrawn themselves long ago, and these maddened children, fifteen-, sixteen-year-olds, flinging themselves like wolves on the women, without really knowing what they're supposed to be doing. All this has nothing to do with Russia, nothing to do with any particular nation or race— it is mankind without God, the apish mask of mankind. Otherwise all this could not affect me so painfully—like personal guilt.

If it were only the Mongols! I can get on better with them in any case. They are simpler, better bred, and therefore by nature less exposed to western influence. Their wildness is not offensive. There are wiry figures among them, with conspicuously slender limbs and a natural poise.

With Czernecki's help I succeeded in establishing a first human contact with a non-commissioned officer of this description. He is going to try and find a command post and arouse some interest in our patients, many of whom are foreigners. I'm setting my last hopes on him; if he gets through and comes back we may be able to save something. Meanwhile we must endure what has to be endured.

Towards evening our courtyard was transformed into an enormous gipsy camp. Hundreds of little carts harnessed to sturdy Russian horses drove up at intervals. Indistinct figures, civilians and a few women among them, were crouching everywhere round little fires, over which, on two bricks, cooking was being busily

carried on. I felt as though I was in furthest Asia, and all this had
been planned long ago. It was all fantastic, like the confirmation
of an ever-recurring dream. They were all busy sorting out their
loot. Among them, unnoticed and dumbly resigned, stood our
patients and their relatives, watching the distribution of the contents of their trunks. My brain reeled when I thought of the
night. But to my temporary relief the crowd suddenly broke up
and dispersed down the Rossgarten towards the town.

Night fell, and our Mongol had not returned. We did our best
to go on looking after our patients. The Frenchmen were still there
and helped all they could. They too have been robbed of everything. One or two of them had managed to rescue some eatables—
a few tins of meat, a little bread—and we shared them out among us.

During the night the operating theatre was a scene of ghostly
activity. In a dim light, fifteen or twenty muffled figures, mostly
younger nurses, busied themselves with a patient lying on the
operating table. Now and then a whole lot of them would be
detailed to fetch another one to be bandaged : there were so many
lying around with wounds two or three days old. The Russians
seemed to find the atmosphere a bit sinister. They stood about for a
while in the next room, coming in now and again to snatch a pair
of scissors from among the instruments, but the nurses were in less
danger here than elsewhere.

Relief was provided unexpectedly by a major, who watched us
for a time and then asked me to remove a tiny wart from his face.
He seated himself on the operating table, and large white cloths
were thrown round him with theatrical gestures, by which he was
obviously impressed; but he suddenly jumped down and ordered
his batman to stand beside me with his tommy gun at the ready.
Feeling safer, he mounted the table again and gave orders to begin
the operation, the need for which struck us as greatly exaggerated.
However, it had the desired result : the major was delighted, and
defended us for a long while afterwards against intruders. Having
taken a liking to us he showed himself a man of feeling.

We took it in turns to lie on the floor and sleep, with the nurses
distributed among the patients. By the morning there was not a
Russian to be seen.

10th April

Trouble broke out again in the course of the afternoon. For a
time our corridors teemed like the inside of a beehive. Women were

heard screaming on every side, and a new tone had crept into the infernal music, the origin of which was not at first clear to me. Up to now it had been possible to shake the intruders' self-confidence by some energetic counter-action. Even Doktora had often been able to save the situation by her sudden intervention. But now? It looked as if the Russians had discovered some alcohol.

Then suddenly our Mongol appeared in the midst of the crowd at the entrance. I nearly fell upon his neck. He had managed to discover some sort of responsible office he was prepared to take us to, and Czernecki and I started off at once, taking another Russian with us who helped to ward off the snoopers that were forever trying to stop and search us. Going down the Rossgarten we got into a denser and denser crowd. On our left the Samaritan Hospital was on fire. I wondered what they would do with their patients, all lying in the basement. All the way to the Rossgärter Markt everything that had not yet been destroyed was on fire; the heat was so great in places as to be almost unbearable.

Up the Königstrasse, over the Rossgärter Markt and beyond, up to the Castle, wound an enormous coil of incoming troops, in which we now became engulfed. I pinched my thigh hard to convince myself that all this was reality and no dream. 'Königsberg in 1945,' I told myself repeatedly. To think that the good old venerable town, which one had hardly taken seriously hitherto, had only been waiting for this grandiose spectacle to expire! How cleverly it had guarded its secret from us when, not so long ago, we had gone trotting about unsuspectingly, with a superior air, among the friendly, static folds of its garment! Not till the assaults of last summer—the two English air raids— was the mask torn from its face, making it outwardly ripe, too, for this moment.

We were swimming in a sea of lava pouring down on the earth from some malicious star. Now it curved round to the right. Why? Of course there used to be houses standing here : just about here was where our dentist used to live. He worked up there—in the air. Perhaps in those days he may sometimes have looked out of the window at the peaceful street below, as though he was waiting for something. Now, between flaming ruins, a wildly yelling throng, without beginning or end, was pushing its way along the street. Was this really today, this very day? Wasn't it two thousand, ten thousand years ago—or as much later? Time was twofold, threefold at that moment.

Indescribable, all that was moving along in the way of people, animals and vehicles. All I knew was : This is victory, victory as it appears, is bound to appear, in the year 1945. The ridiculous and horrible details of which the picture was composed I felt to be compulsory actions, reactions within a uniform physical-dynamical process. The slanting plain seemed to me to play a part in this, and I wondered with a shock whether Königsberg had always lain so much lower than Inner Asia that the grey lava could slide down into it like this. Floating in it, submerging now and then, figures! Figures! No! No! Oneself a figure like that. I saw myself stopping, stumbling on, gaping with a dead, forgotten face. Who was I today? Who were the others? How strange to think that at one time people had stood for hours to watch a march past. Here, perhaps, once, on this very spot. There must therefore have been something worth seeing in it. But this thing here, exceeding everything imaginable, for whom is it happening, who sees it anyway? Isn't it completely purposeless, meant for nobody? Or is God staging something here for his own benefit?

We went on towards the Castle. Out of the ruins, like an exclamation mark, rose the tower, split all the way down, riddled, hacked by a thousand shells. You could see right inside it—the bell was still hanging at the top. And all at once there was a voice inside me, answering me, commanding me : Open your eyes and see, for what is happening here would in effect be senseless, useless, mere diabolical laughter, if you didn't see it. This is not a moment of world history, it is world history at a glance, under your eyes. Look at it therefore, and you will behold the Glory of God. And the dirty, exhausted human worm that I was shivered with profound bliss.

The stream had seized me again. Riflewomen standing in cars came sailing past, at once terrifying and ridiculous. Their gestures showed that they felt themselves to be representatives of Victory. I laughed to myself, although I was aware that my appearance exactly matched what they expected of the conquered.

Right and left among the ruins the remainder of the population was creeping about like half-drowned fowls. One had to look hard to discover them. Now and then they were betrayed by a weak fluttering of the wings as they were started and run down by one of the tireless sleuthhounds. They are probably searching for bread already.

Our little company was increased by a civilian, who was suddenly driven over to the Mongol from another party. In some indefinable way there appeared to be a certain system in the turmoil. The man spoke Russian, had apparently been seized as a spy, and looked like a fox in a trap. A few steps further on an idea occurred to the Mongol. He pushed the man down on a heap of stones and ordered him to take off his boots. Then he held out his feet to him, one after the other, to have his own boots pulled off, and put on the pair belonging to the man. As those left over didn't fit the latter, he was obliged, like so many others, to walk on in his socks. I doubt whether he will ever have occasion, in this life, to wear boots again.

After a time the Mongol made us halt on the left side of the street, while he disappeared down a hole. This was probably the cellar entrance of a former house, the seat of some big business concern perhaps; it was impossible to guess what had once stood there. He was lost to sight for a long while, but in the meantime other figures emerged from the hole, and still others went creeping in. This really seemed to be the command post we were seeking. The ridiculous entrance was being used with inimitable seriousness. Like underground wasps they buzzed in and out. After a time our Mongol came out too, and escorted us back without a word. We gradually got out of him that for the moment nobody felt any interest in us—later on, perhaps, in a few days' time. It obviously pained him to tell us this; he couldn't help knowing all that awaited us.

11th April

Dawn is just breaking; our operating theatre is crammed with people. A small candle-end is doing duty as illumination. We've got through the night somehow or other. Only a few Russians still haunt our basement. On the operating table lies a dead woman, who is always being attended to the moment a Russian appears. Lying on the floor, in a drowse, I can hear Doktora's voice in the next room, comforting somebody. It's a miracle she's come through this hellish night unharmed.

Just as we feared, the Russians had found some alcohol. Right alongside of us in the Menthal liqueur factory lay some thousands of gallons, carefully kept dark, saved up by the irony of fate for this very moment. Then something like a tide of rats flowed over us, worse than all the plagues of Egypt together. Not a moment went by but I had the barrel of a pistol rammed against my back or

my stomach, and a grimacing mask yelling at me for 'Sulfidin!'
So nearly all these devils must have got venereal disease. Our dispensaries were burnt out long ago, and the huge store of tablets lies
trampled to bits in the corridors. It gave me a certain wry pleasure
to be reduced to pointing, again and again, to the havoc wrought
by their fellows. They broke in from Menthal in flocks—officers,
men, riflewomen, all drunk. And not a chance of hiding anybody
from them, because the whole neighbourhood was lighted up as
bright as day by the burning buildings.

We stood close together, awaiting the end in some form or other.
The fear of death, which had hardly played any part since the
days of the bombardment, had been entirely dispelled now by
something infinitely worse. On every side we heard the despairing
screams of the women: 'Shoot me, then! Shoot me!' But the tormentors preferred a wrestling match to any actual use of their
firearms.

Soon none of the women had any strength left for resistance.
In a few hours a change came over them; their spirit died, one
heard hysterical laughter, which made the Russians madder than
ever. Is it really possible to write about these things, the most
frightful things human beings can do to one another? Isn't every
word of this an accusation of myself? Hadn't I many opportunities
of flinging myself between them and finding a decent death? Yes,
it's a sin to be still alive, and that is why none of all this must be
passed over in silence.

On my return from the town a major, who seemed more or less in
his senses, had sent for me to go to the isolation block. Thirty or
forty Russians were rampaging among the patients. I was to tell
him who these people were. Sick people, of course, what else? But
what sort of sick people, he wanted to know. Well, all sorts: scarlet
fever, typhus, diptheria . . . He gave a yell, and hurled himself like a
tank among his men. But he was too late: when the tumult had
subsided four women were dead.

Later in the day I was standing with Doktora among the milling
crowd that always blocked the exit from our basement, watching
the battlefield hyænas busily hurrying past, intent on their
purpose. We were just thinking out how we might fetch my pistol,
which with fifty cartridges I had hidden nearby under a rubbish
heap, when all at once we heard a terrific din overhead, and saw
a lot of Russians making a tremendous effort to roll the dud bomb,

which had been lying above the operating theatre for the last three days, towards the iron staircase. It was much too late to take cover. We looked at each other, laughing, and no doubt both thinking, 'It'll be worth while, anyhow, here in the midst of the densest crowd!' But then the cumbrous thing rolled back again upon itself, and was left lying peacefully on the landing.

When it was dark we succeeded in retrieving the pistol and fastening it in a handy position, against all emergencies, under the top of the operating table. Apart from this we merely carried on with whatever needed doing at the moment. For instance, we found a lot of German officers lying among the patients in the dressing-station, who had not been wounded at all; they implored us to give them civilian clothes because they thought they would be safer in them. Of course we couldn't think for a moment where to find any; then we remembered the dead who were lying on the first floor among the fallen debris. We stole up there and undressed them, as soon as the landings were more or less free of rummaging Russians.

About midnight a Russian doctor turned up in the operating theatre, accompanied by a woman in uniform. A little spark of hope glimmered again. Perhaps he would have a little fellow-feeling for us. But he was drunk too, and only out to impress his companion. He took his stand by the operating table, and went on prodding the knee of the wounded man lying there till the victim broke out into a choice Bavarian curse—'Thou sow's carrion, take thy filthy paws off my hocks!'—and released us from the spell of this atmosphere of dull resignation to fate.

It was obvious that the riflewoman saw through our manœuvre of keeping so many nurses in the theatre. I was prepared for some very dangerous move on her part where they were concerned, and was greatly relieved when she marched off, merely wrinkling her nose in contempt.

The Frenchmen were particularly decent. 'Adieu, docteur!' one of them called out to me, just as I was tackling a Russian who was about to use his tommy-gun in earnest from the middle of the crowd, because I had succeeded in driving him off. He rolled on the ground, and I retreated into the background to remove my white jacket for a time, so that he shouldn't find me again there and then. The Frenchmen must have been carried off soon after, for I never saw any of them any more.

It's touching to see how sorry for us our Russian patients are.

Four men who have been successfully operated on for abdominal injuries feel particularly obliged to us. When other Russians are present they are forced to take a high hand with us and order us about, because they're afraid. But afterwards they always apologise to us in private, and say how dreadful they think all this is.

Towards morning I found a Russian all by himself in our burnt-out dispensary. For some seconds I felt a mad thirst for revenge as he blundered along in front of me. What thoughts flashed through my brain! Moses and the Egyptian! But where should I take the body? It would be found here at once. No matter, things can't get worse than they are. No, leave him alone, he's only a poor, miserable tool.

I had a long struggle with the theatre sister, who wanted to take her own life. I begged her to stay with us for Jesus Christ's sake. No other argument has any effect now. In the end she yielded.

Oh, what envious glances the dead have to suffer! The little woman on the operating table is the symbol of peace to all those around me. What more is there to tell of the night? Now, at daybreak I've nothing left in me but the feeling that I'm standing in an empty station and have missed the last train that could have carried me away to a decent 'other side'. Indifference, the worst enemy of all, creeps slowly into one's bones.

In the forenoon only a few Russians came to bother us, but one of them is horror incarnate. Not an Asiatic, but a type one may meet with all over the world. Judging by his uniform he belongs to the Navy. His behaviour is so outrageous that I noticed him at once, and I'm keeping an eye on him. His ghastly grimacing mask keeps cropping up. Once when I was crossing the yard he was cutting the clothes off a couple of old women with a pair of scissors. They stood there afterwards as if asleep, bleeding from a number of gashes. I fetched my pistol and hid it in the big bomb crater by the main entrance, through which every intruder must pass. This would be the only chance of finding him alone. I hung about there for a long while, feeling cold and apathetic. Then I had to give it up because there was something wrong in the main building again.

When I went into the operating theatre later on I realised at once that something had happened. The nurses looked at me with terrified faces. Doktora was standing by the table dressing wounds as usual. But those eyes! My God! A knife ran through what was left of my soul. I crept out and dropped down somewhere on an iron bedstead. Now sleep, sleep, and see nothing more. It's enough.

After a time I found her standing beside me in her torn training suit, trying to comfort me with her hand. 'Will you please find my Bible for me?' she said. 'It must be lying about somewhere on the landing. It was dragged out of my pocket.' I went looking for the Bible in a purblind daze, and found it. Then we sat side by side for a time on the bedstead without moving. She wants me to get away. On my own, I'd be certain to get out somehow and reach the west. 'There's nothing more you can do here. I've got my tablets, and anyway I know God doesn't demand the impossible.' I was far too tired to answer, and I should have loathed the sound of my own voice. I saw pretty clearly what must have happened in my absence. It could only be that devil she had foundered on—the Power of Darkness, against which there is no defence. (I read the confirmation of this, months later, in the notes she left me : 'I felt afraid for the first time in all those months,' she wrote, 'I knew at once there was no escape.')

The Russian was nowhere to be seen. We walked down a little way towards the edge of the Castle pond, where a number of up-turned boats were lying about on the grass. There was nobody looking. I wrapped Doktora in a tarpaulin and pushed her under one of the boats.

In the afternoon the whole building was full of Russians again; they were starting fires everywhere. A house alongside of us burned so rapidly from below upwards that our own roof caught fire. The experts declared that it couldn't reach us in the basement, but for safety's sake I gave the order to evacuate all the same. To make a beginning, I carried a fat man, with a recently fractured thigh in a stretching appliance, on my back down to the Castle ditch leading from the pond. With astonishing rapidity the house emptied behind me, and after repeated pauses all those unable to walk were dragged over the little footbridge to the opposite slope.

The Russians had become very active again, and were racketing about in our midst. Doktora, who in spite of my pleading had taken part in the transport, was suddenly fallen upon by three quite young lads and carried off. I ran limply after them; a couple of shots from a tommy-gun passing close to my head stunned me for a moment. Czernecki was just going by with a Russian major and tried to intervene, but in vain—the major laughed him to scorn. Doktora soon freed herself—they were only raw, foolish boys— and hid herself among the patients on the slope, content to lie quiet there at last.

Meanwhile I noticed that another caravan of nurses and patients, carried, led, more or less crawling along, was also making for our slope. They belonged to the Samaritan Hospital, which because of perpetual outbreaks of fire had had to be evacuated too. Soon the whole mound was occupied by patients, with the Russians tearing about among them like a horde of baboons, carrying off nurses and patients at random, tormenting them, demanding watches for the hundredth time. Mine is still safe round my ankle, between two pairs of stockings. With my pockets turned inside out, I went in and out among the patients. It was bitterly cold; snow showers fell on us. The patients were complaining, some were getting abusive, a good many had begun talking to the Russians in a none too reassuring manner. The last shreds of internal order were cracking.

I sat by Doktora for a little while. She was lying quite still under a blanket, crying. A Russian had helped her to carry a sick girl, and that had released her tears. I was glad she was at last giving way.

I left her alone again, so as not to betray her whereabouts; the Russian major was on the hunt for her. When he was no longer to be seen I reconnoitred the immediate surroundings. Our buildings were not burning now, but fire might break out again at any moment, and I had to look about for some emergency shelter for the patients, as night was not far off. On the road along the upper pond, which looks like a ploughed field, little carts were being driven to and fro, getting stuck in the mud, working free again, hurrying on. I had to keep reminding myself that this was once Königsberg.

In my once white surgeon's coat I reached the Dohna Tower unhindered; it was swarming with Russians. There are supposed to be some remains of a German hospital about there. I walked determinedly towards the entrance, and was allowed through the barrier unquestioned. In the rooms at the rear I found several German medical officers, a staff surgeon and some assistant doctors. They have a few wounded under their care. They have no idea what is to become of them. The Russians are busy at the walls outside—perhaps the Tower is to be blown up; anything is possible. We cracked a few bad jokes. They fed me with peppermint drops out of a big glass jar they had rescued. On the table lay a Russian, groaning horribly, with an abscess in his knee-cap that had got to be lanced. They were just considering what sort of narcotic they should regale him with. I seized the knife and cut into the abscess with gusto. The Russian, greatly taken aback, was suddenly quiet, and let himself be carried away, quite pacified. As nothing further was happening at the moment I took my leave, inviting my colleagues to pay us a return visit if they were not blown up meanwhile.

As darkness set in, the staff of the Samaritan Hospital got on the move to take their patients to Maraunenhof, where a couple of empty houses are said to have been allotted them. I can't imagine how they will get that far. We were left alone with our lot, and began to move back into our basements. I shouldered a fairly heavy man again, and had just crossed the little bridge when I was stopped by a Russian. He was accompanied by Tamara, one of our Russian nurses of the old Fortress days, already rigged out as a riflewoman and gesticulating in character. I begged her to help me, as the Russian was molesting my patient. She whispered, 'I'm frightened, too, today,' and went on playing the madwoman. I had to let the man drop. The Russian ransacked him, then shot him in the stomach as though by inadvertence, and went on. The man sat there looking at me questioningly. Couldn't I put him out of his misery? I gave him a shot of morphia and left him lying on the path. Before going on I looked up the slope once more, to absorb the sight of it into myself before it was cleared. Up at the top there, against the sky, the Cross should have been standing.

The next moment I went limp. I had cracked my breastbone, a thing that in normal times would probably have bothered me a good deal, but was now a quite welcome dispensation. The others went on lugging their burdens along with the remains of their strength. A new colleague who has lately joined us helped us with a will. Czernecki has left, and so have the foreign patients. On the slope, at midnight, there were only eight figures left lying, all dead, among them our theatre sister.

The town is burning at every point. Aircraft circle over it, continually dropping fresh incendiary bombs into the ruins. Meanwhile our tormentors have suddenly vanished off the face of the earth. A Russian has told us that our district is now being cordoned off to be blown up. It's all the same to us. I've fetched my pistol again, and all the sleeping tablets and narcotics to be found, with the last remaining hypodermic, and deposited the lot in our latest hide-out.

To think we hadn't tumbled to it before! Behind the windows of the bricked-up operating theatre there is an empty space about two feet deep, imperceptible from the inside, in the bad lighting, even when one is standing right in front of it. Behind each of the three windows there is room for two people. Now the nurses sit there by turns, and we quartered Doktora there for part of the night. I sat beside her for a time, reading to her from the Epistle to the Hebrews, which she is so fond of. 'We have an High Priest, which hath pity . . .' We have all grown very quiet. I have promised to shoot them all if we are buried and can't get out. That has calmed them for the moment.

Below us, on the floor, lies Dr. Hasten with severed arteries. He was brought in in the morning from the Samaritan Hospital, where he had been found lying when it was cleared out. One of the nurses who brought him gave me Bothmer's last greeting. She was present when he was wounded on the 8th April; he died on the 10th.

12th April

The night has gone by without any special incident. About five o'clock the front building began burning again. Most of the basements could still be evacuated, only two very sick people were left in one of them. It was impossible to reach them. The fire was so fierce that there seemed little hope of putting it out with our insufficient equipment. All the same we made the attempt, more to deaden ourselves than by way of self-defence. We formed a long chain, starting from the well, along which all available buckets and containers were passed from hand to hand, drawn up by ropes from the depths. The Russians went on throwing in incendiary bombs and firing anti-tank guns from the street, but in spite of this we managed to get the fire under control, taking it in turns to advance with our faces protected. When it was all over, Gudat, our treasurer, who had turned up again from somewhere or other, came to fetch me for a scouting expedition through the town. He had heard of a command post somewhere near the University Clinics.

Blackened with smoke we started off. The streets were almost empty; the main body of the Russians seems to have been withdrawn. Big formations of aircraft are still flying westward : one dare not think of all that is still in store for our people over there. They have receded into such a dim distance that our thoughts can no longer reach them.

We wandered like ghosts through the deserted streets. Here and there a Russian, if we asked him for the 'Kommandatur', pointed towards the Chemical Institute beyond the Castle. There we fell in with a pitiable crowd of people, who had obviously been wandering round for the last three days with nothing to eat and no roof over their heads. Their houses had been burnt down; nobody took any notice of them; there were a lot of mothers with small children among them.

Suddenly three Russians appeared, separated about fifty of us from the crowd and took us along to the former Red Cross shelter in the courtyard of the Medical Clinic. The place has been laid surprisingly open to view since I was there last. Under the impression that this was the command post we were looking for, we waited impatiently to be admitted. After we had stood there for a time a Russian came up to me, hung his loot-sack round me and a military cape over my shoulders, and ordered each of us to take two full tins of vegetables off a pile that was standing there. Then we were surrounded by a number of armed Russians and marched away in close formation out of the town gates. I first tried to protest, then looked hastily round for some chance of escape. Gudat held me back, it was no use. On the instant a heavy stone fell away from my heart. I was a prisoner—free. Free from all that appalling responsibility. I felt like Jonah in the whale's belly, waiting with a thankful heart to see where it would spew me ashore again. My second life had begun.

Loudly whistling, I walked along at the tail of the procession. People looked round at me with disapproval. No, with the best will in the world I couldn't feel sad now. Life was so immense. It would be a pity to let the joy of it escape one; and the only prayer left to me was for a spark of humour and an open eye for all that might come.

We went past the smoking ruins of the Town Hall and the Northern Railway Station. The surface of the road had been torn up by bombs. The Gestapo Prison—that was still standing, more or less—it would be! Down the General-Litzmann-strasse—one huge gutter. Keep your eyes open! Yes, but they simply can't take in any more; seeing has its limits somewhere.

Where could they be taking us? To the sea, perhaps, and thence by ship to Russia? It was all the same to me. My Bible, torn from my pocket a hundred times, was still there—for the moment I needed nothing more.

We came to a halt at the town boundary. Everybody sat down at the edge of the road and dozed. The sun was shining, but it was cold. It crossed my mind that twenty-three years to the day had gone by since we came as children to Trakehnen, where the loveliest time of our life had begun. It was just such a day as this : the starlings were whistling in the bare trees; then they swept away before the wind into the clear East Prussian countryside and took my whole heart with them.

I did not join in any attempt to deal with our escort; it was completely useless. There was no chance of getting any information out of them, only the risk of a hefty blow with the butt of a rifle. Hardly two of my companions belonged to one another; their relatives were waiting somewhere in the vast field of ruins for their return, but there was little hope of their ever seeing one another again. And all this was being accepted with the utmost calm, as a matter of course. What was happening to us wasn't anything out of the ordinary, it was nothing but what millions of people had been going through for years. It was simply the new way of behaving to one another, less out of hatred than—well, lack of imagination. I today, thou tomorrow.

We went through the completely annihilated Fuchsberg district. The towns and villages looked like half-decayed fishes standing up in the air with their bare bones. To all appearance we were being taken to the front. We could see the bombers that came roaring over us circling not far away, calmly selecting a target and coming back again, while over there one smoke mushroom after another went up. So our men must still be sitting there in their dug-outs. What must it be like to see death falling straight upon one in that way!

Because of the fast traffic on the road we were forced to walk in the slippery fields alongside. Vehicles carrying 'Stalin organs' and other heavy weapons were driving to and fro, regular V.I.P.s, with their staff of servicing personnel. 'Gitlair kapoot!' the men yelled in triumph as they overtook us. Hats off, thought I, if it's taken all *this* to bring *that* about!

By the evening we had left Königsberg some fifteen miles behind us. Two old people had fallen by the way, the remainder were still there. To the right of the road there stood a little farm, towards which we were led. A few Poles were living there, probably auxiliary labourers left behind. We were first crammed into the smithy, but there wasn't room for everybody. So then they decided to quarter us in the cowstall, where we should at least have a roof over our heads. It was cold; we pressed close together on the floor. Gudat and I lay at the foot of a flight of stairs running the length of the building.

When it was dark our escort came with bull's-eye lanterns and routed us all up. The women, whimpering or cursing, were dragged out with the help of the Poles. This unending devilry! *'Davai suda!'* 'Woman come!' It has a more horrific sound than all the curses in the world. When that which should signify Life stands under the sign of Death, Satan's triumph has reached its zenith. It didn't matter to them in the least that they were handling semi-corpses. Eighty-year-old women were no safer from them than unconscious ones. (At one time a patient of mine with head injuries, as I discovered later, had been raped over and over again without knowing anything about it.)

13th April

That night, too, went by. To be still alive is a standing reproach. Stiff and bewildered we were routed out in the morning twilight. The ground was frozen hard. We ate the remains of the tinned food cold, and then were made to stumble on in a north-westerly direction behind the front. My heavy military cape weighed me down almost to the ground; other people were lugging all sorts of things along, with the idea of being able to use them again at some time.

The surface of the ground began thawing again in the morning sun. We climbed a long, slippery hill of clay and suddenly found ourselves close behind the front. We suspected that we were to be recruited. I shouldn't have minded, and Gudat said he wouldn't be averse either. I let him know that this was my birthday. Thirty-five, a round number.

But they seemed to be getting on all right without us. The artillery was firing away over our heads from the rear; we saw the heavy clods flying. When we reached the top of the hill the sea lay spread out before our eyes. So that at least is still there! One was prepared for anything. Neukuhren, which lay nearest, was being heavily shelled. We were led a little nearer over the field as far as a narrow, wooded valley, the flanks of which were pitted with dugouts. Our escort appropriated some of these at once, and met other soldiers there, who had a party like ours to guard. We remained in the open at first, sitting at the edge of a little wood, apparently as a target for any German aircraft that might turn up. But none appeared. Meanwhile a whole swarm of Russian planes was circling over the hapless little town in front of us.

After a time I was singled out, with two other men and three women, and led into the wood. We were to stay there and boil potatoes for the whole party. This, all at once! And again as a matter of course! Potatoes were lying about in heaps, there was a big tin pail at hand, and water in a little stream running through the valley. We slipped a rod under the handle of the pail and hung it on two forked branches we had driven into the ground. Then we lighted a fire under it. Going in search of wood I clambered up the opposite slope and surveyed the field. Close in front of me stood a quick-firing gun, from the muzzle of which some hundreds of shots issued every few seconds. I heard the hits re-echoing from Neukuhren like the slow collapsing of a wooden hut. I began ruminating thoughts of escape, but I could see that it would be impossible to get through on this side by daylight.

The sight of the boiled potatoes warmed one's heart. One of the three women shared a piece of bacon with us. The women are going almost barefoot already; their shoes were not made for such marches. After our meal we sat for a while dozing on the slope. Then a Russian appeared with an axe, and showed us how to build a shelter for ourselves out of branches. With our united efforts we erected a hut like those we used to build on a smaller scale, as children, for the Easter Hare. We went into it in the evening. The rain came through, but we had a certain feeling of security.

When it was dark they began all at once to take an interest in us individually. Close in front of us, in a dug-out on the slope, a little square-built Russian had established himself, and now sent for us one after another. Towards midnight it was my turn. Bending double I crept into the shelter, in which a stove threw out an exceedingly pleasant warmth, and immediately resolved to make my interrogation last as long as possible. Apart from the stove there was only room for a short camp bed and a small table. The Russian and I sat on the bed, with a Polish interpreter in front of us on the floor. The few papers I had left on me were thoroughly examined. Then the interrogation started. Listening to the details I was giving about my family circumstances, landed property, and possessions, the number of horses, cows, pigs, sheep, geese, ducks, hens my relations had possessed, the Pole rolled his eyes and asked if I was crazy; it was absurd to tell the fellow all that stuff. He evinced the most touching sympathy for me; he knew what country life was like, having worked on an estate himself for a long while. When the Russian left us alone for a minute he told me he had lived very comfortably in Königsberg for the last two years, and earned no less than forty thousand marks.

The Russian hadn't been able to get all he wanted out of me, and sent for another expert to help him. This one was a bit more cultivated, spoke good German, and questioned me about medical affairs. I asked him what they intended doing with me, and he began talking about big modern clinics in Moscow and Odessa. I was to work there as a surgeon. My over-excited imagination at once transported me to an entirely different world. I saw cube-shaped rooms with walls of black glass, in which a couple of silent men were working. Everything was dark, only their hands glowed. All that had belonged to me up to now was submerged. Nirvana . . . Russia!

When the interrogation was ended—the Pole had long since been allowed to shove himself under the bed—I signed five closely written sheets of a questionnaire. I had no notion what was in them, as I didn't know what sort of lies the Pole had told the Russian for my sake. Then I was led away and shut up with those of our party who had made the most dangerous impression—twelve men, including a public prosecutor, Gudat, and a railway employee on account of his blue uniform. We lay in a little dug-out in two layers, one over the other. There was a barbed-wire fence outside, with two sentries in front of it. The second half of the night was chiefly taken up, as before, with the rape of the women nearby.

At daybreak they fetched us out of our hole again. We rose like Lazarus from the grave—once again, after all. We had fully expected they would blow us up or do something solemn with us; we were gradually getting ripe for some ritual sacrifice.

Cold is much worse than hunger. In one's wet clothes one's main endeavour is to move as little as possible. Facial expression grows benumbed in the same way. One can't laugh any more, except deep inside.

Our procession got slowly under way, we twelve dangerous ones in the van, the other forty, including the women, in the rear. Most of them were already finding it difficult to get along. We went up the hill again and then westwards behind the front, which was already fairly far ahead. The villages were smoking, the inhabitants nowhere to be seen. The farmyards, riddled by bombs, were covered with bed-feathers. Not a fowl, no livestock of any kind except a couple of half-wild dogs. And the smell of burning! I shall never get that smell out of my nostrils again.

After a few halts in the wet fields beside the road we reached the high road to Rauschen towards evening, and turned north-wards along it. Where it forks—to the right towards Kranz through Pobethen, to the left towards Rauschen—there lay two long potato clamps in which innumerable Russians were digging. We were drawing nearer to the advanced lines again. The stretch between the fork in the road and the next town, Watsum, was a terrible sight. There had obviously been strong resistance shown here a short time before. The houses on the right-hand slope, dotted about singly, had not been burnt down but riddled by shell-fire. The trees hung in splinters, the field had been churned up by bombs. There were many dead lying in the ditches or rolled flat on the road. But none of these things impressed us particularly at the time; the longing for warmth was so overwhelming that the sight of the burning town in front of us stifled every other feeling. Just before crossing the Samland railway line we met the first detachment of captured troops. To think that people have actually come alive out of this inferno! With grey, expressionless faces they went stumbling past us towards the east. I made an effort to nod to them, but had to turn my head away again. One dare not look at them.

We dragged our feet at the slowest possible pace on our way between the burning houses, to make the most of the warmth. As we left the place the icy wind met us again, driving wet snow in our faces. Because of a blown-up bridge we bore to the left, and beheld a column of vehicles and guns, lighted by torches, crossing the little marshy valley in front of us. The heavy machines pitched to and fro like elephants through the morass. On the opposite side the troops were gathering round a number of fires. There were some powerful, clean-cut figures among them, the sight of which had something reconciling about it.

Soon after this we came to a halt and squatted down or stood with our backs to the wind. When it was quite dark we went a bit further, to a farmhouse standing by itself, that was still more or less undamaged. A trap-door in the floor was opened, and we twelve dangerous ones found ourselves in the cellar, a hole about six feet long, wide and deep. Because of the potatoes in it one could only stand in a stooping position. A little Russian, who must have had a punishment to serve, was shoved in with us, and then the trap was closed. One of our fellow-prisoners still had some matches about him, and another a candle, so that we could at least inspect our lodging. First we had to portion out the space. Six men could lie on their side in a row, the others must squat at their feet with their backs against the wall or against each other, until they were relieved. The poor public prosecutor was in a bad way; he had a high temperature and frightful diarrhoea, and was horrified at being such a nuisance to us. The Russian horde was rioting overhead with the female part of our main company, which was lodged in the upper rooms.

15th April

The night went by, and the whole of the next day, without any change in our situation. Once, towards noon, we were hauled out and taken to a ditch running behind the farmyard. I ventured another attempt to escape, going a little distance along the ditch, but was driven back by the picket. The next minute found us squatting in our cellar-hole again. We had long ago given up speculating as to what they really intended doing with us.

The Russian was the only one of us to be given any food, but in the evening the Polish interpreter brought us, secretly, a few boiled potatoes. Then a second night went by in this confined state. At least we were not cold. On the other hand we sat there as if in a wet pack. The first vermin made its appearance, and we could do nothing about it. I was glad it was dark, so that we couldn't distinguish one another's faces.

16th April

At four in the morning we were driven out of the cellar. The sky was starlit and it was freezing. We went on in a westerly direction. The public prosecutor hung heavily on my arm for a little way, then he was flung on the wagon at our rear because he kept falling on his knees at every step and was holding up the march.

The renewed cold paralysed my capacity for decision for the time being. I let myself be driven along, but dragged my feet more and more awkwardly to avert any suspicion of flight, for I had gradually come to the conclusion that one need not consent to this folly that was leading one slowly but surely to death, so long as one could feel a spark of self-assertion within.

At daybreak we reached the high road leading to Palmnicken. I now acquired a very accurate picture of a considerable part of the Samland, for a man harbouring ideas of flight sees the countryside with quite different eyes from those of a man driving through it unconcernedly in a car. Every rise in the ground, every clump of trees becomes important and imprints itself on the mind. On reaching the high road we turned northwards again towards the sea. The farms on our left made a pitiful impression; isolated cattle with serious shell wounds stood motionless in the wide fields. A stork, which had probably just come from the south, was fired at with tommy-guns by the Russians at our head. It rose into the air, astonished, and winged its way towards Gross Germau, which lay before us on a little hill. Above the town a volley of a hundred shots brought it down like a stone.

In Gross Germau we turned off to the left and went on to the next village. The Russians appeared to have only recently broken in there. A few old people were running aimlessly to and fro, while their possessions were dragged out of the houses and either destroyed or loaded on to lorries. I took a good look at the surrounding country. A few hundred yards to the north there was a wood running down in a narrow strip to the sea; I should have to try and reach it.

We were driven into a little wooden shed, through the chinks in the walls of which the wind whistled. Every now and then we got a cold douche into the bargain from the pond, which the Russians were splashing up with hand grenades. Through the open door we could watch the looting going on. The most useless objects, sofas, lampshades, life-size photographs and other tasteful pictures were being hurriedly thrown into the yard and carted off on lorries, while old cupboards and tables were broken up for firewood. There were no animals left alive here either.

Our public prosecutor was very ill; he lay on the floor and hardly moved. One of our guards came along with a big black-bearded man, the resident country doctor of the district. He was ordered to examine the sick man, who was then carried off to be housed elsewhere. We were given a couple of fresh people in his place, among them a well-fed farmer of my own age, still in good shape. I took careful stock of him, in case he should be prepared to escape with me as soon as an opportunity presented itself.

The Russians were still busy sorting out the inhabitants. When that was over they fetched us out and shut us up in a partition in the loft, through the lattice wall of which we could have communicated with the less dangerous ones, but we were all far too worn out by then to profit by the occasion.

We were brought down again at dusk and drawn up in two lines in the yard. It was rumoured that some lorries were to come and take us to our final destination. The aforementioned farmer was standing beside me, and I told him in a whisper that I should probably make a dash for it in a moment, and asked if he felt like coming with me. He made no answer. And of course it couldn't be done just so; something else would have to happen if we were to evade the pickets. But I was waiting for that something with my whole strength, like a racehorse at the start.

And then came the signal for our departure. The Russians must have thought the war was at an end, for light-rockets shot up suddenly into the evening sky from several points at once. 'Gitlair kapoot!' yelled our guards, and went quite mad with delight. I broke out of the ranks on the instant, heard a terrified hubbub behind me, got round the pond, thirty, forty paces—still no shot. I vanished behind a wall and ran towards the wood. Far away behind me things were stirring; a few shots fell. Fortunately it was very foggy. The Russians I ran past took no notice of me. I ran on in one of the many defence trenches, clambered out again, became invisible against the dark wood, and dived into it unharmed.

Freedom! Freedom! Like a moon-calf I lived in a frenzy of joy for some minutes, with no care for what might follow. The mouse has escaped—have a care how you catch it again!

Seated on a hummock in the thick undergrowth, I took stock of the tract of country I had left behind me. It was woodcock flighting time. A thousand peaceful memories crowded in upon me. What a miracle life is!

My thoughts turned to people who were no more. My cousin Heinrich Lehndorff stood before me. A year ago, in the winter, we were still going shooting together in his wood by the Mauersee, picturing to ourselves what it would be like to live there together as 'partisans' after the catastrophe. Might not our homeland then reveal its deepest significance to us for the first time?

Half a year later he came to see me one night in Insterburg, and told me about the attempt on the Führer's life that was planned for a few days ahead. What he wanted to know was whether I was prepared to be at disposal if they needed another assistant. As I was already aware that I should be asked this, I had begged a young pastor whom I trusted to go to the railway station with me. Sitting there on a bench for some hours we sought counsel in the Scriptures. The thirteenth chapter of the Epistle to the Romans gave us the most trouble—how could it be otherwise? 'Let every soul be subject unto the higher powers . . . the powers that be are ordained of God.' Must one, as a Christian, responsible for one's country, really put up with everything? Must one go on idly watching a madman dragging the nation to destruction? One thing at least became clear to us: the Apostle Paul gave one no right of appeal to the Epistle, to save one's own soul. He only helped us to realise with what a weighty decision we were confronted. The choice lay simply between guilt and guilt.

Days of frightful spiritual tension followed for me. I kept asking myself where I should find the strength to walk up to a man with an explosive machine in my pocket and kill him with it. Shouldn't I suddenly feel closely bound to him, with the duty to do everything to warn him? Or—still more difficult to overlook—suppose there was a latent possibility not to destroy the man but to make known the Law of God to him in such a way that his eyes would be opened? How terrible, if perhaps one had been unable to conceive of this possibility because of one's own spiritual incapacity!

The 20th June, with its frightful reality, brought this dilemma to an end. And while I myself remained safe from any suspicion, I knew my cousin to be first under capital arrest, and then in flight through the forest—not from the Russians but from Hitler's executioners, until he fell into their hands again through betrayal. Compared with that, all I was going through now was merely child's play!

When it was quite dark I got up and began walking on in an eastward direction. A camouflage jacket was hanging on a branch, and I took it with me. I crept cautiously along inside a young plantation. Firelight was visible in several places, and Russians could be heard felling trees. I came to the older woodland again, and took a path that led further into the main stock. Suddenly I felt that something was trying to hold me back. Pricking up my ears, I thought I heard movements, and then, a few paces in front of me, I noticed the remains of a smouldering fire. I heard myself being hailed, and ran, first straight on and then round through the underwood. Two lights were coming after me. At the next boundary stone I gained on them, turned sharply to the left, tried to shelter in one of the many dug-outs, jumped out again and hid close beside it under a little drooping spruce. My pursuers ran past me, a hand-grenade flew into the dug-out, the sand spurted towards me. I lay at full length, waiting for the next few hours to go by.

17th April

The night passed extraordinarily quickly; I must have slept

without knowing it. Timber was being felled not far from my hiding-place, and heavy vehicles were being driven along a road in both directions. The wood nearest me was too thin to hide in by daylight; I must find a better place before it grew light, seeking cover like a wounded boar. Close by ran a wood-path, and behind it on the left lay a thick fir plantation that was very tempting. But I had to reckon on the wood being combed, and the densest parts would be the first to be searched. The big clearing on the right looked more promising; there were only quite low fir-trees left on it, which from a distance would hardly suggest protection for a human being. I dashed over the path and lay down under a clump of these trees which was surrounded by nutbushes. Two paces away lay one of the many dug-outs, connected to another by a communication trench.

It was hardly light when the hunt began again. A ceaseless rattle of small-arms of every size gave me some idea of the steps that were being taken to clear the wood. The plantation beside me was combed through for hours; there might be some German soldier hidden in it. It was pouring cats and dogs, and this uncomfortable fact became my sheet anchor at the moment when I heard dogs baying; the rain was my only hope against them.

Aircraft were circling close above the treetops; they were going to some expense over this hunt. I'd turned quite cold, and observed all this as if from a great distance. The times when I had wounded game, out shooting, which had haunted me ever since, recurred to me now, no longer as a nightmare but as debts that were being wiped out. There was no longer any distance between myself and the suffering animal.

About midday a series of shots from close at hand swept through the bushes over me. Immediately afterwards a Russian stood in front of the dug-out, deliberating; that is to say, I could just see his feet, which I could have touched by stretching out my hand. I wasn't certain whether I was sufficiently hidden from above, but I dared not move to make sure. A few seconds went by, during which I felt exactly like a hare—then the feet went on again and vanished from my field of vision. A little later the situation became critical again when several Russians pushed through the bushes at the same time. I drew up my knees and waited, ready to make a dash. I wasn't going to let myself be shot lying down. Then even that was over and I was left in peace at last.

Late in the evening the rattling came to an end. I lay on my back and tried to sleep, but the cold and the rain kept me awake. I sucked a little moisture out of my wet sleeve; the feeling of hunger had passed long ago. All round me there was a rustling in the bushes, and blue lights flashed before my eyes. The shadows thickened gradually above me; two great birds with outspread wings rocked on the thin branches. When I made an effort to see them more clearly they dissolved into the indistinct greyness of the night. But then there they were again, beginning to whisper to each other. I wished they would fly away and leave me in peace. But they wouldn't leave off, they entangled me more and more in their confidential talk—till I rose to my feet with a jerk.

It may have been about midnight. The birds had vanished, but without further reflection I started on my way. I crossed the big fir plantation in a south-east direction, left the wood, went through pastures intersected by deep ditches, crossed the Palmnicker high road and landed up on the other side in a little wood. I kept picking myself up without having been aware of falling. Fires were smouldering round the edge of the wood. I made a detour round them and went past lighted windows along a slippery country road towards the east, till another little wood swallowed me up. There I lay down and gave up all attempt to come to any fresh decision. The feeling of that place becoming gradually covered with snow was a last, lingering memory.

I had only lain there for a little while when I heard the two voices talking above me again. 'He must get away from here. We can't leave him lying here in the middle of the road.' It went on like that without stopping, till I could stand it no longer, and forced myself to get up again. I had actually been lying in the middle of a road, right across some deep wheel-tracks. I crawled along a wire fence towards the nearest house and dropped down on the doorstep. My flight into freedom had come to an end.

A Russian in underpants opened the door and called out to me; then he summoned two other Russians, who fetched me in. Sitting on the floor, I was stared at by all three like some curious animal. One of them pushed his billy-can of soup towards me—then for the first time hunger overcame me. I said grace, and began eating, slowly, cautiously, like a child taking its first steps. Eating and being were one and the same at that moment.

Food and warmth set me on my feet again. The man in the underpants led me across the yard to the barn, where by the light of his lantern I saw a lot of people lying in the straw. I lay down among them and slept well into the day.

18th April

In the morning there was a slight frost again. I found myself in the midst of a company of women with small children, elderly men and a few half-grown boys. We lighted a fire in the yard, between two bricks, and boiled some potatoes. The guards let us carry on. The women and children, one of which is still being pushed along in a pram, come from villages as much as twelve miles away. They have been driven around for some days; the soles of their shoes are worn through, their clothes are dirty and quite insufficient for the cold weather. They have brought a few things with them on hand-carts all this way. Some of them are complete strangers to the district; they were living there as evacuees, with relatives, when the Russians arrived. Several little children have died during the last few days; their mothers have no time to grieve over them, they are too busy looking after those that are left. They have been given nothing to eat, but in the intervals of the march they have been able to boil potatoes, which are lying about everywhere.

At midday my new company got slowly under way. Marching eastwards we crossed the high road, and then went on along a deeply rutted muddy track, half under water, towards a village lying on higher ground. Our troop became widely scattered, because the women found their hand-carts getting stuck. When after endless effort we reached the place, we found we were not allowed to occupy it. We turned off towards the north, and reached Craam, a village about a mile and a quarter distant. On the way there some of the women at the end of the line were dragged away from their children into a solitary house on the left, and only set free again after a long while. They are used to it, it's the same everywhere.

Just short of Craam we encamped in a meadow near the village pond. The place is obviously an assembly point for Russian military vehicles. The farmyards are full of tanks and guns. Fresh ones come in, others are driven away. There was no room for us here either; we had to go on again towards the east, this time along the high road. Vehicles went rushing by. We had to do long stretches through deep plough, advancing only at a snail's pace. Towards evening we reached the village of St. Lorenz, lying higher and looking like a menacing skeleton. We halted beside a barn, and in a few minutes a lot of little fires were burning, with something cooking over them. A sack of soaked peas, which I had dragged out of the village ditch, was hailed with delight.

Soon we had to go on again, straight ahead for a time, as far as the road to Rauschen and then in the opposite direction towards the village of Watsum, which I had passed through once before. A great coming and going here too. A woman in a nun's habit was pushing a blind, paralysed man along beside me in a wheelbarrow. I asked where she was going. She was making for Königsberg, because the blind man's house had become too uncomfortable for him with all the Russians about. For a moment I felt I ought to dissuade her from her senseless attempt, to enlighten her as to what awaited her in Königsberg. But then I felt it would be kinder not to deprive her and the man of their illusions. By all human calculations there was no hope of their reaching their goal. She was having to stop every five minutes and set down her burden; it couldn't be long before one of the vehicles hurtling heedlessly past put an end to their misery, and sent her protégé, at any rate, into a better kingdom.

The straggling village of Watsum was a scene of wild commotion. The houses had been shot to bits and the ruins occupied by the Russians. Some of them were still burning. After many vain attempts to find accommodation for our party, we ended up at the railway station in total darkness. Meanwhile we had met with several other parties like ours, coming from Königsberg, looking wild and distraught already. No roof had been found to cover them either.

The station building, which we ended by occupying, had just been accidentally freed. In the basement there were a few sofas, the coverings of which had been ripped off as usual. Here our guard settled in. A few days earlier German soldiers had been sitting there, with Russian shell fire crashing through above them. A lot had happened since.

The two rooms in which we were housed were full of a mixture of straw and unspeakable filth. After clearing out the worst of the dirt we lay down sardine-fashion on the floor. Mutual warmth outweighed all the loathing we have gradually acquired for one another, not so much on account of the vermin, or our scrubby, unwashed, miserable appearance, as because mutual courtesy has been worn away. My only comfort in this respect is a fifteen-year-old lad from Palmnicken, Helmut Z., who treats me with great civility and consideration in spite of my horrible appearance, and has even shared a bit of bacon with me that he had salvaged. He has only been dragged along with our party for three days, and still has considerably more energy than I possess.

All through the night two of us men were made to stand sentry on the stairs. For what purpose, and against whom, we were not informed. We have long ago left off asking for reasons. I myself took a turn at it, utterly frozen in the horrible draught. We haven't taken off our clothes for a fortnight, we've been wet through and frozen for a week, we can hardly walk properly, and yet nobody is actually ill, nobody feels any symptom of a chill or any sort of organic disturbance. Our bodies are behaving far better than we could have expected.

19th April

They let us out by day on to what was once the platform. The men stood about, half stupefied, at a little distance from a cauldron in which the Russians were boiling soup for themselves and those of the women they favoured. As there was to be none for us, we crept away from the wind and drizzling rain into the dug-out under the platform, and lit a fire there between some bricks. Alongside the rails water was spurting out of a drainpipe, and Helmut Z. persuaded me to wash at least my hands and face in it; I couldn't have summoned up enough energy to do it of my own accord. We took advantage of a moment when nobody was looking to climb up the bank on all fours as far as one of the many dug-outs in it. There we found a sack of coarse rye-meal. We emptied out enough to allow us to drag the sack behind us, and reached the platform again unobserved. The men had put one of the cooking-pots that were lying about upon the fire, and we crumbled the lumps of rye-meal into it, accompanied by good advice. I avoided looking round the circle. In their miserable avidity the wild figures reminded me of pictures by Hoegfeldt; and when one is a like figure oneself one lacks the sense of humour to make it bearable.

While the porridge was cooking—during which a dispute arose as to whether it should be stirred or not—it occurred to me that I had been here once before. Twenty years ago, when I was on my way to Rauschen with a jolly crowd, the train stopped at this station. I remembered it quite clearly; it was a hot summer day, the rye was getting ripe. And it seems to me that even then I had felt heavy-hearted, with a foreboding of what is now being fulfilled.

When the porridge was ready it was dished out in every sort

of container. It far exceeded my expectations. How could people have fed only pigs on it before? While we were eating it some of the Russians came past, tied up a cow on the platform and went into the station building. With a big tin in my hand I ran up in all haste to the cow, and while Helmut Z. stood on the look-out I succeeded in drawing a few pints of milk before the soldiers came back. But the tin must have had vitriol or something of the kind in it at one time, and we could do nothing with the milk. Even we men couldn't drink it, and the children's mothers refused it with tears in their eyes. For the rest of the day we went on cooking rye, so to speak on a running belt, and distributing it.

In the afternoon one of the many Russians going past stopped and talked to us for a while. When it was dark he turned up again with a pair of felt boots that fitted me. He couldn't have come by day, he said hurriedly, and made off again. I watched him disappear with a thankful heart, but to the joyful anticipation of warm feet there crept the contrasting feeling : How much simpler would everything be if we had no sort of human contact with him and his kind.

20th April

The second night at the station went by like the first. In the afternoon we men were taken to Rauschen, while the women were left behind. What is to become of them we don't know.

My outfit at the time was composed as follows : a short-sleeved tropical shirt, a pair of underpants, a pair of cotton trousers eighteen inches too big in the waist, which I had found on the road, and over them my own long trousers tied round my ankles, a jacket inherited from a relation, the military cape, the felt boots and a hat I had likewise picked up. In a bag over my shoulder I carried my old shoes and the camouflage jacket I had found.

The weather was a bit better, the sun shone now and again. Traffic on the road was still unusually lively, and the air was full of aircraft making for Pillau. I recognised a lot of East Prussian horses harnessed to the carts, and bestridden by riders, which had grown quite spiritless, broken in to the horrible high-stepping gait always forced upon them—goose-step at the gallop. It's torture to hear them tearing past along the road, necks bent backwards, heads crooked, mouths torn and bleeding.

The big farm on the right before you get to Rauschen is quite undamaged. The new buildings with their red roofs have a challenging appearance in this desert. In Rauschen they quartered us at the rear of a motor repair shop. This spot is familiar to me too : a few weeks before the outbreak of war I got my car repaired here. For the sake of completeness one now lives the reverse side of everything.

Squatting close together on the floor, we were guarded by a kindly, fair-haired Russian who knows a little German. In the middle of the day he cooked some thick porridge for us in a pail, on a brick stove in the front premises. Our hungry eyes gave him obvious pleasure.

In the afternoon we were called up singly for examination. Mine didn't take long. The grim-faced major discovered from the remnants of my papers that I was a doctor, but beyond that he could make nothing of me. He couldn't understand, apparently, how I came to be in this party. I was astonished, as before, that there should be any system in this chaos. Why do they go on making any distinctions? Hardly anybody will come alive out of this sorting-machine as it is. The other details I gave struck the major as exaggerated. I was obviously in a condition that no longer evoked any special interest in my person. He wouldn't believe that I had never belonged to the Party. The interpreter asked 'Why Party bad to you?' I couldn't explain that to him in a hurry, I said. After being repeatedly pressed to give an explanation all the same, I made the sign of the Cross. The interpreter tapped his forehead and nodded to the examining major, who pushed my papers back to me and let me go.

The other men were interrogated for a much longer time. The boy was asked, among other things, how many Russian prisoners he had shot at the Hitler Youth manœuvres. An old man who had been in the police never reappeared.

21st April

To our great astonishment we were simply turned out into the road next morning. 'Go home!' Our guard laughed good-humouredly. 'Home where?' I asked, 'To Insterburg?' 'Yes, Insterburg!' 'Give paper,' I said. 'Paper? Rubbish! No paper!' It was obvious that we should be rearrested round the next corner. Our party started off doubtfully. As a matter of fact nobody paid any attention to us; we could hardly believe our senses. Further along, at the cross-roads, Helmut Z. turned off to the right; he was going to Palmnicken to see if any of his people were still there. As I had no plans of my own I went with him, for I shouldn't have been capable of any longer walk.

We went through the villages of St. Lorenz and Craam again; nobody took any notice of us. Where the road entered a wood, an old man came towards us pushing a wheelbarrow. We sat down with him by the roadside. He was a farmer from the district of Labiau; he had fled with a cart and horses as far as Palmnicken, where he was overtaken by the Russians. Since then he had been skulking about the roads with the rest of his possessions, and was now going to try and reach his native place. He advised us urgently against going to Palmnicken because of the Russians there. My companion decided to go on in spite of this, while I joined the old man, not least because he still had a piece of meat in his barrow. We took turns in pushing the latter, in the opposite direction again. We advanced very slowly. In Craam we were hurriedly overtaken by the Polish interpreter of my first interrogation. I ducked my head involuntarily. He went past without batting an eyelid.

The old man was forced to take over the wheelbarrow altogether, as I couldn't get it to move. Columns of vehicles rushed past; one of them caught the side of the barrow and flung it into the air. It broke in pieces and the contents flew far and wide over the field. Unfortunately, however, there was a tin bath among them, with two handles, and everything was collected and packed into it again, including a meat-slicer, an axe, a hammer and a pair of tongs, very useful things in themselves, but not suitable for lugging about the country as one's last remaining possessions. My attempts to wean the man from his meat-slicer were unsuccessful. I didn't mind the other things : two white sheets, a few potatoes, a piece of meat, a little bacon and several shirts.

Carrying the tin bath between us we toiled on through the field as far as a little coppice on the right of the road. Here we sat down and decided to cook dinner. As I was not quite sure whether I was to be allowed any of it, I made myself useful by lighting a fire. I fetched water from a trench at some distance, which led through a little swamp. As I was dipping it up a couple of bullets whistled past me. I looked round. A half-undressed Russian was standing a long way off beside the same trench and firing at me. He made no attempt to follow me when I retreated.

We boiled our potatoes in peace. When I went to look for some dry wood, a German soldier's head popped up out of a communication trench. Two men of the 5th Panzer Division, a lieutenant and a non-commissioned officer, had been lying hidden there for three days. They belonged to a scout patrol that had got behind the Russian lines. I asked after my cousin Knyphausen, who belongs to the divisional staff. They thought there was a chance that the rest of the division might get away by sea. They themselves had been without food for three days. My companion invited them to our potatoes and shared his bacon with them. They intended going on in a southerly direction after dark.

We started on our way, leaving behind the meat-slicer, the tools and the tin bath. We carried the rest of our things in my bag, out of which I had jettisoned my unwearable shoes. Behind St. Lorenz we cut off a corner and walked over the fields to Watsum. There we hid in an empty house, the interior of which presented the usual appearance. Upholstered furniture with the coverings ripped off lay about in pieces in a knee-deep mass of bed-feathers, bottles, pictures and smashed crockery. Window-frames and doors had been torn out. On a window-sill lay a piece of cheese. We ate it up on the spot. Two Russians came in, turned everything upside down again and departed without noticing us.

The main body of the troops had left earlier, but aircraft were still very busy, from which we deduced that Pillau was still being fought for. From the direction of the sea came a heavy thunder of guns every now and then; and as the wish is always father to the thought, we imagined that the Americans were already advancing against the Russians.

On the other side of the road there was a house occupied by women and children. They were all lying in one room, on the now universally adopted principle : the old women in front, the children behind them; in the background the younger women and girls disguised as old ones. They were all worn out, except one talkative old creature, who thought it highly interesting to be living through such apocalyptical times. We lay down to sleep on a two-tiered truss of straw, left behind by German troops. It was difficult to realise that only a few days ago this was still Germany.

Russians came in the night and shone pocket torches on us. We didn't stir. We were at their mercy anyhow, and lying at full length was so glorious that we didn't want to sacrifice a moment of it. To our joy they soon went away again and left us to sleep.

22nd April

In spite of his seventy years my companion is far more enterprising than I. He ferreted out two lame horses left behind by the troops. These he harnessed with improvised horse-collars to a rack-wagon and loaded two families upon it, who came from the same district as himself and were going to try and get back there with him. I hung on to the back of the wagon, and passed for the third time in front of Watsum railway station, which I shall always specially remember. At the fork in the road we turned left through Pobethen and went on towards the east. Craam, St. Lorenz, Watsum, Pobethen, the sound of those names, so homely and familiar to the people of Samland, echo in me like an endless scream rising up to heaven.

Step by step we drew slowly along the road to Cranz. Anything useful seen lying in the ditches was picked up and taken with us. In the cold, clear, windy weather of early spring a detachment marched past us, singing. All went well for another mile or so; then a patrol held us up, searched the wagon, examined the horses and pulled me off. The wagon was allowed to proceed. I waved to the old man. We had spent twenty-four hours together— a chunk of life.

I lay beside the Russians in the grass. They began by searching me, then they busied themselves with my papers, among which there were still a couple of letters and photographs. I gazed at the sea and took no notice of them. They held a photograph of my sister under my nose. 'Your wife?' I nodded. 'Where your wife?' 'At home!' 'Where home?' I mentioned some place or other. 'Gitlair kapoot!' The usual conclusion, like Amen in church. I made no reply to any further attempts at conversation.

A few hours later they were relieved, and took me with them as the first occupant of their new prison, the living-room of a labourer's house on a landed estate. The windows were boarded up; it was freezing cold. I sat and lay by turns curled up on the floor. Now and then I put my feet up on a milking-stool, the only piece of furniture in the room. That made less of a hollow in my back; one gradually adopts a kind of routine in these things. I laid my handkerchief over my nose and mouth; that conserves a lot of warmth in one's body.

The sentry posted before the door seemed uneasy about me. He kept coming in, staring at me and trying to make me adopt a different position. I lay still, keeping my eyes on his. He might be about eighteen years old, and stood there like a young dog in front of a rolled-up hedgehog. Then he made off again and drew himself up in the doorway like a stalwart. Once when he came in I gave him to understand by signs that I was very cold. He could think of no remedy. Instead, he began teaching me a few Russian words. 'Give . . . me . . . food.' When I had got hold of it I repeated it as a request. He was frightened, became embarrassed, retreated slowly towards the doorway, and from then onwards only peeped in through the chink in the door. Towards morning he brought me a piece of bread. When I tried to take his hand he started back.

23rd April

About midday I acquired a comrade; a young Lithuanian who had deserted from the Russian army was shoved in. He was given a billy-can of soup, which we ate in turns with his spoon. Later on we were joined by an elderly German with a wooden leg, a native of the district, who had just managed to get this far from somewhere else.

Towards evening we three were taken in charge by two guards and brought nearer to Königsberg again. In a village swarming with Russians we were shut up in a pigsty already occupied by ten other men. It seemed that we were to be examined again. One is thrown from one sieve into another. Meanwhile we boiled two pails of potatoes in the pigwash bucket and ate our bellies full.

24th April

We were sent on again without being examined, viâ Fuchsberg towards Königsberg. I was seized by a growing agitation. I shouldn't have had the courage to approach the town again of my own free will; there was too much finality about it, and I had no resistance left.

In the suburb of Tannenwalde we turned left, and were once again sorted out on some unfathomable principle. The Lithuanian was to stay where he was—to be shot, so he declared. When we were led away he started playing madly on a piano that had been left standing on the road.

On we went towards Königsberg. I could only just drag myself along in my felt boots, and felt every minute that I must drop; yet I was intensely alive to the scene around us. The place was like a lunar landscape, crater beside crater, with a sea of rubble beyond. In the direction of the Inner Town a few last fires were dying slowly down to glimmering ashes. The song was ended.

Beside the road, on the right, a Russian had got stuck in the mud in his car—one of those innumerable, hideous little American affairs that look like public lavatories. We were ordered to go and drag it out. I simply let myself drop. The others struggled to no purpose; splashed with mud, they were forced to give up the attempt. We went a little further, along a narrow-gauge railway, and found ourselves on the Cranzer Road in Rothenstein, in front of the Wrangel Barracks. A sentinel let us through the gates. We had reached the camp.

4

ROTHENSTEIN CAMP

End of April to Mid-June 1945

TODAY everybody knows from hearsay what such a camp is like. It's a place where people are put away that one doesn't want to think about for a time, either because one has other concerns in mind, or because thinking about them proves too uncomfortable. In the camp they are automatically subjected to a process of attrition, which has no demonstrable connection with the intentions of whoever sent them there, but is to their advantage in so far as it dispenses them from any further trouble in the matter, or at any rate reduces the need for it to a minimum. The final result of the camp is in any case a condition that calls forth no more than a wrinkling of the nose; one can't be expected to feel any further responsibility for such people.

The feeling that one has been consigned to oblivion in this way is hard to describe; if one didn't know that God casts no one aside, one might fall into despair.

The barracks surrounding us were almost undamaged. We were led down the central roadway; on our left the yards between the garages were guarded by pickets; grey masses of humanity were creeping past them. We were pushed into Hall Number Eight. The floor couldn't be seen for people. Followed by feeble curses we went carefully feeling our way over a mass of legs, looking for an empty spot; but with the best will in the world no room could be made for us. Two thousand people were said to be collected here, all men. Some of them had been there for four weeks, the majority for a fortnight; they were literally living each on his eighteen inches of cement floor. Hardly any of them could lie down; most of them were squatting on their hunkers or standing upright.

I clambered on till a hand held me fast. An elderly man was looking at me as kindly as his stubbly face allowed, and said if I would sit back to back with him, and his neighbour could spare an inch, he could find room for me. With a sigh of relief I bent my knees and assumed the position he suggested. Mutual introductions were superfluous; here everybody was alike, and differentiation was apt to have a painful effect. In the course of conversation, however, I did learn his name, and that he was an engineer and a State Surveyor. He was sorry he had nothing to offer me in the way of eatables: once a day, with luck, they got a cup of gruel and a slice of bread. He had four coffee beans in his trouser pocket and gave me two.

The mood of the broken creatures round us varied from indignant to lachrymose. I gathered from their utterances that they had not yet realised their situation. They still believed they had fallen victims to some unpardonable error on the part of the Administration. As soon as the word got round, among those nearest me, that I was a doctor, I was besieged with questions as to what sense there was in all this, and when they would be let out again. It was really a crime to pack people together like this; it made one ill. And the food that was due to them they never got. I really ought to go to the Commandant and make a serious complaint about this abuse. There was no water at all, and no latrines. The whole thing was a filthy shame, which nobody 'at the top' knew anything about, most likely.

I behaved as apathetically as possible, not wanting to implicate myself in these long orations. Tub-thumping was never in my line. An old man ventured on the ninety-first psalm, which he shouted out to the rest: 'Who dwelleth under the defence of the Most High . . .' Nobody took any notice of him; maybe one or another among them was beginning to see clear.

Towards evening a woman put in appearance, who had evidently assumed a sort of medical service on her own responsibility. She was called over to us, and told to take me with her to the other German doctors. I was to get full information from them and then set things in order.

She went away, came back after a little while, and asked me to follow her. She took me past several patrols as far as Hall Number Two, where we pushed through another dense crowd of people to a room that had been partitioned off. The door opened, and I saw several men in dirty white jackets bustling about. My escort went up to one of them and I followed diffidently. He looked at me, came quickly towards me and shut the door behind me. Without many words I was led to a wide wooden guard-bed and covered over with a big cape. I felt guilty, and moaned ashamedly to myself. One couldn't be better sheltered in Abraham's bosom.

From under the cape I took stock of my benefactors. All three of them had hats on, resting more on the nape of the neck than on the head, and civilian clothes under their jackets. What they were doing, I couldn't see. People kept coming in for treatment. When two Russians appeared the cape was drawn right over my head till they had gone again.

By and by a fourth man joined them, bringing a saucepan of porridge which was shared out among us. I came out of my corner and introduced myself to the others. They consisted of a young army doctor whom I will call Schreiner and two medical assistants, Holter and Klein. They had belonged to a unit posted on the outskirts of the town, and were brought here after Königsberg had fallen. Here in the camp, with the help of a hypodermic syringe and a few medicaments they had brought in their pockets, they had set up a surgery in which even the Russian custodians had begun to take some interest, coming occasionally to be treated in secret. In general, however, the Russians kept outside the patrols and left the restraint of the prisoners to the Poles. The latter made exaggerated use of their rubber truncheons to get good marks—i.e. better food—from the Russians.

As sickness increased among the internees, Dr. Schreiner had enlisted the energies of a few women to build up a volunteer medical service. With a Red-Cross badge on their upper arm they went through the camp halls, listened to complaints, made notes of them and told the doctor where he was wanted. The guards usually let them through without difficulty; they were free to carry on.

Except for the cold, I was feeling fairly fit again; I was merely quailing at the thought of meeting some connection of mine in this place. As there were no latrines, everybody, men and women alike, met in fantastical fashion between the halls, in a corridor some twelve feet wide. There was always a horrible crush there, for some of these people were already suffering badly from diarrhoea. Added to which it rained all day long. It was not unusual for someone to collapse from weakness. To have lived one's life only to end up in this place, literally 'in the shit!' A hymn recurred to me involuntarily: 'Thus far hath God brought me . . .' Was that blasphemy? But who else had done it? Well, if He had stood by one so far, He must surely continue to help one.

In the hall opposite men have been lodged in one half and women in the other. There is a partitioned-off room there like ours. An ear doctor is camping there with two men I knew in the Fortress days—Giese and Röckert. At that time they were working with Bode in the Field Hospital as members of the ambulance corps. Giese had been the pastor of a parish in Stockholm, and Röckert a medical student. They put me up for the night, as there was room for four in the compartment. I lay on a long table, and my comrades on the floor. There was actually a small stove in the room.

Next morning we went on a little expedition. Dr. Schreiner had persuaded a Russian to let us out of the camp, under escort, to look for some medical stores. Somewhere quite near by he and his assistants had hidden a good quantity before they were taken prisoner. Holter directed us to the place he knew; but even here we found that everything had been looted. The little cottages were knee-deep in rubbish. As the only serviceable object I could find, I brought away a somewhat battered coffee-pot for use as a food container.

In the allotment gardens the first rhubarb was venturing above ground. It was barely visible as yet, but I took all I could tear up, and ate it going along. Vitamins! Life is forever assuming astonishing importance again.

In the camp, meanwhile, people had formed into wide queues in the yards and were waiting to be given their food. Behind a tin bath at the end of our yard stood a half-blind, toothless Polish woman, threatening everyone that came too near with a ladle. In the bath there was a thin grey fluid, at the bottom of which lay a few groats. It took hours to distribute the stuff—one cupful per head. People remained begging beside the bath, and had to be driven away by their Polish gaolers. A great many got nothing; the bath didn't hold enough for them all.

Those who had assembled in our yard came from a distant barrack building. They had brought everything with them that they still possessed, because they didn't know whether they would be allowed to return to the same place, or would be housed somewhere else. Many of them were wearing three suits one over another; and as this condition had lasted more than three weeks already, vermin had increased in grand style. Astonishingly few people, however, were really ill. Sister Hedwig, the woman who had taken me to my colleagues, came to fetch me for a walk through the halls under her care. She had found people suffering from fever. I examined these a little, as far as it was possible in such a crowd, and gave them tablets of some kind, leaving the requisite instructions to Sister Hedwig. She dragged me from one to another, and I followed her directions as long as I could. Examining those lying on the floor was no light task; it took me all my strength to get up again. Near the exit I succeeded in escaping when she wasn't looking, and on reaching our cabin I hid from her pursuit with a bad conscience. She turned up after a time, and I pretended to be asleep. Dr. Schreiner sent her away.

A girl turned up one day in our compartment called Erika Fröhlich, the embodiment of the innocent country lass. She had come about a wound in her finger, and when she saw what a mess we were in she started tidying it up unasked. We were surprised to see how much could be accomplished in that way, and asked her if she had anybody belonging to her in the camp. No, she was quite alone. So we asked her to stay with us.

At the end of April dysentery began to spread. Those most seriously ill were brought out of the various halls and laid in rows before the door of our surgery, where the floor had been cleared for them. There were soon a hundred of them; they lay on planks or on doors taken off their hinges, or even on the bare cement floor, some of them only half clothed and without blankets. Over the way, in the other hall, about fifty women were lying in a separate room, nursed by a deaconess, Sister Bertha. She took their temperatures, and assisted Dr. Schreiner when he paid them proper visits.

With us, as over the way, everything was strikingly quiet. The sick seemed hardly conscious. On the 28th April we carried out the first dead. Chaplain Klein and I laid them out like a row of hares beside the sentries. Their places were immediately taken by fresh patients, most of whom were much too weak to move, and simply relieved themselves where they lay. The state of the floor was indescribable; we leapt, so to speak, from island to island to reach individuals, or to retreat into our cabin and throw ourselves on the bed for a moment, covering our faces with a cloak.

Our patients were not all suffering from dysentery; other troubles broke out, quite apart from the enormous number of women suffering from venereal disease, whom it was impossible to examine. I was particularly sorry for one old man, whose bladder I had to relieve every day with a big cannula—in default of a catheter—which of course could not be cleaned. He thought it wonderful, and thanked me heartily every time.

A man was brought to us in the evening, bleeding from the wrist. He had cut his arteries a fortnight earlier; the wounds had festered, and now one of the arteries had opened again. By the light of a little candle I made an incision above the wound and ligatured the artery with the only thread I could find. The man bore it all patiently, without stirring. He had come from the cellar, brought by two young army doctors who had thus managed to escape from the cellar themselves. They hoped to be able to remain hidden with us and not be fetched down to the cellar again. What they told us of the place makes it clear that we've not yet seen the worst.

I have meanwhile contrived to rid myself of my three weeks' beard, which has buoyed me up a bit; washing is still out of the question because one dare not waste a drop of water. Dr. Schreiner has managed to persuade a Russian officer, who turns up from time to time as a patient, to arrange for a little water to be brought to the camp. So now twenty miserable men push a sewage cart out of the camp gates to the nearest pump, some seven hundred yards away. It takes several hours for them to return with their load, but at least the camp gets a few hundred gallons of water in this way.

29th April

The number of dead has increased so much that the Russians, from an instinct of self-preservation, have started some sort of fight against the spread of infection. Schreiner has been appointed head physician of the camp, and made responsible for practically everything else. We have till midnight to move, with the sick from all the halls, into the second storey of a big barracks block, failing which, some of us are to be shot. Holter, who acts as interpreter, translated this to us in a dutiful manner, with a slightly humorous undertone. Schreiner took note of the order unmoved, but explained to the Russians that owing to the large number of patients, exact fulfilment of this plan could not be expected. The result was a loud roar, which we didn't allow to intimidate us. The consciousness of being at their mercy gives one a certain feeling of superiority. They surely can't get much fun out of shooting by now, and they would have nothing to gain by it.

We began by inspecting the place allotted to us, and discovered that the Poles who had been lodged there up to now had no intention of leaving the field to us. Their removal to another barracks block had then to be expedited by the Russian guards. The state in which the place was left was something we had long grown accustomed to. With improvised brooms and a little water the worst of the filth was scraped off and carried down in buckets, the drains being stopped up. We collected about thirty men, still fairly mobile, among them some former medical orderlies, and with their help we managed to lug some four hundred patients up the stairs in the course of the evening. In the gathering darkness we could only distribute them in the empty rooms according to their sex, and not, as we had intended, according to their diseases. They were all having to lie on cement floors again, except for a few who had been brought upstairs on planks, so their situation was not in the least improved. On the contrary, it was even more draughty up there, because some of the windows have been blown out, and others carried off by the Poles.

By midnight everything was so full that the Russian officers, who had been ceaselessly harrying us, were satisfied and left us in peace for the rest of the night. In the smaller rooms stood a few iron bedsteads; in the first one, alongside the entrance, we four from the surgery settled in by order of the Russians, and made everything draught-proof for the night. Holter found a quart glass full of sugar somewhere, probably in the Russian kitchen. We didn't ask where it came from, but let our portions trickle down our throats on the spot. Our helpers and one or two colleagues are bedded in the rooms on either side, and Erika shares the adjoining one with a young woman who had been delivered of a dead child in the surgery and detained there.

The night was very quiet. As our kidneys only function now when we are lying down, we often had to turn out into the passage where the pails stand. There was nothing to be heard there except the soft groping and creeping of all those who were likewise seeking the pails. And we were thankful that there would still be some hours of darkness.

30th April

In the morning we singled out the dead. Several people had died in the passage, one sat dead on a pail. The rest were not easy to pick out because even the living respond very slowly when spoken to or touched. In time there were about thirty-six corpses, all men, piled up in a heap three feet high in the wash-room. (The women hold out longer.) Many were almost naked, their clothes having been appropriated by others against the cold. Only a minority of the patients have any papers left, and they will not be able to keep them much longer, so eventually nobody will know who has died here.

I've given up all attempt at independent thought. I let Schreiner give me orders, and carry them out as best I can. There's no longer any question of getting things properly done; we merely help one another, and here and there somebody is saved from the worst. However hard one tries to do something, it's impossible to tell whether in the end it does good or harm. Up here the sick have been removed from among the crowd, but on the other hand they are bedded even more uncomfortably than down in the halls. Fortunately most of them are so exhausted that they hardly know what is happening to them. We doctors have become co-operators in the death-mill of the camp, whether actively or passively makes no difference.

In some mysterious way Erika has made friends with the Polish woman who distributes the food. She discovered some ailment she was suffering from and took her a few tablets. Now she spends her time carrying one billy-can of soup after another concealed under her jacket, for us and her other protégés. We ask her no questions and let her carry on. In her little room there is now a second woman awaiting the birth of twins.

Fresh patients have been brought to us the whole day long, and there has been friction with the Russians, who disapprove of everything. Fresh committees keep arriving, including women in uniform. We don't know where to hide from them.

As we can't possibly find room for all the patients on the one storey, some hundred men have had to be taken right upstairs to the attics—a frightful business for all concerned. The wind and rain blow through the open windows and the holes in the roof. When it was nearly dark again I went up there once more and found them lying in all directions. I heard faint, senseless talk here and there, and felt the spark of life fading out everywhere. Some of them were definitely dead. I removed their overcoats and jackets and covered others with them.

There are times when I feel that a voice is asking me 'What are you doing here, actually?' Yes, what am I doing? What are we all doing? But it's no longer any use trying to find an answer.

There can be no doing in the true sense of the word, only now and then an attempt. And as I turned round once more before leaving the attic, my arms rose instinctively to bless these creatures consecrated to death.

Later in the night the first twin came into the world, assisted by Erika and myself. Life goes on, as they say so sensibly.

We didn't notice much of the First of May, except that a couple of loudspeakers were blaring away, even more than usual, on and on in the neighbourhood. We still see fighter squadrons flying westward; Pillau seems not to have capitulated yet. How in the world do they still manage to hold out?

It's raining in torrents. Down below in the yard some Frenchmen have been assembled, to be transported to their own country viâ Odessa. A good way round! Two of our helpers, who had given themselves out to be doctors, have joined them in the hope of getting out of the camp in this way. As they don't know a word of French, we have been advising them, from the window, to act deaf and dumb as far as possible.

The people in the halls are growing visibly weaker. A rumour having spread that charcoal is good for diarrhoea, they are all hunting for bits of burnt wood to eat.

A Russian medical student has obtained permission from the Camp Commandant to go round the cellars with one of the German doctors. I was singled out for this and took Röckert along with me. He brought a box filled with dressings and medicaments which had gradually come to light. We knew more or less what to expect down there, and had no illusions about being really able to help.

The cellars under all the barrack blocks are crammed with people, some four thousand men and women, many of whom are examined every night by the NKWD[1] official. The examination is not for the purpose of extracting from people what they know—which would be uninteresting anyway—but of forcing certain declarations out of them. The methods employed are very primitive; people are beaten up until they confess that they once belonged to the Nazi Party. The result is more or less the opposite of what one would expect, namely that those that hadn't been of the Party would come off better. The authorities start from the assumption that everybody *must* have been in the Party. Many people die as

[1] Soviet People's Commissariat, to which the political Secret Police is subordinated.

a result of these interrogatories, while others, who confess their allegiance at the outset, hardly suffer at all. Only the lower classes are involved, anyway, for the higher officials got out of the affair earlier on, either by escaping in time or by suicide. A fairly large batch of these 'partisans' is shipped off to Insterburg or Gumbinnen every day. The cellars left empty are filled up with men and women out of the halls in the following way. A Russian and a Pole appear with a list of German names in Russian script. These names are called out to the crowd by the two of them, one after the other, in a hoarse voice. Not one of them can be recognised; often they are not names at all, but designations of some kind, copied out of the collection of documents. A lot of people answer to them, nevertheless, in the hope of being released from the camp. All those on the list are removed and taken down to the cellars. There all interest in them ceases for the time being; some of them may be examined later up to three or four times, some not at all.

The first cellar the guard opened had just been refilled. Three men were staggering about in the passage and were driven in again with the butt of the guard's rifle, with difficulty, however, because the room was too small and the door could only be closed by force. People had been standing there for three days, waiting to be examined. At the sight of us a senseless hubbub broke out that left me helpless. It was impossible to deal with individual requests. As far as I could gather, the usual senseless questions were being reiterated : Why were they there, and for how long? There was no water, and hardly anything to eat. They wanted to be let out more than once a day, and so on. The guard was getting fed up with the outcry. I had just time to call out to them that they must think out their most urgent requests before the next visit and let a spokesman deliver them. Then the door was banged to on them.

Lest this should happen again I hastily thought out a few introductory words for the next cellar. These gradually became a sort of formula that I rattled out in a loud voice as soon as a cellar door was opened. It went more or less like this : 'People! Keep quiet, otherwise I shall have to go at once. I'm the doctor. We're going to try and get those of you who are most ill out of here and into hospital. Who has blood in his stool?' 'I, I, I!' broke out on all sides.

'No, that won't do. Pay attention, please. Those that name themselves can't be considered. Who is so ill that he's a plague to the others? Choose a spokesman for next time, and have everything ready.' This made things easier. The most serious cases were soon listed; but whether we can really get them out is another matter. Would they even be better off with us in the hospital? It's colder there, in any case. Perhaps it would at least make things a little better for those left behind in the cellars.

In some of the cellars I found people I knew; that is to say I recognised them only when they whispered their names to me. The head physician of the Children's Clinic, and other doctors that I knew slightly, and Pastor Leidreiter in an army cape. Their incarceration was just as fortuitous as my relative freedom. They may quite likely have taken me for a protégé of the Russians. Some of them had tidied up their prisons a bit. We were at least able to leave them some dressings and a few medicaments. We couldn't talk to them for long, because the guard soon broke in with his 'Hurry up! Hurry up!'

A group of cellar occupants was just being led out and taken to the fence surrounding the camp, to the accompaniment of 'Schnell, schnell! Hurry up!' A few holes had been dug there, with two boards laid over each. That was all. In addition, there were pails standing in most of the cellars, brought in from the yard by the prisoners.

Many people have dysentery so badly that they can no longer stand up. In their case we are always faced with the question : Is it worth while putting them on the list, or will they be dead in another few hours? One has come to judge people like cattle. We know that if we put too many on the list we shan't get any out at all. We feel all the time as though we were passing sentence of death, the more so because of course they all think the hospital must be Heaven. I have the greatest difficulty, in any case, in persuading them that I'm not God Almighty. They are still under the impression that they have been wrongly imprisoned and then neglected. They haven't done anything wrong, after all! What is to become of their families if they are kept here? They'd be glad to work for the Russians, and I must tell the camp management so.

Some of the rooms are not so full, and one can move about in them and make contact with individual prisoners. One little broken-down man hung on to me and entreated me to tell the Camp Commandant that upstairs in one of the barrack blocks there are eleven Italian Old Masters he was robbed of when he was there. They are worth many thousands, and shouldn't be left lying there in the damp, or they will be lost to the Russian State.

Touched though I am by his anxiety, that conclusion seemed beyond a joke to me at that moment; and secretly I congratulate the Italian Masters on their fragility, which prevents them from representing their money value at this juncture, while millions of living people are being made to rot unregarded. May they now find a useful end as substitutes for window-panes or in a stove.

Some of the rooms are occupied by women. It is a relief to see them, their behaviour is so much more intelligent and practical than that of the men. When the first of these rooms was thrown open I saw at once that I needn't make my usual speech. The women were sitting back to back, distributed over the floor like a mosaic. At the sight of us, one that I knew—Sister Waltraut of the Nerve Clinic, *alias* Field Hospital—stood up from among them. We greeted each other from a distance, and then she gave us the most important details. Two elderly women and a young one lying near the door, beside the bucket, were unable to get up without assistance; the others, sixty-nine in all, were in better case; they don't give in as quickly as the men. As I was leaving, the Sister gave a signal, and the whole company broke into a cheerful song. One is perpetually astounded at the things people find the strength to do. Where order reigns within, help from without can find a starting-point; the little we can do is not useless here.

We couldn't get through anything like all the cellars that day. I was held upright only by my felt boots, and was thankful when the guard prevented us from going any further. But I had hardly got back to my berth when a Russian came to fetch me again. Chaplain Klein was roped in, and we returned to the cellars. We were halted before a door at the end of a passage, and supposed we were now to be shut up inside ourselves.

A pitch-dark, windowless space opened before us, with a sloping ceiling at the back. The Russian made us go in. This was obviously a room that had been forgotten. We drew one body after another out of the darkness into the light. There were fifteen men, and we examined them as expeditiously as we could. Seven were definitely dead, and there was not much life left in the other eight. We were allowed to take them all with us to the hospital. Four of us carried them away, one after another, the living and the dead.

We were left in peace with our patients for two days; then there was a fresh upheaval. A Medical Commission came to inspect the hospital, and raged round the building like elephants, as though they would have liked to trample us all down in their fury at the conditions they found. We doctors were to blame because a proper hospital service had not been organised long ago. What a pigsty! And the Germans were still pretending to culture! No chloride of lime even! And all over the barrack blocks there were cupboards that we could long since have used as beds! Worst of all, we had no office, with lists and registers of medical supplies! We were seized with a slight shudder at the thought of what they might understand by a 'proper hospital service'. It was useless even attempting to explain to them why we had not yet been able to make all these praiseworthy arrangements. They were not concerned with reasons but only with conditions, they themselves being solely responsible for the health organisation.

Schreiner was given the latest orders: The place was to be evacuated with all possible speed, and the entire three-storey block opposite taken over instead. Besides which, all necessary installations were to be carried out, failing which we doctors would be shot —the usual refrain. Faced with Schreiner's dilemma I should probably have thrown up the sponge at this juncture, but he could still draw on his reserves for this new battle. We had first to procure an enormous number of workers from among the internees, which of course was only possible with the assistance of the Polish gaolers. For it was not merely a question of occupying the building, which the Poles quartered there up to the last minute had left in the usual state, but of carrying out all sorts of improvements such as building latrines, installing a sort of field kitchen for boiling water, laying on a water supply, and fetching bedsteads and cupboards from the other blocks, to which we had hitherto had no access.

There is a blank in my memory concerning the events of that day. I had the impression afterwards that I had been chiefly intent on avoiding notice, and always having some chloride of lime at hand. Six big barrels of this were suddenly at our disposal. Chloride of lime was the charm with which to soften the ferocious looks of our tormentors; whosoever throws chloride of lime about shows that he is not insensible to Russian culture.

I have no idea, therefore, how Schreiner contrived in the end to get everything done. At any rate we settled in after dark on the ground floor over the way, in a room just big enough for our four beds, which could only be reached through an adjoining one, in which we intended to set up our 'office'. Somewhere quite near us Erika was encamped with the two women in childbed, one of whom had had her second twin two days after the first. Opposite us, separated only by the central corridor, Giese and Röckert have settled in. They guard the wash-room, which is to be used for operations. Some twenty hospital orderlies and a lot of women from the cellars, including some trained nurses, have been taken on as nursing staff. The cellar with the singing women has been evacuated, and Sister Waltraut has taken over one storey of the so-called surgical department.

The greater part of the block has of course become an isolation department, right through all the floors, including the ground floor and the cellars, for the patients coming from the cellars are to be housed in the cellars here too. This means that the cellar lights must be cleared of the earth that had been shovelled against them by way of defence against air attack.

I got into conversation, standing at our window, with one of the men engaged on the work. He was the owner of the big farm near Rauschen that had struck me by its undamaged state when I passed it a fortnight ago. Less than a year ago Goerdeler[1] had been staying with him, and was later, after the affair of the 20th July, looked for there by the Gestapo. We talked of the events which, a few months earlier, had concerned us even more deeply than the approaching Russians. Now they seem like happenings in some other life.

Seven doctors are at work in the isolation department; Schreiner and I are in charge of the general and surgical cases. Schreiner has thankfully surrendered his post as head physician to the eye doctor, who knows a little Russian and is not entirely dependent on the Polish interpreter when making his daily report to the Commandant. The house has been divided in two from top to bottom by cupboards on the landings. All sorts of bedsteads, mattresses, palliasses and cupboards have been collected from the other blocks, so far as they are not occupied by Russians, by permission of the Commandant, and distributed throughout the house. Many of the patients are now lying on overturned cupboards, placed either singly or rammed together like a barricade, in the middle or in a corner of each room. The majority are still obliged to lie on the floor, and all of them still have to suffer from the cold, because the windows can only be gradually re-glazed or filled in with cardboard.

A special squad has been formed to collect substitute materials

[1] Carl-Friedrich Goerdeler, 1930-1937 Chief Burgomaster of Leipzig, selected as Chancellor of the Reich by the Resistance Movement. Executed 1945.

for repairs. They are actually allowed to go into the town, under escort, and fish out anything at all useful from among the ruins. We even get dressings and medicines from the recently opened Russian pharmacy. The leader of the squad is a certain Schäfer—as we may call him—a tall lad, not bad-looking at a distance, who was probably a soldier at one time but now wears civvies. It would take too long to repeat all the tales with which he regales his astonished audience about his past. However, he's an expert in everything, good at organising, and knows to perfection how to wheedle the Russians, so his usefulness can't be denied.

On the 8th May we heard that the war was over. The loud-speakers blared even more piercingly than usual. In the halls some dubious-looking German soldiers were holding forth about our liberation from National-Socialism and the blessings of Bolshevism. Outside the Commandant's door a floral trophy had been erected —from what source in this desert? Otherwise there is little to mark the final victory, as far as we are concerned. The official food situation has not improved; there is still nothing but gruel to eat, with now and then some dried bread, brought in sacks. The hospital has, however, this great advantage over the rest of the camp, that we can fetch our rations, and prepare and distribute them ourselves. In addition to which, patients and staff are given a dessertspoon of sugar per head every day.

Our chief trouble is still the cold. In the first half of May it blew and rained almost without interruption, and the temperature at night was around freezing point. Most of the deaths at that time were the result of lowered body temperature, and occurred silently, with no sign of any death struggle. Movements became feebler from day to day; people still spoke if they were prodded, and then one was glad when at last the time came to remove them from the row with a clear conscience and lay them on the heap in the cellar that was daily buried, since there were many waiting for the places they left free.

The only warm spots were the kitchens, one of which had been installed on each floor. Iron ranges and stovepipes were collected from the barrack yards; the pipes were led through the windows and the openings stopped up with cardboard. Everything combust-ible was burnt. As a rule the whole room was full of smoke, especially on the windward side; but the warmth made up for everything. Besides which we could now make the bread eatable instead of breaking our teeth on it. It was soaked in water and then roasted. All other eatables had to be procured secretly. By way of a spread on the bread we used Vitamin-B extract out of a big tin, which the indefatigable Erika had found lying on a rubbish heap. Schreiner and I discovered the remains of some semolina, flour and rice, which had been used as object-lessons, on a scouting expedition through what had been the lecture-room of a block that had just been evacuated. We were as delighted as children with this unexpected booty.

The fence surrounding the camp is open in several places, and the gaps are only superficially guarded. In spite of this, hardly anybody dreams of escaping. What one hears of the town doesn't tempt one to go there; anybody showing himself in the street is seized and taken to work, or into another camp. As for running through it, right out of the precincts, nobody has enough courage and strength left.

A few days after our move, Giese, Erika and I buried the twins near the camp fence; fortunately they had soon died of the cold. Giese read a text out of the Bible and added a little address. The burial of the other dead takes a very different form. The young Chaplain Klein, who has been condemned to this heavy duty, because in the opinion of the Russians he must obviously be an expert at burying, never says a word to us about it, although we are living together. When I asked him discreetly whether he was able to pronounce a few religious words while it was going on, he waved the question aside without a word. Once he lay on his bed for two days without speaking, and Giese had to take his place. Giese described the proceedings to me later almost in the guise of a confession. In the field at the rear of the camp, close to the fence, a long hole was dug, into which the dead were thrown, fifty or sixty every day, mostly naked; their clothes are used to bribe the men out of the halls to do the digging, as the only means of doing without the Polish gaolers. As the men are all very weak, the excavation of the heavy clay takes the whole day, and if one of them collapses it is difficult to persuade his comrades to carry him back after work. The burden of one's own body is heavy enough of itself, and one literally risks one's life with every additional effort.

One day the guard was reinforced and the fence repaired; we might no longer go more than fifty yards from the house, just as far as the latrines. The reason was this : two dentists had escaped, using the last of their strength, in order to avoid their impending examination. But they didn't get very far. They were tracked by dogs and shut up in the crematorium. The older one, who had climbed up into the dome, was shot down. The younger one was taken back to the cellar.

As a consequence of this occurrence the Camp Commandant came to our block and summoned a meeting of all the doctors and nurses. Supported by an old Polish interpreter armed with a crutch, he gave us an endless lecture on the uselessness of running away. It wasn't in the least necessary, either, he said, for nobody need fear the examination. It was merely concerned with statistical enquiries, and if one gave the right details at once, nothing would happen to one. We couldn't believe our ears. Was it possible that this man, who had been living in the midst of the camp all this time, had no notion of what went on there? That night after night people were beaten to death, merely for telling the truth? In the dim candlelight I tried to get a clear picture of him. His appearance didn't in the least resemble that of the other Russian officers we were used to. He looked like an old English colonel, tall and spare, really distinguished, with an expressive face and a definite air of kindness. I simply couldn't believe he was lying as shamelessly as the others. He concluded his speech by repeating what he had said earlier about the state of our nerves. National-Socialism must be a very emotional affair, he said, to have shattered people to this extent; otherwise it wouldn't have been possible for so many people to fall ill and die.

When he had finished I felt I must answer him, more for his sake than our own, since he could doubtless do nothing to alter our situation even if he had wished to. But he had shown himself so humane that one could not leave him to his mistaken notions. I begged therefore to be allowed to speak, and only realised when I began that I could no longer collect my senses sufficiently to make the situation clear to him from our point of view. With a friendly nod he took his leave, promising to come and see us again some time. We watched him go with a certain emotion, wondering how any man of his sort could possibly hold out in such surroundings. That such a man should be Commandant here makes the condition of the camp more grotesque than ever.

It's frightful to see the intensity with which every thought and action of those that can still stand upright is centred on their own dwindling vitality. These tortured people turn to horrifying masks, grey monsters burdened with the remains of former passions as if with a wet fungus. They babble such a hotch-potch of rubbish that one doesn't know whether to laugh, scream, or lay about one. In the end one can only keep silent, telling oneself that as long as one's own stomach has a chance of snapping up something now and then, one has no right to say a word.

But we too are very low, and have adopted a creeping gait. We hesitate before taking a step, for our blood pressure is so reduced that theoretically we ought not to be able to stand upright. Our legs go numb when we walk upstairs, and our ears feel stopped. The skin on the outer and inner surfaces of my thighs has become insensitive to touch. One's whole bodily consciousness has changed; one often has the sensation of floating. One can only think seriously when one is lying down, and every opportunity of stretching oneself out is seized for making one's next decisions. One's kidneys only function at night, and the pail is the most important object in our room.

Of all the doctors in the camp, I personally have the least exacting work. In my so-called surgical department there is very little occasion for treatment. What the patients need is food and warmth, and as I can't procure them either, I feel that my activities as a doctor are more or less of a fraud. Their sufferings merely give me the right to play the doctor and enjoy the attendant privileges. I've tried all sorts of ways of prolonging their lives, but I can't say that I've ever succeeded. Many of the men end by dying of erysipelas. With the women the most painful symptom accompanying hunger and cold is a sudden atrocious pain in the basal joints of the toes. One woman's feet turned black and fell off. Fortunately we have at least a good supply of narcotics.

The only moment of the day when I feel that I'm doing something useful is when I'm distributing cod-liver oil. We've been given a whole barrelful with which to prepare a remedy for the itch. Since then, of course, the whole building has been reeking of cod-liver oil, because something or other is being fried in it over every stove. I've secreted a gallon or two myself, and go through the ward twice a day to shove a spoonful into each patient's mouth. As I dislike cod-liver oil, and distributing it has therefore no temptation for me, I've taken on the job of my own accord. All the same, the desperate greed with which I'm awaited is hard to bear; the gaping mouths, the grunting and the smacking of lips— a sound film of all this would horrify the world.

What I find most painful is going through the cellars, which is allowed every three or four days. One is really completely powerless there. Sister Hedwig, the armour-piercer, who can even impress the Russians with her gift of the gab and always gets her way, comes to fetch me in an enterprising mood. She distributes medicine here and there, manufactured by ourselves with a lot of water, delivers lectures, in a convincing tone, on the general situation, and lays down rules of behaviour to all and sundry. I never feel sure that she's quite right in her mind, but here, at any rate, she's irreplaceable. And no survivor of the camp but will remember her with gratitude. The fact that she's almost a skeleton obviously matters little to her.

Things are very quiet in the operating room. My two assistants, Giese and Röckert, who camp in the room alongside, keep guard over the bandaging material. We can't really operate because we have no instruments; we can only make a few unavoidable rough interventions. If a leg has to be amputated, it's done with a garden saw. Neck carbuncles are lanced, and the many swollen legs, covered with sores, are dressed. There is a terrible lot of vermin. Many people are so covered with lice that they look quite grey from a distance. But delousing is feared almost to the same degree, because it means parting from their clothes for the time being, and they are not sure of getting them all back again. Some patients die every time, if not at once, then later on, owing to the great change of temperature they are exposed to.

Sometimes Russians come for treatment. They are not really allowed to, but they come in secret, and always leave food of some kind behind them. One young Russian woman helped us particularly in this way; she came once, and sent for me several times afterwards. She told me that her three years in Germany had been the happiest in her life. When the Russians came the same things happened to her as to all the other women, and now she was ill as a result. In the camp she is forced to live with one of the guards. This means that she has at least plenty to eat, like the German women who are held prisoner in the other guards' huts. She insisted on giving me a really good meal at her place, and then presented me with half a pound of margarine to take back with me—the occasion and foundation of our first banquet, which took place at night.

Only when darkness has fallen on the manifold misery of the day can we breathe again. At dusk, when one can still just see to read, I go to the operating room, where my two assistants are awaiting me, and we take it in turns to read the Bible chapter for the day, according to the 'watchwords', which I still have about me. In the darkness we may let fall a few words, unsaid by day, querying the significance of all that we are living through here together.

Before we creep into bed, Erika usually has a surprise for us. The margarine came most opportunely on the day when she had succeeded in begging some potatoes off a Russian. Now there could be potato soup for eighteen people—an exciting affair in the pitch darkness. Erika sat in the kitchen crying for joy; it was a red-letter day for her.

The Russians have given us a female major as superintendent of the hospital, a little, deformed, pitch-black woman, from whom one is never safe. She has been trained to a primitive form of disinfection, and chloride of lime is the only means by which we can divert her attention for a time from the worst of our offences. She was very severe with us at first, especially when she discovered that we kept no night watch. But she soon cast an eye on the afore-mentioned Schäfer, and now her interviews with us usually come to a rapid conclusion with the words 'Go to work. Send Scheffair!' He seems to have a special attraction for her, and is now the coming man in the hospital. He has set up a private establishment, with a little furniture, in the isolation department, and lives there with a woman who displays much the same doubtful characteristics as himself.

Two fellows hang around Schäfer, employed in so-called special work in the camp; in other words they earn better food for themselves by denouncing a lot of people every day as having belonged to the Nazi Party, or for some other transgression. One of them, who often crosses our path and likes chatting with us, makes himself out to be a foundation member of the Communist Party, shortly to be appointed Burgomaster of Königsberg. The other is of uncertain nationality. Both are in the service of the NKWD. They appear to have been given a free hand in everything. Wherever they make their appearance one may be sure that in the evening so and so many people will be fetched by the guards to undergo examination. From this, those concerned will end up in the cellar, or else we have them brought back to us in the middle of the night, beaten to death. Both these men have hundreds of victims on their conscience.

One day they organised a grand police raid with Schäfer and

his lady friend through all the wards; they undressed all the patients, robbed them of everything they had left that could be of use, and beat up a lot of them with their cudgels. We were fully prepared for it to be our turn. But their laundry basket was full, and after dividing the spoils they made off for the time being. As they are officially appointed spies we can do nothing to protect ourselves from them. The guards merely laugh, and we haven't the physical strength left to cope with them ourselves. We should have to kill them outright if we did, anyhow—a thing we have seriously considered, of course. (I shall never forget the moment when the worse one of the two came to me to have two teeth extracted, and made me give him a shot of evipan.)

But our Camp Commandant's reaction took us by surprise. The eye doctor had managed to report the incident to him, and as a result the two were forced to return their loot, and were themselves sent to the cellar, while Schäfer was left to our jurisdiction. Although we might easily have got rid of him in consequence, he was let off once more by the eye doctor. He was no sooner out of this scrape than he came to me and offered me a mackintosh, which he had probably kept back out of his swag, reminding me that I had always wanted one. I seized the opportunity to tell him what we all thought of him. This did not prevent him from offering the eye doctor the selfsame mackintosh a moment later. A man without an atom of conscience. He kept a lot of people busy after this, and then vanished altogether from Königsberg. I sometimes wonder what became of him.

We have one or two other remarkable characters on our so-called hospital staff. Among the women, Wanda, as we call her, plays a prominent part. She forced herself upon us in the early days of the camp, and as soon as we were installed in our cabin she burst in with a determined air, made straight for me with a piercing look in her eyes and addressed me in a strident voice without giving me a chance to interrupt. With unmistakable pride she gave me to understand that she held all the records with regard to rape; she counted up to a hundred and twenty-eight times. Unrepeatable details followed one another in a breathless stream. I failed to understand why all this was being poured out for my exclusive benefit, and I saw Erika's eyes fixed on me pityingly. My friends were nearly bursting with laughter. For once we had an authentic caricature of this devilry, signed and sealed. The outburst gave us a feeling of relief. At the end she looked triumphantly round her;

she had marrow in her bones still, anyway. We harnessed her to the nursing service, regardless of the incidents she might still be involved in.

What a lot of different sick and dying people have passed through our hands! I shall always remember Pastor Lubowski, who on account of his origin had to live as an outlaw in Hitler's day and fell into Russian hands as a sick man. We had fetched him into the hospital in a pitiable state and put him back on his feet sufficiently for him to undertake the keeping of the lists ordered by the Russians, before his life was suddenly cut short by an attack of pneumonia. And there was an old man, brought to us from the cellar, so covered with lice that he looked like an ant-heap. I took his fur coat and hung it on a line in the attic to air. In a hardly audible voice he told me he had been the manager of the Cranz and Samland Railway, and was therefore afraid of being examined. He begged me not to pass this on, for Heaven's sake. An hour later he was dead. It often happens that they die as soon as they reach us. Suspense has kept them alive till then, when it is over they fall asleep in peace.

Not till halfway through the month has May at last remembered the spring. Dandelion plants are beginning to sprout, and are used with enthusiasm as salad, for our food still consists of gruel, though this is gradually becoming a little thicker.

20th May, Whit Sunday

The sun has shone all day, for the first time, out of a cloudless sky. The Commandant gave us permission to hold a service; he even showed a personal interest in it, and asked the interpreter if he might be allowed to attend it himself. There was no God, of course, and in Russia people became priests only for the sake of idling. Was it the same in Germany? To which our interpreter replied that it might happen so, but in general such was not the case, because God was decidedly against idling—a view which the unbelieving colonel promptly and benevolently confirmed. But in the end he didn't turn up at the service, so we took it that his interest was not yet as warm as we had supposed.

Sunlight and warmth flooded in through the two wide-open windows of the operating room, the walls of which were hung with fresh greenery. Right and left near the altar table, in stone jars, stood tall branches of laburnum, in full bloom. Even a crucifix had been unearthed, and our nursing staff had managed to put on clean linen. What a festive sight! About a hundred people pushed their way in. We had written out the hymns on sheets of paper and had them distributed. Pastor Reiss, who could hardly stand, took the liturgy, and Giese preached the sermon. For the space of an hour we were released from all earthly burdens. Afterwards, when the room was emptying, I chanced to see the Commandant outside, stealing away from the window. Had he been standing there all the time? What unhappy creatures they are, these conquerors!

Going into our bedroom lost in thought I started back. What did I see? Sheets on all four beds! My three friends were standing there in ecstasy. We didn't enquire out of what rubbish heaps Erika and Waltraut had dragged these riches; eyes like theirs can always discover something where other people have given up looking. We just ate our dinner and then lay, still and blissful, in the coloured check cotton. The door into the next room stood open, and we could see the radiantly beautiful laburnum spray in its stone jar. 'Cloven tongues, as of fire.' All Pentecost was there.

Our tongues, too, seemed released from the spell that had lain on them so long. That evening, and on the following days, Giese and Klein held services in several of the wards, where people had asked for them. I myself gained courage again to talk to the patients on a text from the Bible. In the dysentery ward in the basement the ward sister—no trained nurse, but a woman of great strength and warmth of heart—had arranged a little table with two candles on it, and set up a crucifix. My shadow fell like that of a giant into the room. It was easier to speak in the darkness, and the Gospel story of the rich man and Lazarus the beggar occurred to me as a fitting text, for many of those that lay dying now on bare boards were formerly wealthy people. I said that we were not being punished by God, but that in his goodness he was turning the rich man into Lazarus while he was still alive, to give him a chance of beholding His glory and opening his heart to it. On going through the rows afterwards I found two of the men dead already.

At the beginning of June I was told that somebody from outside wished to see me. What could this mean? Some sort of trap, for certain! Who could have penetrated into the camp of their own free will? A few days earlier somebody had pushed a letter for me through the fence, from some person entirely unknown to me. I went hesitatingly down the stairs. There stood Doktora, unchanged, neatly dressed, in far better form than we camp inmates. She had somehow discovered that I was in the camp, and had forced her way through the guard.

It was not easy to pick up the threads again after all that must have happened since we were parted. She had become ethereal, hardly of this earth any longer, I felt. I couldn't find anything to say at first. We sat outside there in the sun for a time, on the ruins of a wall. She had come from the Treasury, where the remaining doctors and patients from the hospitals, as well as some of the nursing staffs, had been assembled at some time. What had happened up to then she passed over with a smile. (Six weeks later, after her death, I read about it in her diary.)

There are about a thousand patients now in the Treasury, which has finally been turned into the main dressing station. Doktora herself has a ward on the third floor, and still has some of the nurses from the Municipal Hospital with her. They have had peas, bread and a little sugar given them since she has been there, and they have also managed to secrete other food, so they are not too badly off. But the general atmosphere is unpleasant, the house is full of spies, nobody trusts anybody else, everybody tries to please the Russians. Doktora feels that her chief task now must be to help those that still have enough strength to escape, for she considers the future development of the situation to be hopeless. She can still think very realistically for others. She stayed with me and my colleagues for some time and we ate some pancakes she had brought us.

Three days later she came again, and again I couldn't believe my eyes when I saw her approaching. She had a rucksack with her —my rucksack—filled with things that had remained undiscovered in her cache between the pipes of the burnt-out engine-house. She had salvaged it all and taken it across to the Treasury, and was now bringing me all that had belonged to me, in case I got a chance of escaping. It was a puzzle to me, how she got through the camp guard with it. The sentry wouldn't let her through at first, but took her to the Commandant at her earnest entreaty. There they had wanted to take the rucksack from her, but she tendered it so willingly that she was allowed to take it with her.

I unpacked it bit by bit. My companions were quite envious when they spied my highly elegant trousers. At the bottom of the rucksack a curiously heavy little rubber cushion came to light. Doktora had used it as a pillow up to now, she said, but thought it better I should keep it by me against all emergencies. Against all emergencies? I couldn't think what she meant. I picked the thing up and turned it about; it rattled a bit. I gave her a meaning look, and she nodded affirmatively. I glanced sideways to see if my friends had noticed anything. It was my Russian Kommissar's pistol with the fifty cartridges. I gave a little moan. How was this to end? She was like a child playing at the edge of a precipice.

I heard later that the pistol had been the subject of much perturbation since I parted with it. It had never been used, but its mere existence was enough. Doktora had asked a colleague, whom we knew well, where it might best be hidden. He nearly went out of his mind, and began by reporting it to his chief. The latter begged her for Heaven's sake to do away with the thing, and is still in a fright about it, although Doktora has told him the matter has been settled. I took charge of the so-called pillow and stowed it, for safety's sake, in the wall of the attic.

Doktora told us how things were in the town. A sort of Isolation Hospital has been set up in the old Nerve Clinic, under the superintendence of Professor Starlinger, who seems to carry weight with the Russians. But he has a lot of trouble with an old, fat nurse, well known to me, who because of her extraordinary girth is looked upon as a prodigy by the Russians and is protected by them. She makes use of this involuntary advantage to tyrannise unscrupulously over her unfortunate countrymen.

After the entry of the Russians almost all the staff of the hospital we had worked in were removed from the Nerve Clinic, including Brother Martin and Doktora's sister. What became of the wounded nobody knows exactly. Some were taken along with the staff, the greater half probably perished. Many are said to have been shot out of hand.

The chief trouble in the Isolation Hospital is a fever resembling typhus, the exact nature of which is still undetermined. Many people have died of it. Dysentery has not yet made its appearance there. Not long ago fifty of the older nurses and Professor Joachim were turned out of the Treasury and sent to Insterburg. Some of them returned on foot after days of horror. Professor Joachim, who had held out that far, hanged himself in Insterburg behind the barbed wire.

Doktora comes nearly every day now to give us the latest news. They seem to be taking an interest in me at the Treasury, because they are short of surgeons. They have already tried unsuccessfully to get me out of the camp. I am in no hurry about it myself, for what Doktora tells us of the goings on at the hospital is not very inviting. Here in the camp we are at least sure of one another. Doktora would do better to stay with us.

At the end of May another female major was sent to the camp to superintend us, the old one having departed on private business, in which looted carpets play a part. The new one is her exact opposite, quiet and friendly, almost pretty, rather shy—again a source of many conjectures on our part. We persuaded her to take us for a drive through the town, to search for medical stores in various places among the ruins. She ordered a lorry, in which we were driven at a crazy speed down the Cranzer Allee, now like a succession of waves, to the town. One of our party disapproved of my hat—I had picked it up somewhere on the road during my involuntary tour of the Samland—really one couldn't go to town in *that*! I couldn't believe my ears. The town! A grandiose rubbish heap. And oneself: a little dung-beetle that had just been run over by a steam-roller and couldn't yet understand why it was still alive. But the old ghost is walking again, prescribing the kind of headgear the Herr Doktor is to go to town in. Life is one unending joke.

The town is really an incredible sight. The eye no longer attempts any reconstruction, but lets itself be absorbed, overwhelmed, by the utterly transformed aspect of things. The sight is so accusatory that one can hardly believe there are still people capable of taking this obvious judgement of God for a nasty accident.

The former Power Station by the Northern Railway Station, in which Bode's hospital was housed in the Fortress days, is outwardly fairly well preserved. Inside, of course, everything is devastated and turned upside down. In my search for objects that might be useful to us I came upon a number of corpses still lying on their mattresses in the knee-deep rubbish, and fresh details came to light at every turn, with which to fill out the picture of the capture of the hospital. Where Bode's room was, the walls have been torn out; in one corner I found the red-rimmed glasses out of which we drank his allegedly last Martell. What became of Bode himself, nobody has yet been able to tell me. I can't imagine him still alive among the Russians.

My search among the ruins of the Municipal Hospital was far more rewarding. I freed myself from the others, so as to be able to go alone through the basements and inspect our caches. The walls were so black with soot that the light of my small candle was almost swallowed up. I climbed over indefinable rubbish—there must certainly be many corpses lying about here too—feeling for the places where wall cupboards had been built in. Most of them had been torn open, but one had remained undiscovered and was full of the most valuable things : dextrose capsules, morphia, bandaging material and—a special surprise—castor oil, which can be used for frying. I packed everything in a wastepaper basket and laid the bandaging material on top by way of camouflage. Then we went back to the camp.

By the beginning of June conditions had become almost comfortable. We had fewer patients, because some were removed by lorry to the Treasury every day, and very few new ones came in, because the camp was being gradually broken up. Many internees were sent to Insterburg, where there appears to be a camp for Nazi partisans. Others are simply left on the road because they have suddenly become uninteresting. The cat-and-mouse game goes on.

We that are left behind sometimes have nothing to do. We sun ourselves by the open windows, contemplating our conquerors. Several of them are still detailed to guard the building. They walk up and down, or lounge on the easy chairs they have dragged in front of the doors for the purpose.

It's most amusing to watch them bicycling, which obviously has the charm of novelty for them. Wildly ringing their bells they tear up and down the road, preferably through the puddles, of which there are many because all the drains have been stopped up. When the water spurts up they shout for joy. Many of them had never seen bicycles before and would only gradually trust themselves to them. They are afraid of anything unfamiliar. Trusses, for instance, strike them as very mysterious; they tear them off people, hold them to their ears, try to break them, and if they don't succeed, fling them high into the air in a wide arc. They evidently take them for secret radio transmitters.

They are utterly insensitive to noise. Some of them stand the whole day in the garages, working all the available motor-horns. The radio blares without a stop in their quarters, until far into the night. Electric light has to be as glaring as possible too. Lighting circuits are installed at top speed, and where there is glass left in the windows, holes are shot in the panes so that the wires can be led through. One is repeatedly astonished at the rapidity with

which they hit on the simplest way of attaining their purpose; the
immediate moment is all that exists for them; everything must
serve it, no matter whether what they ruin in the process is something they will be in dire need of the next minute.

One is perpetually dumbfounded by their total lack of any relation to things which, to us, are a part of life itself. One ends by
giving up thinking of them as creatures of one's own kind, and
gradually assumes the attitude of the lion-tamer. This happens
quite automatically, for even before one is conscious of one's own
behaviour, one is exposed to their extraordinarily prompt reaction
to any form of resistance. To show fear is to fare worst of all with
them, it provokes them visibly to attack. Audacity, on the other
hand, can get one a surprisingly long way. The most hopeless
policy of all is to try and make them like you. We often observe
the fruitlessness of such attempts by our countrymen with a certain
wry pleasure. The Russians have no use for such arts; they use
people of that sort for their own purposes and openly despise them.

It is when they sing that we realise most clearly that they come
from another world. They form a community then, and include
us as hearers, in some immeasurable expanse. They are living over
here, for the moment at least, and everything here is as unreal to
them as some circus they have been led into. When they return
home later on, all their experience here will seem to them like a
mad dream.

That is why it never occurs to them to look upon us as anything
resembling themselves, and our claims on their humanity find
hardly any echo in them. The fact that they drive cars, fire rifles,
listen to the radio, and are trained to many other of our tricks,
still creates no living bridge from man to man. Of course it won't
always remain so. They will get used to things; we know how
teachable they are. The excitement of the circus will die down. But
then they will be useless for the purpose they are meant to fulfil;
they will be thrown away and replaced by others, with whom the
dance will begin again. It's not exactly fear that one feels at this
thought, but helplessness, as though one were lying under a heavy
wet blanket.

Compared with this uniformity, the diversity of one's own
countrymen strikes one all the more; one is perpetually astonished
at the difference between one human being and another. Under
so-called normal conditions this is not so noticeable; there are written and unwritten laws which most people observe. But here, where

no law runs, every characteristic comes glaringly to light. The fact that one can be seen is no longer a reason for not doing what one likes. Everything is permitted because there is nobody left to forbid it. And one asks oneself seriously whether good breeding and morals are not merely peace-time luxuries.

Meanwhile the camp is shrinking more and more in size. One day I found myself left with a few nurses and medical orderlies, and the patients, about fifty in number, who have still to be examined if they are ever able to stand up again. All the other doctors and patients have been transferred to the Treasury and to the Elisabeth Hospital, part of which is still standing. Schreiner has been sent there, and—to Schreiner's sorrow—Schäfer too, this time as an architect.

Except for Erika, the only member left of my little party is Chaplain Klein. We haven't much to do, and have decided to read something together. The Bible suggested itself at once, but as a Catholic he has had to take a little leap to step into the Old Testament with me. We started right at the beginning, and were relieved to find that light was created independently of the heavenly bodies. So it won't perish along with those bodies, as Mephisto declares. It evidently merely makes use of them as a disguise.

The medical superintendence of the hospital has now been taken over by a woman whose character we learnt to appreciate at the beginning of the camp period. A tall, very lively, good-looking young woman from Riga, she presented herself first as a nurse, but now gets people to call her Dr. Natasha. I saw her first as she passed us in the crowd on one of the staircases and exchanged a few hurried words with Schreiner. I asked him who she was. He only knew her Christian name, and that we ought to try and keep in touch with her. Several times during the next few days she sent us something from her dinner, or asked one of us to come and fetch it. I went to see her once, too, and was allowed to sit in her room for a little while and begin to eat. She lives in a barrack room with two children, six and three years old. She had been living among Germans ever since the taking of Riga in 1941, and her life is probably in danger for that reason; but we don't talk of that. She doesn't know much about medicine, but she can get along with a hypodermic syringe she carries about with her, with the help of which she gives medical treatment to the Russian officers. They can stand a big dose, and if they feel thoroughly dizzy afterwards the effect of the remedy impresses them all the more. She has collected large quantities of capsules and tablets, and finds plenty of opportunities to use them. She has also invented a species of massage which her patients are ready to undergo.

Once she actually asked me for advice. One of the dreaded NKWD leaders was in a high fever, and demanded to be cured on the spot. When we entered the ward the man was sitting with a cap pushed to the back of his neck and the radio going full blast, behind a bottle of vodka, in a cloud of tobacco smoke, coughing at the top of his voice. Before him on the table lay a heap of tablets of every sort, red, yellow and white, that he was to take in a certain order. He asked me if it wouldn't be better if he swallowed them all at once, then he might get well more quickly. I took a closer look at them; there was no sublimate among them, he would be able to stand all the rest. One or two, however, which looked to me like sleeping tablets, I coaxed away from him and Natasha. I advised him to take the others at intervals. Then he asked me if massage would be any good. It could do him no harm either—he appeared to have influenza. Natasha was fairly pleased with my advice, but as her patient had not recovered next day she gave him a few injections, to be on the safe side. And these will no doubt have been helpful too.

It is certainly no easy game that Natasha has to play here; but she plays it with courage, and we benefit by it as well. On this last day of the camp she has actually become my chief, and I am only too glad she should enjoy this little intermezzo in the farce. We visited the wards together, and the patients were all delighted with her. Fortunately she is thrifty in the matter of prescriptions. When I am finally transferred myself I shall feel quite easy at leaving the last patients in her care; she has more means of helping them than I, and will make use of them.

Our departure from the camp was so informal that I was able to smuggle into the lorry the whole of the dispensary that we had set up for ourselves. Doktora had taken the cushion with the pistol in it back to the Treasury somewhat earlier. I wanted to leave it behind, but she insisted on carrying it out of the camp like a handbag, under her arm; the sentry hadn't held her up for some time now. She found it more difficult than I did to part with the thing.

Just as we were leaving, the Commandant appeared and bade us a really friendly goodbye. When the camp gates closed behind us he was still standing there, watching us. We almost felt like waving.

GERMAN CENTRAL HOSPITAL

Mid-June to Mid-October 1945

WE entered the Treasury as late-comers. I had been there a week earlier, accompanying patients, and had three hours in which to inspect the hospital. The building is one of the few left standing. On the yard side, however, it was damaged by a heavy bomb—at the same moment, as it turned out, when the heaviest bombs were falling on us at the Municipal Hospital. Staff Surgeon Temme, who was working with Bothmer, was killed at the time, with some of the soldiers. They had just moved in here with their main dressing station, after the post office beside the Main Railway Station had been destroyed by artillery fire. In the gateway of the courtyard, Bothmer himself was hit by a bullet the following day, when the Russians were marching in. The reception office is on the left of the gateway, and there I found junior surgeon Brichzy, still in uniform. He received me very kindly and gave me his dinner—two platefuls of grey pea soup, a typical East Prussian dish that they have been enjoying for the last six weeks. The kitchen is right alongside. I found the courtyard crowded with patients waiting to be admitted; even those we had brought with us from the camp had first to be laid down on the ground outside; the house is over-occupied, and not so many die as fresh ones come in.

On my way about the house I found quite a number of nurses with whom I had worked in the Fortress days, and many patients who had once been mine. They all had mask-like faces, and moved very slowly about. To my surprise, the liveliest among them was the dentist from the Samaritan Hospital. He was fit to work again, and had organised a dental ward. He drew me into his room at once, and handed me a ball of horse-meat that one of his Russian patients had given him. He warned me earnestly against his fellow-worker, a pleasant-looking young man, as one of the most dangerous of the official spies. In any case, he said, one must be very careful what one said in this house.

That was my first impression, too, at our reception in the main entrance on our final moving in. A great lanky girl was standing in the doorway looking me up and down. I pushed her aside a little, to get through the doorway with my dispensary. She seemed about to speak to me, but I took no notice of her, and made my way towards a woman I knew, who was sitting on a trunk in the vestibule. She had noticed the little incident, and adjured me to beware of the creature; she was in the service of the NKWD and was feared by all alike. On the score of a big, ugly operation scar on her neck, she had had a certificate made out to the effect that the Russians had freed her at the moment when the Nazis were trying to cut her throat. Armed with this she had free passage everywhere and exercised the most frightful terror.

I looked round the reception hall, and thought it was not exactly comfortable to sit about in in any case. There were flowers on a table, it is true, and a couple of state chairs out of the Committee Room, but in addition to these I was aware of more than one pair of eyes appraising me. I felt like some object in a shop window to which the price had not yet been affixed.

To my surprise I was given a little room to myself on the top floor. Dr. Hoff, whom I had known at the Municipal Hospital, had occupied it hitherto, but had been fetched away recently by the NKWD and had not returned.

Giese and Röckert, my trusty allies, I found somewhat at a loss. They hadn't discovered any place to settle in, and during the three days they had been there they had been given food only at their urgent entreaty. They helped me to stow the dispensary in safety and then brought their luggage along to my room. It's fairly cool there in spite of the broiling heat outside. A chestnut tree rears its roof of leaves and countless flowers right above the window; we look out into a green world.

All at once a heavy thunderstorm blew up, and for several minutes we sat like Noah in the Ark under a downpour of rain. When it was over, Doktora came to take us on a tour of inspection through the building. But we had hardly reached the big window at the end of the corridor when we were held up by an extraordinary sight. Down below, against the black background of the departing storm, lay a whitely shimmering, turbulent sea of ruins, lighted up by the evening sun. From the midst of it rose the riven tower, like an exclamation mark, and over it, in unique perfection, stretched a rainbow, like the gate of Heaven over the desert. We held hands. When the apparition began to fade we turned and went back to our room without a word, struck dumb by what we had seen. 'Shouldn't we read the watchwords?' suggested Doktora. I fetched the book out of my luggage and handed it to her. She opened it at the 13th June and read : 'God said : I do set my bow in the cloud, and it shall be for a token of a covenant between me and the earth.' She left the second text unread. We stared at the floor in silence, and we seemed to hear the Angels of God ascending and descending.

Next day I was put in charge of the men's surgical ward, so called because the patients there are suffering from wounds in addition to their other troubles. A deaconess from the Samaritan Hospital is my Ward Sister. In the operating theatre downstairs on the courtyard side there is constant activity, consisting almost entirely of operations on purulent wounds. The surgeons working there are old Professor Ehrhardt and Dr. Ody, a staff surgeon from Bothmer's field hospital. Dr. Rauch has now started work again, too, having recovered, under Erika's care, from the hardships of the walking tour through the Samland. Dr. Keuten, who until recently had been operating alone, is seriously ill with typhus, and so is his wife, who is a doctor herself. Two deaconesses, Sisters Lydia and Martha, are acting as theatre sisters.

Another member of the theatre staff, a medical orderly named K., thinks he knows exactly where Bothmer is buried. I made him take me to the spot, and resolved to disinter the body, as it is probably only lightly covered over with earth. I should like to give my friend a proper grave, for it would be unbearable to be running around here, taking life seriously, knowing all the time that that man was lying somewhere quite near, just under the surface of the ground. Giese came to help me. We began by searching the top floor of the house for something to serve as a coffin, and found a narrow cupboard that would do. Then we went to work with our spades. In the communication trenches dug in the slope above the railway lines during the Fortress days, lie several hundred dead from the time of the Russian entry, lightly buried in layers one over another. The orderly marked out the place for us exactly —here the head and there the feet, barely eighteen inches down. However used to this sort of thing one may be, one is never quite hardened to it. Reaching from here to there, then, as well he may, considering his height ... and then the scar over his eye, and the mortal wound; it must surely be possible to recognise him even now, after two months. It was on the 8th April that he was shot in the gateway. The Russians had already broken into the building and made the doctors and nursing staff line up outside. Then came a German counter-attack. A rifle bullet tore his chest open. When it became possible to attend to him later on, he made them give him a looking-glass and showed them how to patch him up. They did their best, but the attempt failed and he died two days later.

We found the digging very difficult; he must lie deeper, anyway. I remembered our standing together that night, only a few hundred yards from this spot, while the cranes flew over our heads. How good it is that there should be moments one can define so exactly. They are the hooks on which we can hang the tangled weft of our life.

While we were in the midst of digging I was suddenly called away. The entire Treasury building is to be evacuated at once, and I have been selected to go as advance guard to the fresh asylum they have allotted us : the remains of the Samaritan Hospital. Giese didn't feel like going on digging alone, and contented himself with making a little grave-mound over the spot. Meanwhile I started off with the first of the lorries, which were loaded with bedsteads and mattresses. The Russians have allowed us twenty-four hours for the move. Anyone that is not over there by then will have had it. Fifty lorries are to go to and fro, transferring all the equipment and about a thousand patients.

Late that afternoon I was unloading in the yard of the Samaritan, along with Erika, a number of nurses and a few men acting as assistant staff, when, while my back was turned, the lorries started off, and the men who were to have helped us drove away in them. I stood there alone with the nurses. We scattered quickly over the building, to get at least an idea of the place before dark. The nurses had worked here before and soon found their way about. The new concrete building is still mostly intact; only the upper storeys have been hit here and there, and the roof has been ripped off in several places. But nothing else is left, of course, as the place has been empty since the evacuation on the 11th April, except that some Russians appear to have slept in the basement. There we found the usual sofas with their leather coverings torn off. Not a window is unbroken; the doors have been lifted off their hinges and left lying about the passages. All the drains are stopped up. The lighting wires and water-pipes, useless now in any case, have been torn out of the walls. We gave up all attempt to figure out how we were to live there; like everything else, it will happen somehow, we shall live to see it. For the moment the heavenly evening sun made up for all the impossibilities awaiting us. We didn't even hurry to drag things upstairs. Tomorrow the whole of the narrow courtyard will be chock-a-block with them; then perhaps everything will be shoved upwards of itself. The little strength my nurses have left doesn't go very far anyhow. They pitched camp on the floor on the third storey. Erika is there too. On the fifth floor, where my Men's Ward is to be, I looked for a room for myself. Right at the rear, at the end of the corridor, there is one, unsuitable for patients but more or less answering to our personal requirements. I marked it there and then and barricaded it.

Next morning things started in earnest. To avoid thinking out how everything was to be organised, I set to at random. Beds, furniture and patients came pouring in together, covering the entire premises. In the morning the Russians worked with us, and things were not too bad, but in the afternoon they merely hung about on the stairs and in the doorways, laughing at the chaos. We sought consolation, as usual, in the thought that this too, like so much else, would be over some day.

One of the seriously ill patients lying on stretchers on the floor of the crowded entrance hall caught hold of my leg as I was passing. I was horrified to recognise a man I had long ago thought of as dead. He had been in the dysentery department at the camp, and used to be fetched every night to be examined. He returned severely beaten every time, because he refused to admit that he had been a Blockwarden. One night I was called to see him. He appeared to have a twisted bowel, and was so ill already that an operation, even if we had been able to perform one, would probably not have helped him. I gave him morphia. Immediately afterwards he was fetched again for examination. I pointed out his condition, but it was no use. Giese and I then asked to be allowed at least to carry him, but the guard would not allow this. We were, however, permitted to go along with him, while he pushed the unfortunate man in front of him. The Kommissar took no notice of our declarations either; on the contrary, he almost flew into a rage on account of the morphia we had administered. And then the man was once more examined. Standing outside the door we heard him collapse several times under the blows. We waited there, expecting to be taken to task ourselves on account of the morphia, but the man was simply kicked out again at our feet, and down the stairs. Not till we were alone with him were we able to carry him back. His expression, when I saw him more clearly at day-break, made a deep impression on me : a mixture of hatred, impotence and greed of life. He even showed me a photograph of himself. Nothing was left of the fat, self-satisfied face but the eyes, although these now stood out from their orbits from fear, fury and emaciation. In the afternoon we sent him by ambulance to the Treasury, and reported him to the Russians as dead. Professor Ehrhardt then operated on him after all, but was unable to remedy the bowel condition. And now, three days later, he is still alive and has withstood the second move. He is a mere skeleton now, but he won't give in; it makes me shudder to look at him.

Towards evening the whole of the road was blocked with patients and equipment. Over the way, in a part of the old Municipal Hospital, Doktora is settling in. As ill luck will have it, she has been put in charge of the tuberculosis department. Along with the nurses allotted to her she goes tirelessly dragging one bed after another up to the second floor, while her patients stand around without lifting a finger. There are one or two veritable devils among them, who are probably not ill at all, but go roving about everywhere, doing duty as informers to the Russians.

The hurly-burly went on for another whole day; then at last all the patients were accommodated, and the first dead buried in the graveyard of the Altrossgärter Church. The Russians have sent us a lot of glass, with which some of the windows can be glazed as a start. I have moved up to the top storey with my 170 patients, and am living with my two faithful friends in the aforementioned corner room. Erika has taken over the little anteroom, so as to be able to keep an eye on us. We are glad to be living so high up, and are beginning to breathe again.

June 1945

Some 1,500 people have found shelter in this building, a thousand patients and at least five hundred nursing staff, male and female. Many of these have never had anything to do with nursing, but they make every effort to retain some link with the hospital because this affords them more protection and a better chance of surviving. Outside they are at everybody's mercy, and for this reason we can hardly discharge any of our patients. Having no home, death from starvation on the road is what normally awaits them. As far as possible, therefore, we fit them into the machinery of the place. Actually, the need only rarely arises, for nearly all those admitted as patients die after a shorter or longer period without having shown any improvement. Every day thirty or forty dead have to be carried down of a morning, wrapped in black-out paper, and piled up beside the rear gateway. From there they are conveyed by degrees in a two-wheeled timber-cart to the ground beside the ruined Altgrossgärter Church, where they are buried in common graves under the supervision of Pastor Leitner.

The two topmost storeys now constitute the surgical department, as they did before. My men are right at the top, the women a floor lower. These used to be in Dr. Ody's charge, but he was suddenly removed by the Russians and sent to Wehlau. His place has been taken by Dr. Rauch, who has now more or less recovered from the effects of being dragged about the country. We work side by side in the operating theatre, and relieve each other on occasion. Things are lively there all day. The premises are in good condition, as the outer walls have remained intact, and we have any amount of instruments, medicines and dressings, because enormous stores of these have been laid up in the town. But what use is all this, when one can't give the people anything to eat? They've pulled through somehow up to now—longer than one could have expected—but after all there is a limit to starvation.

The people they bring us are nearly all in the same condition : skeletons above, heavy water-skins below. Some come by themselves, on shapeless, swollen legs, and sit down outside the entrance door, where many others like them are lying on improvised stretchers or on the ground. When their turn comes they often give some trifling ailment, such as a bad finger, as their reason for coming, for they can no longer feel their legs. That is evident when we lay them on the table and slit the greasy, glassy skin from top to bottom with a knife, without their reacting in any way. We wonder then, every time, whether there is any sense in amputating the legs, or whether it wouldn't be better just to let these people die. And as a rule we decide on the latter course.

This death from starvation is a strange way of dying. There is no revolt. People give you the impression that they have left their physical death behind them already. They still walk upright, one can even speak to them; they reach for the stub of a cigarette—

more easily than for a piece of bread, with which they would no longer know what to do—and then all at once they collapse, like a table that has stood up to the heaviest burden until the additional weight of a fly breaks it down.

Apart from these legs our work is mostly concerned with bad, sometimes very bad, inflammatory tumours, including neck carbuncles, which often stretch from one ear to the other. If they are swarming with maggots we consider this a good sign, for then there is some hope of a cure.

Even the women are beginning to give way now. Many a one we came to know in the camp has passed through our hands again, a mere shadow of her former self. The most terrible thing about them is often the trash they talk—so completely unconnected with the present emergency, as though all we have been living through in common for so many months was merely a delusion, not brutal reality. Shortly before she collapsed, a woman in her forties, held together only by the shell of her former coquetry, asked me where she should apply for her maintenance. She'd worked long enough in the Gauleiter's office, she said, to be entitled to it.

It was only by degrees that we managed to discover her real reason for coming to us. She had spent ten days in an allotment garden, feeding on nothing but unripe currants. Now her bowel was choked with seeds. The measures required to free it again nearly cost her her life.

Occasionally, however, we have normal surgical interventions to make, for which we wash according to rule, and which give us the heartening illusion that we are still bona fide surgeons. They are mostly concerned with impacted fractures, convoluted bowels due to the twisting of the shrunken mesentery, and now and then an appendicitis. Besides which we come across things that otherwise hardly exist today, such as gangrenous stomatitis (noma), in which the part of the face affected falls away after a few days, with the jawbones, teeth, lips and cheek, leaving an enormous hole.

In addition to the men's ward I have taken over the surgical service of the children's ward, a particularly difficult and depressing task, because we know the children are being even more defrauded than the rest. The Russians deal out a certain amount of fat for them every day, with which we might be able to keep some of them alive, but it never reaches them, it is diverted at the last minute, and somebody else hoards it up for themselves. I had an encounter at the very beginning with a woman working in the children's ward, in which we nearly came to blows, and she is not the only one of her kind. We are surrounded by a swarm of shady creatures, police spies of every age and degree of dangerousness, who make their living by betraying their countrymen to the NKWD. For this institution, strangely enough, makes use of traitors even here, although it could render us all harmless if it wanted to, without any intermediary. But the appearance of justice has to be preserved in some way. Or else it is considered expedient to demoralise as many people as possible by accustoming them to betrayal. In any case we always shudder when certain people turn up in our department and go rummaging through the wards, taking notes with the greatest effrontery. That night one or more unfortunates are sure to be fetched away, never to be seen again. It's difficult to guess what the civilian occupation of these people used to be, except in the case of a man named Schmidt, whom we know to have been active in the SD.[1] How is it, I often wonder, that these devils don't get murdered? But then, would I have the pluck to do it myself? Don't we all continue to look on patiently, always hoping the cup may be removed from us?

Facing the back door stands the Frischbier School, the building in which the kitchen is now installed. Twice a day, in pails and tin cans, our soup is fetched from there, made alternately of oatmeal and sugar-beet peelings. In addition, we get a spoonful of sugar each and a kind of bread, which tastes of paraffin and contains a lot of water. People scramble to carry out this duty, for there are some fairly well-fed compatriots in the kitchen, and there is sometimes a chance of picking up an extra morsel, so they will cheerfully carry the heavy pails up to the fifth floor. They are less anxious to carry down the full latrine buckets, which are emptied in the ruins nearby. But we always find people to do that too.

At first the water was drawn from the Castle pond, in which lie countless dead. Then there was a sudden rumour that water could still be obtained from a hand pump in the yard of the lemonade factory, not far away. Ever since then people have been queueing up all day with containers of every kind. If a gap occurs, the next-comers wait till a group has formed again, because to advance singly is to invite attack. We are like jungle beasts at the drinking pool. Down in the factory cellar there are still a lot of barrels of lemonade extract, which nobody bothers about because of the lack

[1] Sicherheitsdienst = Security Service.

of nourishment in it. There is also a bath-tub down there, in which I sometimes have a furtive wash.

As we can't, of course, live on the regulation soup, every free minute is spent in the search for food. The early morning is the best time for this, because there are fewer Russians about. At five o'clock by Russian time—three o'clock by ours—I sally forth, accompanied by Erika. In the Municipal Hospital on the other side of the road Doktora is waiting to join us. As a rule we begin by the suburbs of Karolinenhof and Maraunenhof. There, in the neglected allotment gardens, currants are growing in profusion, and the thick bushes offer good cover. Many people have taken up their quarters in the little huts standing there, for this reason. We do an exchange trade with them, taking them some of our beet soup and getting currants in return.

After the allotment gardens it's the turn of the deserted houses in the Cranzer Allee. Although they have been ransacked over and over again, one may still find a potato or some other edible thing here and there. What we always bring back with us is orache,[1] which grows as rankly as a weed everywhere. We eat it at every meal.

These excursions are often emotionally disturbing, not only because of one's constant awareness of the danger lurking near, but because of the enormous contrasts they bring to mind. The race-course affects me most of all. There was a time when it represented the peak of existence. We always arrived there in festive mood, to gaze enraptured at the horses and to see other people and be seen by them. Everything was so beautifully kept and organised. One leaned on the fence, held a short conversation, nodded to this person, followed that one with one's eyes, feeling at the very top of one's form. And now I lean on the fence again, clad in a canvas jacket, frayed trousers, foundling boots, without shirt or socks, watching a little bunch of cows guarded by a Russian sentry, grazing between the old hurdles. If one of the cows comes near enough I shall try and get some milk from her. All around me nothing but weeds, rubbish and ruins. Only the sky is still the same. And I ask myself which of these two realities is the one to which we actually belong.

Our hospital possesses some cows, three to be exact, which between them produce seven quarts of milk. They are guarded by Professor Urbschat, specially appointed to this duty and occasionally assisted by other workless university teachers. It is no

[1] A kind of spinach.

sinecure, for of course the cows are greatly coveted in spite of their leanness, and one day one of them, the best milker of the lot, fell a victim to assault. Two men drove her into a cellar and cut her throat, but were frightened away by the shouts of the cowherd. In our communal soup next day we saw an indefinable object floating, light yellow and soft, as to the nature of which we speculated for a long time, till Giese suddenly declared it must have something to do with 'the Herr Pastor his coo'. (Pastor Stachowitz, the institutional head of the Samaritan, is regarded by the Russians as the owner of the cows.) He was right; it was the udder of the murdered cow.

We have no meat as a rule, although seventy pounds of it is officially delivered to the hospital several times a week. As this consists mostly of the heads and feet of cows, complete with hide, hooves and horns, it is obvious that none of it reaches the patients.

Our two remaining cows give three quarts of milk between them, which trickles away somewhere. The matron of the hospital is supposed to have some of it every day. She is ill in bed in a cubicle alongside the dispensary, calmly and graciously facing her end, after having successfully protected many of her nurses from the worst during our most terrible period of all.

From my ward on the fifth floor an iron staircase leads to the flat roof, from which one has a grandiose view over the ruined town and the surrounding country. Late in the evening, when all is quiet in the building, we go and relax in the infinite peace one feels up there. We take chairs with us, and read something stimulating and inspiring together, indulge in conversations for which we are too much on top of one another by day, or fall into contemplation of the sky, across which long lines of wild duck go streaking, and one half of which remains light the whole night at this season.

We have no lack of literature. Everywhere, in all the houses, books have been left untouched—except for a few carried off and thrown away again—and lovers of books have been able to set up quite respectable libraries in their quarters.

We are kept busy enough by day, either by Russians descending on us suddenly for the purpose of a raid, or by intrigues among the various groups in the building. Or window-panes may come flying about our ears because some other building is being blown up nearby. There are dramatic human episodes, too, in which we get involved. Over the way, for instance, in the tuberculosis department, a madwoman was brought in, who kept everything around her in a commotion with her screams. All at once she managed to escape from the empty room in which she had been shut up, by climbing out of a window more than six feet above her on to the roof, which itself lay far above the window. There she sat, with her hair hanging down, leaning forward at a giddy height, on the little railing above the gutter, singing at the top of her voice the first thing that came into her head, down into the dead silence of the road below—hymns, popular songs, Hitler songs, a mad pot-pourri. After a time the Russians got fed up with it, and prepared to shoot the woman down. But meanwhile Doktora and the delousing orderly had set to work. We saw the two of them climbing out of two different mansard windows and making their way from right and left along the railing towards the runaway, Doktora armed with a syringe. How lightly and surely she moved up there! She is definitely bent on skirting the abyss. To everybody's astonishment the woman allowed herself to be pulled inside again through a window.

One day we were told we had to report to the police. A number of us were assembled and marched through the streets, led by a Russian. After crossing the whole of the town he found we had been going in the wrong direction. We then described an enormous half-circle, marched along the edge of the Upper Pond, through Maraunenhof, and finally across the fields and over a level-crossing to a military hut standing all alone in the landscape. Several fierce-looking officials were sitting there, with the usual yelping female interpreters, prepared to hack us in pieces. Convinced that this was just another of the traps into which one falls out of one's own stupidity, I slipped out of the ranks, with one or two others, and hid in an overgrown garden. There we awaited developments. It took hours for our comrades to pass through the locks. In the end they had not been given any papers, nor had their names been registered; they had merely been shouted at. The whole affair had obviously been got up, as usual, for the entertainment of the NKWD.

The 1st July was a radiant Sunday. Doktora came across and persuaded me to go with her on a reconnaissance trip to Preyl. Barefoot, and very scantily clad in other ways—somebody has made me a pair of shorts out of two towels—we attracted no attention, and got safely out of the town. The country was inconceivably deserted; we walked for an hour without meeting a soul. We picked cornflowers at the edge of the fields. When the corn is ripe we ought to come with scissors and cut off the ears. The big pond in Preyl, from which Königsberg's drinking-water used to be drawn, has been drained; the Russians were standing about in the mud, looking for fish.

My relations' house has been burnt down; all that is left is a part of the foundation walls and the ground floor, which a couple of women were engaged in clearing out. We got no answer from them to our questions. The stable buildings are still there, and I was tempted to go and see what had happened to the part where the racehorses were kept. The moment we entered we were stopped by a Russian and led with pride to the Commandant, who has taken up his abode in the trainer's flat over the stables. I held out my empty wallet and begged for some potatoes, upon which he let us go again. Where the garden used to be we found a Russian in the act of cooking his porridge over two bricks. He gave us some of it with a friendly gesture, and we sat by the edge of the pond to eat it. Opposite us, on the hill in the wood, lay the family graves. We went there to see if they were still to be found. They were unharmed, but partly overlaid by the haulms of potato-plants, which had sprouted out of the German defence post alongside. The potatoes underneath were still very small, but we filled our bags with them all the same.

Suddenly Doktora began to cry. I was greatly alarmed, for I had hardly ever known her to do this before. The midges were tormenting her, she said, and she begged me to take her out of the wood as quickly as possible. I knew there must be something else the matter, but couldn't get her to say what it was. When we were out on the road again she seemed better. We went to look at Warglitten Farm, on which the Russians appear to have started work, and were given a lift in a Russian cart that was going in the direction of Königsberg. We got out at Juditten, and Doktora made an attempt to look at her house, which is still standing and is occupied by Germans; but on entering it she was roughly attacked and had to retreat.

On Wednesday Doktora came to me in the operating theatre; she wanted me to look at the nape of her neck, which was itching horribly. I found a mass of lice, which had eaten their way deep under the skin. When I told her, she broke down. I tried to calm her, while Dr. Rauch helped me to cut away the hair and expose the spot. She recovered herself, but seemed so changed that I didn't know what to do. Her vitality must have come to an end long ago, I thought; she had been going about among us as if in a dream. Only her obedience to our Lord's command to love can have given her strength to be an example to her fellow-workers and to care for her patients, who all rely on her so fervently.

Next morning I was fetched across to see her, because they couldn't wake her. On her table lay a note saying she had taken some of her sleeping tablets because she hadn't been able to sleep for several nights, on account of the terrible itching; she was not to be woken unnecessarily. We left her to sleep. Although she would not have brought death to her aid with her own hand, I knew how gladly she would pass over now in sleep. But when that evening her condition remained unaltered, everything was set afoot, almost without reference to me, that has to be done on these occasions. All emotion was benumbed. I went about my daily work as if I had no concern in the event. I am perhaps dead too, inside, since I cannot summon up any desire to be consulted?

On Friday night her heart ceased to beat. The patients in the tuberculosis department fetched a coffin from Kalthof, where there is said to be a whole store of them. A militiaman, who works in the building, brought me a wooden cross he had made. We wrote her name on it, with the dates of her birth and death. And on the back of it we wrote the closing words of the Scriptures: 'Amen. Even so, come, Lord Jesus.'

The grave is there where they all lie, beside the Altrossgärter Church. In Doktora's Bible, as a bookmarker in the eighth chapter of the Epistle to the Romans, I found a little book in which she had made some notes: thoughts on certain texts, hints as to what had happened after the barriers were broken through. 'Russia—and there was a time when I wanted to go there. Now it has overthrown me.' I read the words over and over again, like a testament. And through them I heard those others sounding: 'These are they which came out of great tribulation and have washed their robes and made them white in the blood of the Lamb.'

All through July, in the intervals of work, I went for long walks alone, ransacking cellars and gardens, bringing back all sorts of gear, and sometimes flowers—once a blue clematis plant with innumerable blossoms. On these walks I often came upon people who had fallen by the way, both dead and living. Getting the living into the hospital was no simple matter, and meant coming to a fresh decision each time. I had never been so often reminded of the parable of the Good Samaritan—not without shame, for in most cases the salvage operation proved easier than I had expected.

I came across Russians in the cellars too. I once saw one leaning against the wall in front of me after my eyes had become accustomed to the darkness. He stood motionless, with one finger pressed to his lips. He was no doubt under a threat of death.

Erika is untiring in her search for provender. She lost all fear long ago, and always has tales to tell us of the nice Russians she has spoken to. One of them is going to bring her some potatoes; she is convinced that he will keep his word. (He did, but somebody snatched them away from him as soon as he appeared and refused to deliver them up again.)

Cooking goes on in the room alongside of ours. A corporal has put up a stove there, which he had dismounted elsewhere; and although he declares he knows nothing about it, the pots and other cooking utensils of at least twenty other parties simmer day and night on the stove beside ours. Erika often has to stand by for ages before she can get near.

A long way out, in the Schleiermacher-strasse, among the ruins of the Hans Schemm School, there are thousands of capsules lying under melted glass—narcotics, and drugs for heart and circulatory diseases. I discovered them on a scouting expedition with Erika, who had been in domestic employment near there for a year, and wanted to see if the family was still anywhere to be found. We returned with all our pockets full of these things, and I made the children who were playing about there promise to collect some more for us.

A few days later I set out in a little cart belonging to the hospital to fetch the stuff. Our old theatre sister Ida went with me, and we first made a detour to the Surgical Clinic in the Drummstrasse. We had worked there together at the end of January, and although six months of wild confusion had swept over it meanwhile, Sister Ida hadn't a moment's doubt that she would be able to find what she had hidden there at that time. And so it was. Out of a wide crack beside the side entrance door she drew several large pots of ointment, a mass of bandaging material and several cans of alcohol and petrol, much to the astonishment of the out-patients' department now installed there. We loaded our booty on to the cart in all haste and drove away before anybody could dispute our right to it.

Many a drama had been enacted in the clinic since we left. As Doktora told me when she came to the camp, my former Czech orderly had practised dental treatment there in grand style after the entry of the Russian troops, who made him crown their healthy teeth with gold from the rings they had looted. He was said to have grown so rich on what was left of the rings that a Russian murdered him for the treasure.

Every time we go out we look round not only for medical stores but for bedsteads and mattresses. My walking patients—five people camouflaged as such—have formed themselves into a gang to fetch these things and distribute them among the wards. We have designs, in particular, on the ruins of the Castle. These are guarded by a sentry, which suggests that there is something there worth digging for.

One morning at five all was ready. My scouts reported that the sentry was off guard. We broke in at once, and in a big room on the left of the gate we found several cases of dressings and other useful material, enough to load our barrow with several times over. A couple of heavy cases, bound with wire and addressed to Moscow, we had regretfully to leave behind. But we took a picture—packed up and marked 'Breughel'—with us as a curiosity. When we got back we found that it consisted unfortunately of hundreds of wooden fragments that couldn't be pieced together again. It had obviously been hacked to pieces with an axe and then laboriously collected again. In the afternoon the sentry was at his post in front of the Castle gate once more.

Not far from us, on the other side of the Königsstrasse, Professor Starlinger is acting as governor of the so-called Isolation Hospital, which includes the Yorckstrasse and Elisabeth Hospitals. Some 2,000 typhus patients have been assembled there. They lie two to a bed, the children four to a bed. We hear a lot about the place, but I had never yet found an excuse to go there, until one of the spies in the tuberculosis department informed me that Starlinger was at the head of a clique that was seeking my life and that of various other people.

I found the professor in a sort of monk's cell, lying on a narrow bed beside a table with books on it. He was holding in his hand—I couldn't believe my eyes—the very book I had been trying to find : Bismarck's thoughts and recollections, volume three. This led us at once into a delightful conversation, despite the difference in our views. I said nothing of the nonsense that had brought me there, and didn't even ask the professor whether he really had typhus, as the notice said on his door. Perhaps he was merely doing what he could to be rid of the Russians for a time. At the end of an hour I left him, feeling greatly cheered by the meeting. The whole organisation of the 'Isolation Hospital' has a certain style. In spite of some singularities of detail, it suggests a will to orderliness within the limits of moderation, and compared with the chaos in which we are drifting this has an extraordinarily beneficent effect.

As I was leaving the building I met the dreaded corpulent sister earlier referred to. I had known her in the Fortress days, when she was still quite harmless. 'Come and have tea with me!' she called out, and I accepted the invitation. Right in front, beside the entrance to the hospital, where she can see everything that goes on, she has appropriated two rooms, with the help of her Russian major, and fitted them up with the furniture left by the head of the Nerve Clinic. Although I knew every stick of it quite well, she referred to the whole installation as the dying bequest of her late brother; but out of sheer greed for her tea and a bit of bacon I espied in the background, I held my tongue, and put up with all the humbug till I had attained my object.

Near the Elisabeth Hospital there is a pond full of fairly clean water, in which I bathe sometimes. It lies in open country, surrounded by high ruined walls like stage scenery. One is quite alone there, for there is nobody living now in this maze. I only once met anyone there—two children who had likewise come to bathe. They leapt into the pond, diving, and spouting whole fountains of water out of their cheeks. Where they got all that energy was a mystery to me. I called out to them that they'd better not swallow any of the water because of the danger of typhus. But they wouldn't listen, they merely shouted, 'Ach, what does it matter what we die of? We're not going to survive anyway!'

It's a bit nerve-racking, going to the hairdresser who has set up shop on the ground floor of our building. The police spies give one another rendezvous there, and the mirrors and bits of broken glass lying about are so arranged that one can't look up without meeting watchful eyes.

Towards the end of July my strength began to fail. I felt slack, I couldn't breathe properly, or remain standing for long, and had to keep reaching for support. It was nothing much; but one day Schreiner turned up, alerted by somebody, and took me across to the Elisabeth Hospital. There I just lay in bed and bothered my head about nothing any more. Endless peace lapped me round. I lay beside two Catholic priests, one of whom had typhus, while the other, or so I suspected, was merely in hiding. We looked out on the white walls of the chapel, through the lancet windows of which faint singing reached us at regular intervals. I let myself go entirely. Schreiner took charge of me, Professor Starlinger came and examined me, Sister Raphaela was a perfect angel . . .

After a fortnight I felt better again, and could begin to make myself useful about the hospital. The Sisters here are lucky; they were never entirely burnt out, and still possess things that are no longer procurable elsewhere. At the time of the Russian entry they had flooded the cellar so that all the tinned food was preserved; they even contrived to keep a cow concealed in one of the upper storeys for a while, owing to their good team spirit and the blessed absence of internal treachery.

At the end of August Schreiner disappeared. A Russian to whom he had given one of the usual treatments had agreed to take him with him. Sister Raphaela and I were the only people to know this; one can't say goodbye to everybody, unfortunately, however much one would like to. The Russian was taking him as far as Stettin; how one went on from there we had no idea. But more than one of our friends had managed to slip away by then, doctors included, and we had only heard of one or two being recaptured.

I was moved into Schreiner's room. Brichzy was living alongside and doing duty as a doctor himself. Assistant Surgeon Ott, who had belonged to my group at the Field Hospital, and Pastor Gross, with whom I had lain ill, came over occasionally from the Isolation Hospital of an evening to play skat or chess with us, or to take part in a nocturnal potato feast for which we had to thank some Russian patient or other. In the corner of the room stood a roll of canvas six feet high, which we sometimes unrolled for fun. It was a special piece of loot, a big oil painting from the Committee Room of the Treasury, which Brichzy had hastily ripped out of its frame when we were forced to leave. Although in spite of its gigantic size it represented nothing but a miserable little forest scene with a puddle in the foreground—an obvious symbol of future impoverishment— its sudden disappearance caused the Russians a lot of trouble, and they made every possible effort to find it again. Up to now, however, nobody had known where it had been left. Later on it served more than one good purpose : Erika was buried in it, and rucksacks for escapers were made out of the other half.

At midday I often went up to the roof and sunned myself. Autumn was near. Crows were flying over the dead city and set me wondering how they might be caught. In a lime-trap, perhaps, but they wouldn't venture into one yet. Not till the winter . . . But we won't, and can't, live through another winter here, it's simply impossible. People are all dying, as it is. And then the cold, and the endless months in which nothing grows, not even weeds—it's not to be thought of.

In the middle of September Erika was brought to us at St. Elisabeth's, suffering from typhus. She was very ill, delirious all day long, with an irregular pulse. Whenever I went near her she saw spooks, warned me against false friends who were after my life, and entreated me to escape. Thank goodness, she has a bed to lie in and is well looked after; the nurses do all they can for her.

I moved over to the Central Hospital again, where Dr. Keuten, now recovered from his attack of typhus, had been attending to my men's ward in the interval. He and his wife had lain long in danger of death at Schreiner's place at St. Elisabeth's, almost pulseless for days at a time, until at last they slowly took a turn for the better. Two other young doctors, Thiele and Arndt, died of typhus at that time.

Soon after I resumed my post at the Central Hospital Dr. Rauch went down with typhus. He was not removed, however, but remained in his own room. All our wards were so pervaded with typhus cases now, that isolation no longer had any point in it. The only advantage of this was that the Russians kept away from us more and more. They came up to the fifth floor only in exceptional cases, and left again very hurriedly. Dr. Keuten had taken over the women's ward. Giese had diphtheria, Sister Martha Wolf of the operating theatre had died of it, and been buried in the courtyard of the hospital. The delousing orderly, too, a young, strong country lad died. And how many others that one had known! More than one could count. Of the evangelical pastors who had remained in Königsberg, only half were still alive; I think only five. Two of them, who had always held together, and were now living together, came to see me : Pastor Beckmann and Pastor Müller of Haberberg. They had made definite plans for restoring the church services, and had got as far as seeing the Town Commandant in connection with this.

By the beginning of October I felt strong enough to pay the pastors a return visit. They were living in Ponarth, in one little room, looked after by the deaconess, doing a lot of visiting and holding services. Hardly anybody dared attend these, however, because there was always a risk of having their last possessions stolen while they were out.

The road to Ponarth was beset with difficulties. On the wooden bridge behind the 'Dominsel', the only one left over the Pregel, there was a sentry who was most unwilling to let one pass. Further on, at the main railway station, one had to clamber over the embankment because the bridge over the road had fallen in. Half-grown youths belonging to the Russian families now swarming in Ponarth lay in wait there to attack women struggling painfully over the railway track. Men usually banded together for protection on the journey; I always carried a piece of iron with me for safety, and swung it to and fro.

October brought cold and rain with it. Our hospital had begun to look like some enormous gipsy caravan. Out of every other window a smoking stove-pipe protruded, sealed round with cardboard. Fresh troops had arrived in the town, and attacks and acts of violence were increasing. Every now and then shots were even fired at the hospital windows.

Famine was leading to excesses here and there, and human flesh was being eaten. One couldn't wonder at it, or even feel upset about it. How horrified we had been, not so long ago, when we heard the same thing about the camps for Russian prisoners of war in our own country! We imagined that only Asiatics were capable of such a thing. Now the Russians were getting upset about us in their turn. Poor Dr. Rauch, in particular, was having a bad time; he was forever being ordered to attend post-mortems and exhumations, to give an expert opinion on pieces of meat, and ghastly things of this kind. He won our deep gratitude by a demonstration he gave at one of the higher education lectures demanded by the Russians on what they choose to call the 'oedematose disease'. After the first speaker had meandered anxiously round the subject, he demonstrated this disease, which the Russians and their friends take such a particular interest in, on the corpse of a young girl, showing us all the organs and tissues in turn, and describing them with dignified calm and expertise. Then he turned, in conclusion, to the Russians seated in front of him with the words : 'Give them enough to eat, and the disease will disappear of itself.'

A vague rumour which had been circulating for weeks—that we were soon to be transported to the West—suddenly assumed greater distinctness. Swedish ships were said to be on their way to fetch us; the people from the western parts of the town would be the first to go, and then the rest of us along with the inmates of the hospitals. No wonder the news ran like wildfire through the suffering population.

And as nobody can ever resist adding a trifle out of their own imagination, we soon knew exactly how big the ships were, what they looked like inside, what there would be to eat on board, and other details on which our primitive wish-dreams could flourish. In Pillau, where the ships were expected, the Red Cross was already setting up a camp. And as the transportation was to be effected under international supervision, we need have no fear that the Russians would carry us off elsewhere.

Freedom became more palpable every day. And although not one of the earlier rumours had been confirmed, people began drawing on their last reserves in order to hold out in the interval before their departure. The last woollen jacket was bartered for six potatoes, one's only overcoat for a tin of meat, and many a carefully concealed object came to light. The swindlers took full advantage of the situation; they offered people tins filled with mud and leaves, and those that fell into the trap nearly lost the remains of their reason when they opened them.

Meanwhile the winter was steadily approaching. The rain fell in torrents and the days were growing visibly shorter. In the evening, when it was so dark that one could no longer distinguish the patients, we gathered in the little corner room where Giese and Röckert were still living, and sat snugly round a 'Hindenburg candle'. Only Erika was missing : she was still dangerously ill. When we dispersed I often decided to go and visit Dr. Rauch, who was in a high fever, and had such exciting tales to tell that one could listen to him for hours; fantasy and reality were subtly intermingled. His thoughts, too, were revolving round our departure, and one evening he described thirteen ships to me, in which we were to start the voyage in a day or two. According to him, however, they were not lying off Pillau, they had reached Königsberg harbour already; one ought to be able to see them from the roof. He asked me to look for them first thing next morning and report to him.

I always enjoyed climbing the iron staircase to the roof. Up there one felt as free as a bird that only needed to spread its wings to leave all misery behind it. And when I climbed from the roof to the little cabin at the top of the lift-shaft, I had reached the highest point in the whole district. It was true that one could see the harbour from there. Far away in the west, at the edge of the field of ruins, a strip of water gleamed; but however hard I tried, I could see no sign of a ship. How could one have got that far, anyhow? The harbour channel, as we knew, was not yet navigable.

Dr. Rauch received my report with an indulgent smile. I couldn't have looked properly; it required some effort; it wasn't so simple as all that. I promised to go and look again later, when the weather had cleared a bit, and consoled him meanwhile with the latest news from the Isolation Hospital. Plans for the transport of the 2,000 typhus patients were being worked out there. Two men, who claimed to have a radio set, were delivering a running commentary on the position and internal arrangements of the ships in question. Professor Starlinger had asked the doctors to settle in good time who was to share the two-berth cabins with whom.

My own feelings were strangely divided. On the one hand I was giving myself up, in spite of all doubts, to the same illusions as the rest, if only to avoid thinking of the winter; on the other, the ground on which we were living here was so heavy with the dead that it almost hurt me to think that our troubles might now be solved in some happy fashion. What should we look like when we met people over there and they began asking us about those we had left behind? We should have to gloss over the sufferings of the dead if we were not to blush for shame ever after under their reproaches. 'What!' I could hear them saying, 'And here you are, coming back, and even wanting to go on living! What sort of creatures are you? You must evidently have kept yourselves alive at the expense of the others.' How could we answer such accusations? I could see no possibility of beginning a new life without betraying the dead.

But then there came a day when all these considerations were thrown to the wind. On the 18th October, towards evening, just as I had come to the end of my distressing round of visits, our friend Paula met me, greatly excited, and whispered to me as she passed, 'Herr Doktor, you must get away, they are going to arrest you to-morrow. I've just heard it by accident. If anybody guesses, I'll be in for trouble. Get everything ready; I'll come again when it's dark.' I watched her as she ran off in all haste, and felt the spark of life reawaking in me that I had long since written off. To be free once more from our grave-digger's task, to stand once again on my own feet! I had yearned for this moment so long that I was hardly prepared for it now. I packed up a few things in a hurry and took them to the Grey Sisters[1] in St. Elisabeth's Hospital. Then I told my two allies. I should have liked to take them with me on the journey, but they couldn't make up their minds so quickly, and were still hoping, moreover, to get out of the place in a legal way.

[1]Franciscan nuns = 'Poor Clares'.

When it was dark Paula reappeared and told me what she knew. She had happened to hear a Russian having my name spelt out to him, so that he could arrest me next morning. The man that had betrayed me was one from whom I had often obtained some medical stores, which he had collected in a drawer. I knew he was an informer, and could quite believe I was on his list; but I had always been on good terms with him. What could have induced him to deliver me up to the NKWD now? No matter, I was heartily grateful to him.

I had no doubts about Paula; she had been an ardent admirer of Doktora, and would go through fire and water for me. We had known her for a long time; she had worked hard for us in the Municipal Hospital at the end of the Fortress period. On the second day after the surrender she had robbed the Russians of one of their horses, slaughtered it, cooked it and fed the patients with it. Later on she fell very ill, and was nursed back to health at the Treasury under Doktora's care. As she behaved and dressed in such a way that nobody really knew whether she was a man or a woman, she was able to lead the Russians by the nose better than anybody. Everything she obtained as a result was for the benefit of those she had taken to her heart. She often brought us things to eat, and for my sake she also supplied two young men lying very ill in my department, whom I had lodged in a little room by themselves. They were still comparatively strong, and all the more in need of help for that reason. I commended them to her now afresh.

I spent the evening with my two friends. They read to me out of the last chapter of the Bible, and as a parting present they gave me a picture they had cut out of a monograph on Raphael : the angel delivering St. Peter from prison. Then I slept soundly and dreamlessly for a couple of hours until the morning.

When I woke, everything was greyly shrouded in fog and rain; the few trees left standing in the hospital yard were dropping their last leaves. I dressed noiselessly and went out into the passage. Dr. Fincke, with whom I had been sharing my room for the last few weeks, looked at me in astonishment. I hesitated for a moment, then told him hurriedly what was up. I should have felt I was betraying him if I hadn't. In the passage, outside the doors of the wards, lay the dead of last night; they flicker out in the early morning most easily, without any struggle. All that lies far behind them by then. There were only a few left for whom I have any hopes, among them the two that Paula was looking after. Life runs its course now only between the lines.

On the floor below, the theatre sister was already about. We exchanged a few words, and then I told her my time was up. She understood me at once, and said a kind word by way of godspeed. I wouldn't burden anybody else; by the time they learned of my flight I must be far away.

It was fairly light already when I left the building, but without any luggage I should attract no attention. And then there was the rain, helping to veil all that went on. Now may God be with you, all you dear and dreadful people living together under this roof! How many of you will yet be among those carted out daily through the dark back gate, the few paces to the Altgrossgärter Church, and then round to the left to the spot where since June five thousand inmates of this building have been buried in common graves?

As I went by, I took leave, too, of Doktora's grave. She had always wanted to travel through the East Prussian countryside by hidden by-ways, more for the sake of the ways than for the journey's end. If she had still been alive she would have been going with me now.

Erika had been up for some days, and came towards me beaming with joy, steadying herself by the beds. 'Look, Herr Doktor, how well I can walk now!' she called out. And then I had to tell her, too, why I had come. She was on to it at once. 'Oh, that's fine!' she said, 'I'll get dressed straight away—we can start in ten minutes.' It was useless to tell her she couldn't possibly walk for miles that day. 'Just let me do as I like,' she said, 'I can do anything if I choose.' What was I to do? For as long as I had known Erika, her life had been a constant sacrifice for others; she had never wanted anything for herself. Now I should have to let her go with me as far as her strength would allow her. It was madness, but I knew that nothing would cause her such a mortal injury as my refusal. She too was standing now on the further side of a frontier, from which she was hardly likely to return. So I agreed, at the risk of wrecking my whole undertaking.

Sister Raphaela, to whom we could safely confide our most secret plans, brought my rucksack, in which she had stowed a lot of good food taken from some hidden corner. Brichzy put in appearance, and then we waited a long while for Erika. Meanwhile a messenger came from the Central Hospital, little Frau Passarge, who worked in my department as a domestic servant. She was to tell me to hurry, for the Russians were there already, looking for me.

By about ten o'clock we were ready to start at last. Far too heavily clad in things inherited from the dead, and heavily laden as well, we set out. Erika had to lean her hand against the ruined wall as she walked—a wholly grotesque flight. People watched us from the windows, shaking their heads. There could be no doubt as to how it would end; somewhere by the roadside Erika would be left lying. We were used to that, they lay about everywhere. It was only to be hoped that this would happen within the precincts of the town, for then there would at least be a chance that somebody would help her back again. A little cart came that way every day, bringing patients to the hospital from Schönfliess.

We moved at a snail's pace through the moth-eaten city. Few Russians crossed our path, none took any notice of us. The pouring rain was once more our ally. The first big snag was the crossing of the Pregel; in the middle of the bridge stood a Mongolian sentry. We had nearly got past him when he challenged us and demanded our papers. We showed him a slip of paper on which our discharge from the hospital was entered in Russian, and gave one of the suburbs as our destination. That sufficed him, and the next moment we were able to submerge ourselves among the uniform skeleton houses on the left bank of the river. Even here there seemed to be people still living at the end of long alleys that wound in and out of the ruins that looked like theatrical scenery.

At the next rise in the road Erika had to stop. She sat at the side of a flight of steps, gasping for breath. I must be patient, just a moment, she said, then she would be able to go on. A lorry stopped in front of us, drawn by two tired horses. Three old men were loading fragments of sledges and carts upon it, which had been lying about ever since the flight. They helped Erika on to the lorry, and went on, stopping every few steps, while I helped them to load the lumber as best I could. I felt my scanty strength failing me, and the hope of getting out of the town that day grew ever smaller. The one advantage was that nobody took any notice of us.

Near the Friedländer Gate there were more people on the road; a few fairly undamaged houses were still standing there, and Russian troops were engaged in turning out the people who had made a temporary home in them, a thing that had been happening, over and over again, for the last six months. They were allowed to take with them as much as they could carry; the rest was to be left for the soldiers who were to move in there. No emotion was visible in the deathlike, torpid faces; and to those that had not shared the experience that had gradually brought people so low, it would have seemed quite natural to be treating them like cattle. Now they were standing about on the road, mostly women of uncertain age, clothed in sacks, legs and feet swollen to shapelessness and bound round with rags. There was nothing left for them but to camp among the bushes in the allotment gardens, now in the winter. The Russians paid no further attention to them; they may have been merely stopping here on their way somewhere else. There is no peace anywhere for them either.

Where the road leaves the town in the direction of Löwenhagen our lorry turned off to the left; it belonged, apparently, to a farm on which the Russians had assembled people as labourers. Erika got down and we went on on foot. I intended making for the part of East Prussia that was said to have been handed over to the Poles, because I should probably find it easier to escape detection there. The Polish sector was said to begin just beyond Preussisch Eylau, but nobody knew for certain; in any case I thought it advisable to steer southwards for the moment. We had to be careful not to stumble on the detention camp at Eylau, against which we had been warned; as far as one could judge that was the main danger point.

In the middle of Schönfliess suburb Erika's strength finally gave out. She dropped down on a heap of stones and couldn't get up again. The whole hundredweight of misery hung about my neck once more like a wet sack. Wasn't it worse than murder, what I was doing here? I was almost prepared to turn back and let fate do what it would with me. A Russian came towards us. I thought he was going to arrest me; but he merely asked the way and went on. I stood for a while waiting, ready to yield to the over-fatigue of my heart. But then Erika pulled herself together again, and said in a tone of command, 'Now you must go on, Herr Doktor, I only wanted to see you out of the town. Greet the people from me, and tell them to take care things don't happen to them as they did to us.'

As she spoke I suddenly realised that I had been haunted for days past by a glorious old hymn: 'And if you do not stake your lives . . .' I had rediscovered it by accident only recently. What was there left to say or protest? What was I waiting for? Was there not an angel standing between me and Erika already? And I began to walk away, hesitatingly at first, then faster and more resolutely. I looked back once. She was sitting there, upright, and waving to me. It looked like a gesture of triumph.

6

GRASNITZ

19th October 1945 to 20th January 1946

19th October 1945

BEFORE me, the rain-sodden road to the south. I suddenly felt fresh vigour in my deadly tired bones, and my feet moved rhythmically of their own accord. 'Quick, before the mood evaporates!' One runs out into the miracle of life, when after many deaths God gives one this chance once again. Wet to the skin, the rucksack dragging on my all too emaciated shoulders, shoes blistering my feet—what was any of that to a man heading for freedom with all sails set? But slowly there, slowly . . . Russians were coming my way again. 'Go on, my dear, they don't look at you.'[1] Involuntarily I uttered spells like this to myself, as I let my free gait sink to a hip-shot hobble. They passed me by. Lucky once again. I should have to keep up this sort of mimicry in my gait for a long while yet, for men of my age didn't run free about there. It was best, too, to walk in the middle of the road if one didn't want to attract notice; side paths would not be advisable by day. Now a car was coming—from behind me, this time; that was worse still. But luckily they drove at such speed along these smooth roads that they would think it a pity to slow down. This happened repeatedly; Russian cars raced past me from opposite directions. Perhaps people really didn't see me.

Gradually the town receded, further and further behind me. Deserted countryside. In the fields to right and left, the unharvested corn like grey-green felt, stretching as far as eye could see and dripping wet. Bomb craters on the road, mutilated trees, military vehicles in the ditches, burnt-out villages. In a half-ruined house I sought temporary shelter from rain and wind. Something stirred beside me. I heard bricks squeaking, and found a handful of ragged creatures standing there, half asleep. They had children with them.

[1] English in the original.

144

They surveyed me with hostility. They too had tried to leave Königsberg, and had been held up here; the Russians had captured them and prevented them from going further. Now they could go neither forward nor back. The last food they had eaten was a few potatoes they had been allowed to take from a lorry that stopped here for a short time. I didn't ask the price they had paid. From the way they spoke it was obvious that the women had had to bear the brunt as usual. Who in the name of Heaven can still find pleasure in such spectres? If this goes on there will be no salvation for anybody.

The next place I came to was Wittenberg. Even here there was hardly anyone to be seen, till suddenly, round a corner, I found a lot of motor vehicles in front of me on the road. It was too late to escape, there was a Russian close beside me, obviously engaged in searching the empty houses; I should have to play a bold game. I limped painfully on and halted beside the lorries. They were full of captive German soldiers, and had come from a camp near Tapiau; they had been three days on the road looking for potatoes, and were now going on to Preussisch Eylau. The guards had found nothing here either, and were getting in again. One of them looked across at me. 'What sort of a chap is that?' I heard him say. I took the risk, and asked him to give me a lift to Preussisch Eylau. What did I want there? 'Look for family . . . House kaputt.' Childish talk, but escape is escape. He made a sign to me with his hand—I might get in. Before starting, the drivers threw the prisoners the ends of their newspaper fags. The men were waiting for them and caught them eagerly, their mutual understanding appeared quite good—provided one didn't compare it with old times.

I took stock, furtively, of my terribly scrubby compatriots, wondering which of them I could take with me when the chance came, but unfortunately they were all too weak, and their shoes wouldn't have lasted out. They plied me with questions as we drove at mad speed through the desolate land; but I answered evasively—there was no point in telling them things.

Eylau came in sight. A turnpike. We stopped at the entrance to the town as if at a word of command, and the guards got out to deal with the sentry. I pointed joyfully to one of the empty houses on the right as mine. They let me get out and go into it. I ran out again at once by the back door, out of sight behind bushes and trees along a narrow field path into open country. Through wire fences and hedges, past a little manor farm, and then to the left through tall grass as far as a hidden ditch, in which I could count on sufficient shelter. I was safe for the time being.

A road ran westwards at a stone's throw from my hiding-place. The rain had stopped; it was beginning to get dark. I took out my watchword book to write a few notes in it; the text for the day was 'Noah found favour before the Lord.' Infinitely comforting to feel protected . . . While I was writing, my motor column went past. They can't have had any luck with potatoes here, either. I watched them go by with a grateful heart; they had helped me along a good way. Then with a great rushing sound, growing louder and louder, a flock of starlings flew over my head, thousands upon thousands—rose, fell, and were lost to sight over the wood in the west. The clouds parted slowly, single stars twinkled in the openings; a milky light suggested that the moon was about to appear. There was a sudden noise again on the road. Out of the wood, at a furious gallop, came a carriage full of drunken Russians; one was hanging over the side, another shouting and flogging the horses. When they were gone, it was night.

I got up, and crawled like a drowned rat through the yard-high grass, crossed the road and wriggled on the other side through a tangled rye-field to the nearest rise. The moon had suddenly come out of the clouds and was making the place far too light. A sandy field-path, beside which stood a few willows, led me on. But soon I had to turn left through old standing corn, meadows and reedy ditches, so as not to lose my southerly direction.

Soon I could no longer blink the fact that it was growing lighter and lighter in front of me. Could that be the Russo-Polish frontier? Nobody knew what it looked like. I saw myself in imagination crawling through barbed wire under a brilliant light. But as I came nearer it turned out to be only a brightly lighted village. I could avoid that. Between alders and poplars flowed a winding stream; I found the bridge and turned away to the right. The last house lay far away on the left; but a dog had noticed me all the same, it started barking behind me and coming nearer. I had to run a little way through wire fences and hedges, and as I ran I took my amputating knife out of my wallet and threatened the dog with it. It ended by turning back. Shots fell in the village behind me, but I had reached the wood by then.

After a pause for breath I went on along muddy forest paths. The moon shone between the trunks and made the reedy grass gleam like silver. Where the wood came to an end I found myself on the highway that traverses the country, recognisable from a distance by its ancient trees. As I could see by the stars, it ran in the very direction I wanted, but I thought it better to go across country so as not to fall into the arms of a sentry. So, off again through barren fields, watercourses, fences and hedges; then along slippery field-paths, past solitary farms and built-up areas—not a sign of life anywhere. Just as I was passing a deserted settlement my legs gave out. I stopped in front of one of the little cottages, taking stock of the place, looking for footprints . . . No, nobody could have been there for a long while. The moon was hidden again, rainy squalls raced up the bare hillside; it must have been after midnight. The wind rattled in the rafters. As I opened the door of the cottage something collapsed inside with a great crash: a chaotic clutter of boards, broken glass and paper. I lay down on the living-room door, which had been taken off its hinges, and tried to sleep. But it was no good; the shutters banged incessantly in the gale and the garden door creaked on its hinges. It was too dark to see anything, and I expected somebody to come in at any moment; I couldn't stay in this deserted place, whose very name was unknown to me. The village signs were still standing, but the name had faded out.

I found it increasingly difficult to keep my balance. The mud was a foot deep, and the water lay in great puddles on the paths; all the drains and sewers must have been choked up. I nearly despaired when I found I had lost my bag with the dried bread in it. I grudged having to turn back for it, but luckily I soon found it under the last signpost, which I had tried to decipher with the help of a match. In my joy I took a good pull at the flask that Sister Raphaela had filled with delicious lemonade.

Soon after this I drew nearer to the main road again, which I had kept in sight. Whitish spots shimmered over there in the fog; some large place, no doubt. I felt my way slowly towards it, then waited to listen lest a guard should be stirring. I could hear the welcoming rustle of the old trees; then suddenly, eerily, a church clock in the middle of the town struck three. By way of precaution I crawled over the roadway on my stomach to get to the other side. There stood a big, freshly painted road sign. I managed gradually to make out the Russian lettering: L a n d s b e r g . Landsberg! I couldn't have hit it off better, for here the road forked to Wormditt. I knew the place well. And there was the second sign in Russian script: W O R M D I T T . Wormditt 22 miles. That was too far for the present, but the direction would suit me very well.

Inside the town something was moving. With a loud rattling noise, which re-echoed from invisible walls, an ancient steam tractor drew slowly nearer and drove past on the highway. I crouched down in the marshy ground beside a little meadow, and there I discovered several rows of potatoes. I dug out a few and slipped them into my pocket. Who could have planted them there? Certainly nobody in a position to harvest them, or they would have disappeared long ago.

The Russians didn't seem to be going to Wormditt very much; the road looked almost untravelled. So much the better for me, for I couldn't face the fields any more. Without worrying now about the noise, I let my shoes squeak on the surface of the road. The moon was already low in the west. The bank of clouds below which it would soon appear was becoming gradually lighter. Another step or two—then I started back in alarm. A black monster barred my way. I waited some minutes in breathless suspense, but nothing stirred. Very cautiously I described a curve round the mysterious object, to investigate it from the side; then, close behind it I espied another black colossus, and the solution of the puzzle slowly dawned on me. Two heavy tanks stood there, like frozen elephants, shot to pieces long ago. But even now I couldn't pass them without feeling my hair standing on end. A little further on the same thing presented itself, then the road was clear for a long time.

By and by I came through a village where the houses still looked in fairly good condition. Standing far apart, they were aligned on both sides of the road under old chestnut trees. I took off my shoes and carried them, so as to make no noise. There was no sound of man or beast, but over there by a garden gate, those two little red flags—that was the Russian guard-room. The sentry must have seen me long ago. Come out from under that tree, you there! But he didn't; he must have been indoors, sleeping. Who was likely to be wandering through the night?

A mile or so further a road branched off to the left. Hanshagen,[1] 3 kilometres, said the signpost. The name sounded promising; I must get there before daylight. I found walking more and more difficult. The sinews at the back of my knees grated and refused to stretch. Up one more little hill; then the road ran down into a silent village.

20th October

Hanshagen, my salvation. There were no Russians in the place.

1 'Hans's Close.'

The Kommandantur was in Petershagen, a good distance away. They come over from there sometimes and poke about among the houses. Some Poles cropped up once and went away again. Only a few women and children were living there, mostly unrelated to one another; they had grouped themselves into families as they saw fit. Some of them had landed up here as fugitives, others had joined them as stragglers; none of the original inhabitants was left.

I found myself lying in a real bed. It belonged to two old women living in a house at some distance from the road. My wet things were drying on the stove. They were keeping a look-out on the village road, to be able to warn me if any Russians appeared. I had been so kindly and readily welcomed there on leaving my look-out post at the top of an empty house, that I could hardly fear betrayal. My hostesses were busy cleaning mushrooms; there were masses of them this autumn, they said, the whole village was living on them at the moment. The people certainly looked much less famished than in Königsberg.

Now and then I heard a scratching noise overhead. 'Are those rats?' I asked. No, two fowls were kept hidden in the attic. So fowls still existed! I had seen the last one six months earlier, just as it was being killed. After a long chase, a Russian had flung himself upon it, on his stomach. What a lot of stratagems these old women must have invented to have preserved the creatures up to then!

At dinner-time they fed me on mushrooms in bed. Then I tried to sleep, but it wouldn't work, the strain had been too great. It was not till the evening that my legs began to feel a little relaxed. I kept my knees stretched as much as possible, so that they shouldn't stiffen in a bent position.

When it was dark again I got up and dressed. My clothes were more or less dry. The Russians hadn't been there that day, fortunately. To our common supper I contributed a little of the dripping in a screw-top jar that represented my iron rations. The three of us ate our mushroom meal sitting by the fire, while the women told me their story. At the time the Russians came one of them broke her thigh and the other nursed her, after which they remained together through all their troubles. They had heard nothing of their relations since they were forcibly separated from them.

In return I told them a little about myself. Meanwhile it was growing lighter and lighter in the room. The full moon peeped over the roof of the shed and climbed into the cloudless sky. Time to be off, no matter how hard it would be to leave this warm nest. Before parting, we gave thanks to God for his wonderful ways, and when I left the house the two old women were kneeling by their chairs.

A stormy night; the moon drove through white tatters of cloud; the bleak road to Wormditt seemed endless. In Frauendorf I heard a rattle of chains, then a dog barked at me. I hurried on as fast as I could; nothing stirred in the houses. Further on, the road ran under trees again; the ground out there was already covered with yellow maple leaves. I dragged myself from stone to stone, from tree to tree, counting my steps; I was obliged to lie down more and more often—I shouldn't get far that night. The cold alone drove me on.

The next village looked very suspicious again. I waited for a cloud to cover the all too brilliant moon, pulled off my shoes and went noiselessly through the narrow lane between the houses, where I could have touched the windows on both sides. And then—here again were the two little red flags nailed to a tree. If one of the guards were to look out of a window it would be all up with me. It's almost laughable, the way they sleep. Go on, go on, don't get weak; isn't the whole village holding its breath till you've got past? Coming out of the village I found the road curving to the right, and I had open country before me again. The fields were all lying waste here too, though there had been some attempt to make hay here and there in the meadows; a couple of ricks were standing beside the road, obviously dating from last summer.

Now the road lay through a wood, for the first time in the course of the night, and of my whole journey up to now. Here I could throw caution to the winds, for there was plenty of cover should danger threaten. The distance to Wormditt shortened very slowly on the milestones, but I was determined to get that far before daybreak. When at last I turned into the avenue, at the end of which the first signs of the town appeared, there was a slight morning mist in the air. After a time the railway station came into sight on the left.

I turned off the road because it ran under the railway, and the passage struck me as unhealthy. Going along the embankment I came to an empty shed beside the rails. There was no light in the station, and nothing to suggest that any trains were running. All the same I thought it advisable to give it a wide berth. A deep gravel trench ran beside the track for a couple of hundred yards and afforded me good cover as far as a spot where I could cross the line in safety. Now I had reached familiar country. That wood over there—a wonder that it should still be standing, for since I was here last, just after Christmas in 1944, a whole age must have gone by.

21st October

By the time it was light I was sitting in the main plantation, under a spruce fir, the branches of which reached to the ground. I had filled in the gaps with other branches. In front of me lay the line to Mohrungen, bereft of rails, as I had ascertained with satisfaction; so it will be a long time before a train runs through this lovely wood again.

What a radiant autumn day! Here in the main stand most of the trees were still in full foliage. I gathered some edible boletus and ate them raw with sugar and dried bread. I felt curiously cheerful; during the last stage of the journey all fear had left me. I had felt as if someone was walking in front of me, keeping watch on the road. It had begun by my seeing a dark object in front of me in the morning twilight, which struck me as rather uncanny. I wanted to avoid it, but a voice said, quite distinctly, 'Go straight on and don't be afraid, for beside the bush in front of you there is a black pool, from which some wild duck will fly up.' And I went on, reassured, twenty or thirty steps, saw the water, and the ducks flying up. There was nothing surprising about it, it was just the fulfilment of something that had happened before. After that I went on as though I was looking at a picture-book printed on transparent paper, so that before I turned a page I could see what was coming on the next one. Don't we live our days like a disconnected sequence of right and wrong notes? And yet there is a tune in it. Only God knows the tune, and is aware of the last note when he sounds the first. And sometimes he lets us join in the singing for a little while.

I chose another place for the afternoon, lying in the sun at the edge of a clearing, staring at the deep-blue autumn sky. Gossamer threads floated past me, jays flew from tree to tree, golden leaves kept falling. And this was Poland now? I thought of all those whose home it had been only a year ago : what wouldn't they have given to be there beside me, even for a moment!

It grew cold in the evening. I heard voices in the distance; children were marching along the road, singing a strange, wild battle song. I waited a little longer, till the sound had faded out towards Wormditt, and then started on my third night of travel.

Near Oberheide station I took the road to Mohrungen; I was forced to walk still more slowly this time, and the wood seemed endless. The long bridge over the Passarge valley was no longer there, of course; a winding road, deeply churned up by tanks, led down the steep slope to the river and up again on the other side. The railway bridge was still standing, very rickety, but apparently used by pedestrians. Halfway over it, above the river, I stood and let my thoughts wander downstream with the water. What might it look like, now, where this river went meandering through woods and parks? Were all the fine old houses still standing, in which generations had grown up in peace, and were free to tend the land? One could hardly dare hope they had withstood the bulldozer of the war. And back there, too, where the water came from? How many had I known of those living there and loving their home! Now the stream of life was flowing through devastated country, which perhaps none of them would ever see again with their old eyes.

The next station, Sportehnen, had been burnt down. I was finding walking more and more difficult—hardly really walking any longer. At a bend in the road I sat down and began looking over my luggage, for I must definitely discard some of my ballast. In doing so I happened to prick myself on a sharp knife. It bled hard, and this put fresh pep into me; I scrambled everything together again and went on. At last the bold tower of Liebstadt rose in front of me. On the right, across the river, a faint light shone; otherwise all was dark and silent in the town. Many houses in ruins, others still standing; on one of the latter, two little red flags. I saw all this drift past me as if in a dream.

Once beyond the town I simply had to come to a decision: my luggage or myself. The sinews of both my knees were on the point of cracking. I sorted out some heavy objects intended for barter, and most of the contents of my surgical instrument case, and left them lying on the grass. The polished knives glittered provocatively in the moonlight; whoever found them would be delighted. But it was worth while: walking had become that much easier.

Around midnight I reached the spot where the road branches off to Ponarien. Surrounded by its fence on the triangle of grass stood the old signpost, just as it used to. I debated for a long while whether to go on, as far to the west as I could, or to turn off here and see if my sister's and brother-in-law's house was still standing, and what was going on there. It wasn't far—less than an hour's walk—and the opportunity might never recur. Something was glistening and sparkling all over the grass and leaves; I drew my hand over them, it was freezing! That meant that I must find somewhere to sleep, and anyway my curiosity was too great.

Before the village of Royen my road turned left towards the wood. Here I saw women's footprints, and in the fields the first signs of cultivation I had met with since I left Königsberg. Some ploughing had even been done at the edge of the wood. Ducks flew up from the carp pond in the paddock, just as they used to do. I made a last halt by the big beech tree on the road to Hermenau, wondering whether anybody in my situation had ever leant against its huge trunk before. No doubt, without knowing it, it had inspired many a one before with confidence and hope.

A silvery moon. Beside me in the chestnut avenue single, stiffly frozen leaves loosed themselves from the twigs, grazed one another with a scraping sound and fell to the ground. In the nocturnal silence it sounded as though pigeon-like night-birds were busy up there, and I kept trying to get a sight of them.

The farm was only a few yards ahead. I hid my luggage in the bushes by the head ranger's lodge and pushed on, sheltered by the old trees. Wide tracks showed that someone had driven in here on rubber tyres. I must be prepared for a guard post. But even here nothing stirred, neither man nor beast. The houses to right and left of the gateway stood there as of old, and behind it—no illusion—the old manor house, wide, white and perfect. The park was there too, and behind the trees the shining surface of the lake. I seemed to hear a mocking voice: 'What more do you want? Isn't everything in perfect order?' Oh, there couldn't have been such an enchanted night as this in a hundred years! It was only hard to realise that one must behave like a thief.

I didn't risk knocking at a door, but began by looking for an observation post. In doing so I came upon two red-painted American tractors, obviously the originators of the wide tyre tracks. The smithy stood unlocked behind them. I glanced at the hearth; there was no fire there, unfortunately, not even enough to warm my hands by. I sat down on the anvil and waited.

Sitting there half asleep, I was roused by a slight noise. I sprang up and pressed close to the dark wall. A footstep by the door: the door pushed silently open. Outside in the moonlight stood a man with a black beard. He hesitated for a moment, then shot a question into the darkness—in German! I detached myself from the wall and went towards him. He drew back a step, looked at me searchingly and quickly realised the situation. We exchanged explanations inside the smithy. It seemed I was occupying the usual post of the night watchman, who had apparently not waited to be relieved, but had gone off earlier to his warm bed. The tractors belonged to the Poles, who had been farming here since the summer. The bailiff was living in the Manor; I was lucky not to have run up against him, he had intended lying in wait that very night by the big beech tree, to shoot a wild boar.

The general situation was a desperate one, my informer said. He himself was not a native of the place, but he couldn't escape because his wife and children had been detained here too. He had let his beard grow to make himself look older, and thanks to this they hadn't carried him off to Russia like the others. I asked him who it was that he was supposed to be relieving here, and found it was old Preuss, the old family retainer. 'What! Is Preuss still here?' I said, 'Can you take me to him?' We crept cautiously up to his window and rapped lightly on it once or twice. The shutters opened, and Preuss stood there in his night-shirt, with snow-white hair. A wave of warmth seemed to issue from him. His eyes started out of his head when he recognised me. I ran back to the road, to fetch my luggage out of the bushes; then I crept with unutterable thankfulness into his warm bed.

22nd October

It was about four in the morning; Preuss and his wife had moved a little to one side, so that the three of us had room to lie side by side, and Preuss took up the tale as follows: 'The Russians came on the 23rd January. Of course they robbed us of everything and were after the women, but otherwise the first three weeks were not too bad. Then the Kommissars came and rounded up all the people in the district, asked them endless questions and carried off the younger ones to Russia. Frau Gräfin [my brother-in-law's mother] stayed on here, and was fairly well treated to begin with. She even managed many times to protect the girls. Then she was made to clean the rooms for the Russians. She stood up to that too. But all that trailing about the roads was too much for her; she had just fallen ill when that began. Somewhere near Reigau she refused to go any further, and they shot her there in a little wood.

Somebody there wrote on the backboard of a sledge that was lying in the ditch : "Here lies the countess from Ponarien."

'Frau von Stein [my aunt] and her daughter arrived here on foot the evening before the Russians came, out of the Allenstein Gestapo prison. She was wearing her convict's clothes, with trousers, so the Russians took no further notice of her—merely asked her "Man or woman?". Her daughter was carried off and we never heard anything more of her. Frau von Stein remained here and looked after the cattle, first here and then in Reichau. In Reichau eight of us men lived with her in a cellar. On the 5th June, early in the morning, she disappeared. She wanted to try and get home. We've heard nothing since. Perhaps she's there. After a time they let us come back here. The Poles mean to start farming; there are only a few of them here. We've always had something to eat—potatoes, anyway. Nobody has actually starved. But during the summer nineteen people died of typhus. I'm keeping a diary about it all. One forgets so quickly, and then later on nobody really knows what happened.'

He asked me about my sister and brother-in-law. The Russians had told people here that they had been caught while escaping and taken to camp—my sister to Hohenstein and my brother-in-law to Russia. I was able to tell him none of this was true : they had both got through to Holstein. Since then, of course, I had heard nothing of them either. Preuss told me they had both ridden away when the Russians were almost in the village. It would have been much too late for a trek, and a few people, including the ranger, ended by making their escape on foot. Preuss himself was maltreated by the Russians to begin with, because he wouldn't say where 'the gold' had been buried. Even here there had been some very unpleasant customers among our good countrymen, who had tried at once to get into the Russians' good books at the expense of their fellow-creatures, but they too were soon carried off to Russia.

I lay in bed all day nursing my sore legs, even sleeping for a few hours. Nobody had noticed my being there; the black-bearded man had held his tongue. But I couldn't stay there any longer without endangering these people, and my plan for the coming night was to go to Grasnitz and look for my aunt there. The thought of seeing her again made me quite restless with happiness and anxiety.

Replete with bread and potatoes, I started off about half past ten. Another radiant, glittering moonlight night. Just past the head ranger's lodge a sounder of wild sows trotted quietly across the road, their black backs gleaming like silver. Here too everything appeared to be in perfect order. I went through Reichau and turned right on to the high road, catching repeated glimpses of Lake Narien until the road swerved left in Willnau. There was no guard in this town either, and I felt my assurance increasing. I had plenty of time now, a whole night for a distance of barely fifteen miles.

I walked slowly through the beautiful Tomlack Forest, stopping more than once for a long while. Where it came out into the open again, the road ran downhill in wide curves, avoiding a little round lake lying like a mirror at my feet, on the far side of which, at the water's edge, stood two farm buildings, thatched with straw and overhung by silver-grey willows. Their roof-ridges streamed with moonlight.

Gallinden, another straggling village, lay before me. When I reached the middle of it a shadow detached itself from a dark doorway and stepped in front of the wall of the house. As all means of escape was barred on either side, I walked quietly towards him. He was an old man in civilian clothes, armed with a fowling-piece. I asked him the way to Locken, and pointed to the Red Cross armlet on my left arm. He didn't understand, and looked at me suspiciously, even a little anxiously; he was evidently alone on duty. I made some ambiguous gestures and went straight on. He didn't know whether to arrest me or not, and ran beside me for a little way, then dropped behind. I took the longest strides I could until I was out of his sight, and then ran to the end of the village and hid behind a hayrick in case I was pursued. But nothing stirred, and I was soon able to go on.

I avoided Brückendorf entirely, out of caution. Beyond it, the road to Locken was covered with fallen leaves, which crackled at every step as if I were walking on parchment. Just as I was going past Ramten a single shot fell quite near me. I thought it best to take cover in the bushes and walk on along the side of the road. Then I took a short cut by a field path that swerved left before reaching Locken and afterwards rejoined the road to Biessellen. There were lights burning in Locken, and I caught the sound of voices. Morning was not far off.

Worleinen had been badly damaged; remains of carts and sledges lay along the roadside again, and the trees showed marks of shell-fire. I suddenly had the feeling that somebody was coming along behind me. I hid in a bush beside the road, and two minutes later I heard hurried footsteps approaching, and two men went past, pushing bicycles. I followed them at a distance. Lake Eissing came into sight on the left, with the first shimmer of dawn on the water. The sawmill appeared to be deserted.

Now my road crossed the Passarge once more, far upstream, where, hidden among limes and alders, it flows from one lake into another. I should have liked to go straight to Grasnitz, another twenty minutes from there through the woods, but I reflected that my aunt was less likely to be there than in Langgut, the next village along the road, which used to belong to Grasnitz. I had better look for her there to begin with.

I found Langgut lighted up already, with a hubbub of voices in the farmyard. It was no use dithering; I walked along the back of the first labourer's cottage and knocked at every window in turn. The first two figures retreated at the sight of me and didn't show themselves again, but the third, a young woman, held her ground. She looked me up and down, appeared to recognise me, laid her finger on her lips and opened the window. I had seen her eyes once before. 'Is Frau von Stein here?' I asked. 'Yes, she's in Grasnitz. But don't go through the farm, there are Polish soldiers there; go round by the mill, then you'll be safe. She's living in the gardener's cottage.'

Back to the mill again, round the lake and through the wood. Excitement made me run, although my legs were giving out. Finding someone that belonged to me, once more, after all that had happened between, would be like a foretaste of the meeting in heaven.

One last pause for breath. The first rays of the sun were glittering over the lake, the chestnut avenues hung like golden bridges from the wood up to the rising ground that was my goal; the old lime trees on the slope still hid it from my sight. A little further —then to my delighted surprise I saw the house standing safe and sound upon the hill. I walked up the wide, metalled road, deep in thought, past an untenanted Russian sentry-box with a turnpike, and stopped in front of the erstwhile gardener's cottage. I drew another deep breath, then I opened the door and entered the living-room. Three women were sitting at the kitchen table. We eyed one another uncertainly for a moment, then one of them sprang up and we were clasped in each other's arms.

End of October

Heavenly security! Up in the attic my aunt had rigged up a

spare room against emergencies, with furniture she had dragged out of the surrounding rubbish heaps. I lay there in bed all day, nursing my feet, while she came up from time to time to bring me something to eat or to sit by my bed and tell me about the events of the summer.

As I had already heard from Preuss, she had escaped from Reichau early on the morning of the 5th June, to find her way here. A nail in her shoe had chosen to make the journey as painful as possible, but she didn't dare take the shoe off to see what was the matter, lest it should prevent her from going on again. Here in Grasnitz she had found most of the old tenants still alive, and had been kindly received by Fräulein Jokuteit, her former house-keeper, who had settled into the gardener's cottage with the gar-dener's wife and two eighty-year-old spinsters, who had also be-longed to her household. In addition, they had taken in a man with frostbitten feet, who had been on his way somewhere else at the time of the Russian entry.

The rest of the village didn't know at first how to treat my aunt; they didn't quite like her coming back after a period during which, by force of circumstance, a certain *modus vivendi* had established itself with the Russians and Poles, which seemed endangered now by her sudden reappearance, and they held aloof. Gradually, how-ever, they got used to her being there. She went to work with the other women, and like them was given flour and a quart of skim milk a day. At the beginning she had to do a few days' work in her own house, in which the Russian Commandant was living with a certain Frau Schmidt, whom he had brought with him from Pomerania. There she started clearing up after a fashion that didn't suit the said Frau Schmidt, at any rate she was soon dis-missed. Since then the couple had moved to Langgut, and the house was standing empty. There was nothing left in it but an enormous wardrobe. Everything else was lying about on rubbish heaps, or scattered far and near throughout the neighbourhood. Some of the furniture was being kept in a shed at Langgut and gradually burnt up by the Commandant. He would let no one deprive him of the pleasure of chopping it up for firewood himself.

The Russians had been farming here up to the summer. In June, hundreds of dead cows that had been lying about everywhere were hauled away and flung into the ponds till they overflowed, after which some hay and corn were harvested. By that time, however, the Poles had taken over the management of the property. At first they could think of nothing sensible to do, but now that the frost had started they had at last begun to lift the potatoes. Up to then the women had all been sent into the woods to gather edible fungi for Warsaw. They liked doing this, because they could collect all sorts of other things for their own use at the same time. The fungi, which were still growing in enormous quantities, were piled several yards high in a shed and left to grow mouldy.

One day in September my aunt had gone to Januschau[1] to try and get news of my mother. She went by goods train to Deutsch Eylau and walked from there. Arriving late in the evening, she spent the night under a tree in the avenue, and waited till the morning to go into the village. She found only Russians there. They took her into the house at once, gave her something to eat, and wanted to keep her there to work for them. She succeeded in escaping, however, ran straight back to Eylau and got on to the next goods train. In the wood, near Jablonken, she had to jump out because a Russian was attacking her. She reached home in the evening with a sprained foot.

My aunt had no complaint to make about her treatment by the Poles. They had beaten her once, and that wasn't pleasant; but otherwise all that had happened so far had been like a period of convalescence compared with the half year under the Gestapo in Allenstein. Besides, the old Grasnitz was more beautiful than ever, this autumn. Inconceivable, the colours! And the game was so tame. A little while ago a wild sow had come past the door at night, with her young, and stayed for a long while on the grass under the window.

As for myself, my aunt thought it best I should stay where I was for the present. We could manage somehow. The Poles might be quite glad to know there was a doctor in the place; there was none in the neighbourhood.

My aunt knew nothing of her family. Her husband and two daughters were said to have been seen in a camp, and to have sent her greetings. Some of her sons had been on active service at the time the war came to an end. We gave up plaguing ourselves with conjectures as to what might have become of those we loved; being together was happiness enough for the present.

After two days in bed my feet were sound enough to put shoes on. My presence was not yet known, evidently, for neither the Commandant nor the Polish soldiers stationed in Langgut had

---

[1] The birthplace of the author's mother.

enquired about me; but prepared for surprise at any moment, I remained in the background and stayed in the house while the women went to work in Langgut.

When I came down in the morning I found living-room and kitchen floors scrubbed, the barrel filled with water, the socks they had worn the day before darned, and breakfast on the table. After breakfast I was left alone with the totally deranged old Ili, the survivor of the two Fräuleins, and tried to make myself useful. I chopped wood, fetched water from the little stream some thirty yards further down the hill, and boiled potatoes—everything strictly in accordance with my aunt's directions. It was important to remember how and when the fire was to be lighted, how many logs must be brought in to bake the bread, not to throw away the potato water because it would be needed for soup, and much else that had proved necessary if one was to keep alive.

Towards evening I went to meet the women on their return from work—a little further every day. After all, my presence couldn't be kept secret for ever. Each of the women brought two baskets of potatoes back from the harvest. We emptied them on to two different heaps in the cellar, strictly separated according to their kind, for the sake of introducing a little variety into our daily fare. Then we ate our supper at the kitchen table—potatoes and a kind of pumpkin soup—while the wet socks dried by the fire.

At the end of October the village seethed with rumours of a transport to the West. Nobody knew whether to apply for it or not. These transports entailed a great deal of hardship and danger; one was not allowed to take anything with one, one was even stripped to the shirt more than once on the journey and robbed. The journey itself, by cattle truck, took days and sometimes weeks in any case, and there was no means of keeping warm or getting anything to eat on the way. Nor was there any guarantee that one really reached the West. One might very well land up in one of the dreaded labour camps.

For all of which reasons my aunt thought it wiser to hold aloof. Nevertheless we thought we might try and find out more about the scheme, and decided to walk to Biessellen, three miles away on the railway line.

On the way there we met two poaching dogs in the wood, which had just killed a deer. We succeeded in chasing them away, and then secured the deer to a tree, to be picked up on our way home.

In Biessellen we first called on an old couple named S. The wife was well-informed, thanks to her knowledge of Polish, and warned us urgently against applying for the transport. After she had given us something to eat, we made for the Polish registration office, near which I remained in hiding, while my aunt went into the hut. She came out again after a time, accompanied by a Polish woman who was talking excitedly to her. They came to my hiding-place and I was introduced to the lady, now known as 'Doktourka', a former nurse, who had taken upon herself to attend the sick in the neighbourhood. When she heard that I was a doctor she wanted to have me to support her in Biessellen. I answered evasively, for I couldn't quite see how to manage it. All the same, my existence can't be concealed any longer now, and I'm curious to see how things will turn out. On our way back we took the poached deer with us, to be shared with those who, like us, had seen no meat for many a day, for want of 'connections'.

At the beginning of November the rumoured transport actually left. Carts drove up suddenly, and whoever had applied for a place was made to get in. Several hundred people were said to have assembled in Osterode, and from what we heard, they very soon came to grief. In any case we were very glad not to have been among them.

After the village had calmed down again, the women went back to work. In spite of all warnings, orders had been issued to cart the beautiful potatoes from the field into the empty cow-house, where they were piled up to the ceiling. As they would inevitably freeze there, the women set about carrying away as many as possible, semi-officially, to their own cellars. For the same reason, we started secretly making a little private clamp of our own on the Fünflindenberg. We dug out a rectangular hole before sunrise, and filled it with about a ton of the finest potatoes. This was covered over with straw and earth and camouflaged to some extent. Just as we had finished, two Polish soldiers came along the ridge between the fields, hesitated for a moment and then went on.

That evening three soldiers fetched me to Langgut in a very rattly cart. I went quietly, but was much relieved when I discovered what it was all about. Frau Schmidt had taken something, for intimate reasons, that had violently disagreed with her, and I was to give her some advice. The Poles didn't take the affair very tragically; they even brought me back again in the cart.

The fact that I had been called upon as such a matter of course encouraged me to move about more freely. I got in touch with the

Doktourka, and visited patients on my own account in the neighbouring villages. Soon my day became organised as follows : I went
to Biessellen in the morning to hold consultations in the little out-
patients' department organised by Doktourka, was given my dinner
there, and then set out for the villages on the right and left banks
of the Passarge. I gradually became known, and was allowed to
go my way unhindered. Even the dreaded militia occasionally
asked me for advice, which helped of course enormously to in-
crease my security.

Nevertheless this period was still full of all the strains that one's
little, defenceless life is subject to. We parted of a morning, never
quite sure whether we should meet again that evening. I went
down the steep hillside to the little stream, over the footbridge
from which we drew our water, to the wood, and along the side
of the lake as far as the high road, where caution was called for
on account of the Russian troops that might be marching through.
Once out of the wood, I followed an overhead light-cable for a
mile and a half over the fields, which brought me straight to where
the old S.s lived, who had been so kind to us at our first visit.
They would see me coming in the distance, and always had something hot for me to eat—a sufficient reason for remembering them
forever with gratitude.

The out-patients' department had been set up in a house beyond
the level-crossing, together with a couple of bare rooms in which
stood a few primitive beds. Down below in the cellar the Doktourka had stowed away the remains of some German army
medical stores, from which not only our own needs were supplied,
but those of the dispensaries in Osterode and Allenstein. By way
of patients we had a few typhus cases, both Polish and German,
nursed by two girls from the nearest village, who had had the
disease before. Besides these we had occasionally to admit
casualties : Poles who had burnt their front-sides while making
schnaps, an old German who had been found half-starved beside
the railway track, having probably fallen, or been pushed, out of
a transport taking people to Russia; a young Pole who had had a
fight with some Russians between Osterode and Allenstein, had
been shot through the breast and flung out of the moving train;
and a nice Polish soldier who had broken his leg below the knee
and wanted me to attend him. I was hard put to it to know how
to treat him, for I had nothing with which to immobilise his
broken leg properly. After I had failed to make something out of

straw bottle-covers bound round with strips of paper, I begged one of his comrades to find me some plaster somewhere. He took the train to Allenstein and returned in the evening with a paper bag of cement. With this I was able to make a somewhat more compact, tolerably immobilising apparatus. Unfortunately the patient was transferred sooner than he should have been, and I never knew how the dressing behaved, nor, above all, how it was later removed.

Most of the walking cases coming for treatment were women and girls, all with the same terrible symptoms before which we were helpless, because we had no means at that time of treating them properly. We gave them a sort of pretence treatment, more for the solace of both parties than with any hope of success.

At dinner-time I was given a princely meal—considering the circumstances—consisting as a rule of potatoes with some sort of tinned food sent by America. After this I set out on my rounds through the surrounding villages, trying each time to extend the circle.

I had never had an opportunity to get to know a country district, together with its people, so well as at that time. And as a doctor is usually welcome, there was always a special attraction about these walks. They often amounted to a round of fifteen to eighteen miles, viâ Gusenhofen to Mittelgut, thence over the Passarge at a place called 'Von Ferne',[1] through Penglitten, Leissen, Dietrichswalde, Woritten and home viâ Langgut.

On the right bank of the Passarge, in what is known as Ermland, many more people had remained behind than on the left bank. They were all Catholics, could speak a little Polish, and thought perhaps that they stood a better chance with the Russians and Poles on that account. But they had become just as impoverished as the others. The fact that a greater number of younger men were to be seen about did, however, suggest that on this side of the river one's nationality could be to some extent disguised.

Some families still possessed a little poultry, and there were a few goats about; one or two privileged people owned an old horse. But apart from these there was hardly any livestock left, although many caches had remained undiscovered for a long while. A woman with three children had even managed to keep her cow concealed for several months; she had walled it up in one of the rooms so that it could only be reached through the window.

[1] 'From afar'.

Another, also the mother of small children, had succeeded in hiding a milch ewe between a door and a cupboard until it betrayed its presence by bleating. Pigs had been kept in the cellars for quite a long time.

Even people had been hidden. Just recently a woman had brought her newly married daughter out of the cellar where she had kept her hidden from everybody, even her own sister, ever since January. In another village the Russians had discovered two girls that summer and carried them off, upon which their desperate mother had betrayed all the other girls that had been hidden in the place.

Even here there had never been any lack of informers, most of whom, however, were not actuated by despair, like the mother, but rather by some unsatisfied desire for vengeance or some other impulse that springs to life, uncontrolled, from the dark depths of human nature in times of chaos. Almost every village had suffered from this devastating spirit. Many of these people went so far that even the Russians were sickened and put an end to their activities in some way or other.

I had a curious encounter with the wife of one of these individuals, the mother of many sons, some of whom had actually served in the German army. I was the guest of an old man who was held in great respect as a minister of the East Prussian Prayer Association, and we were talking about the sufferings of the village, which led me to mention this inhuman creature, whom I knew by report. The minister suddenly became evasive and tried to turn the conversation. I didn't realise his intention at once, and pursued the subject until a woman sitting at table with us gave a deep sigh and said 'Ach ja, that was my husband.'

Among the people I visited there were some who had been imprisoned by the Russians, either in camps in East and West Prussia, or even in Russia itself. Most of these were candidates for death. Two elderly men, brothers and common owners of a farm hard by the Passarge, had returned from Russia at a few hours' interval, and probably by the same transport, completely dried up and inwardly benumbed. One of them died in a few days, the other a month later. A girl who returned from a camp by the Polar Sea was benumbed in the same way; she could sit at table, and one could converse with her. She described in a cold, hard way all that she had suffered at the hands of her own countrymen; it sounded like somebody talking who was already dead.

Some days I went my rounds on the other side, more to the west and north, to Rapatten and Dlusken, beautifully situated at the edge of the wood and mirrored in the lake, and thence through Wönicken, Pupken and Worleinen round Lake Eissing to Pulfnick. The population in all these places is entirely evangelical. I found some children who had not yet been baptised, and took the opportunity of repairing the omission. This was always the occasion of a little celebration, attended by the neighbours, and this led me to reflect on the nature of baptism as a sacrament and our peculiar attitude towards it. I was particularly struck by the answer I received when I asked a woman if her two-year-old child had yet been baptised. 'No,' she said, 'it's been vaccinated, but not baptised.'

Encouraged by these celebrations, I decided to hold Sunday services in the little empty church at Langgut. The first one took place on All Souls' Day by permission of the Commandant and under the supervision of an armed sentry. I suggested that today we should let God's word detach us from the thought of the dead and the missing, and think of life and of those that had remained to us and with whom it had been granted us to live; and that we should be thankful for everything we were still undeservedly able to call our own. A lot of women had come from other villages, and they begged me to hold services in their homes too.

On Sunday afternoons we went on scouting expeditions, partly to make the most of being outlaws and partly to add a little variety to our diet. By way of addition to all the dried mushrooms, berries and tea-herbs that my aunt had piled up already, we helped ourselves to a couple of hundredweight of cabbage turnips from a deserted field in Worleinen, to make syrup with, and experimented with lupins and things of that kind, which nobody took any interest in. We got wood for burning from the forest, and coal, illicitly, from the cellar at the Manor, where it was still lying unheeded.

On one of these occasions we took a look round the Manor, the door of which was only secured with a nail. There was nothing left in it but a pair of antlers and a huge wardrobe, disregarded no doubt on account of its size. Everything else had long ago been used as firewood, or else I found it scattered far and wide in the houses of the Germans and the Poles on my visits to the sick. Over and over again I found shirts bearing my relations' initials on my patients' bodies.

At the end of November we acquired a lodger in the person of

Gross, the former chauffeur. He turned up in Biessellen one day, after his release from a prison camp in Graudenz. Owing to his bad state of health, and because we had no means of transport, we kept him there to start with, in our little hospital, and only brought him home when he was able to walk again a bit. He soon recovered, went fishing, and was finally commissioned by the Commandant to see to the damaged sawmill and do his best to set it going again. We lodged him upstairs in my room, and I moved down to my aunt's, where we slept along with old Fräulein Ili, who rambled on incessantly about the days at the turn of the century when she was living as a governess in Vienna, evidently with some very distinguished people. She was forever preparing to alight from some carriage or other, getting tied up in the bedclothes and falling forward on the floor. She often made very grim remarks, too. 'O Lord, thou art our refuge for ever and ever,' we would hear her recite, and as an immediate afterthought, 'A nice refuge, I *must* say!' In spite of all the trouble she gave my aunt, we couldn't help being amused by her; we had many a good laugh at her expense.

The women were still going to work in Langgut. They now had orders to cart the huge pile of potatoes lying frozen and rotten in the cow-house out to the field again and bury them in a clamp. They were no longer eatable, and handling them was horribly dirty work, but they were now to be made into alcohol, and some 200 hundredweight of wheat had been procured with great difficulty for the purpose—I fancy, from Korschen. As this wheat was now stored in a granary with a leaking roof, the work had finally to be carried out in great haste. The distillery was set going as best it could; but when things had got to the point at which the mash might begin to ferment, the wall of the distillery collapsed outwards and the first big barrel emptied itself straight into the river.

I often visited patients in Langgut. Once, in the bailiff's house, I fell in with a high-ranking Polish officer, who had evidently come to inspect the troops stationed at the farm. When I entered the room he made a grimace and looked sharply at me. 'What's this man?' I heard him ask. 'This is the doctor,' replied the bailiff. 'Papers?' he shouted at me. If you only knew, thought I, that I'm prepared to run twenty miles this minute, to where you'll never find me! Meanwhile I thrust my hand carelessly into the breast pocket of my canvas jacket, pulled out a scrap of paper that happened to be there, and made as if to hand it to him. That sufficed him. He waved it away and took no further interest in me. I was free to depart, greatly relieved.

When visiting Poles I was usually made to drink schnaps and was given something to eat as well. But most of them were living in extreme poverty too, in almost empty, barely weathertight rooms. People in the militia and the secret police, known as the UB,[1] were better off, because they had more means of procuring supplies, and they sometimes gave me good things. Once the Commandant in Locken sent his carriage for me in a snowstorm. He had an abscess in one of his tonsils, and would have liked to keep me for a few days. I stayed one night with him. Next morning I managed to persuade him that he was better, and after a lot of hemming and hawing he sent me home again with his horses, after giving me some money, eggs, white bread, stockings and a shirt, the latter adorned, as usual, with my uncle's monogram.

I owed my good relations with the dreaded UB chiefly to the Doktourka. Right at the beginning she once gave three armed men who appeared to be about to search me such a dressing-down that they made off again, half stupefied. Moreover, she was zealously engaged in 'polonising' me. She kept asking me if a Polish name hadn't played a part at some time in my family. In the end I let myself be persuaded, and told her that before the Thirty Years War the name 'Mgowski' had occasionally cropped up in connection with my own. She was delighted, and a few days later she handed me a sort of certificate, in which to my astonishment I found myself entered as 'Jan Mgowski'. Sad to say, this interesting document was lost on one of the later occasions when I was being searched.

I often had considerable booty to bring home. Once it was thirty pounds of wheat flour from the mill, where some Polish soldiers had called me in professionally, another time I was given a live fowl by some people whose entire family were down with typhus. The flour was particularly welcome in view of Christmas : with the fowl, whom we named Lorchen, we struck up an intimate friendship.

The Doktourka had long had a mind to introduce me to her friends in Allenstein and Osterode. She took me with her one day, greatly daring, to Allenstein. For fourteen zloty we were permitted to take advantage of the morning train, consisting of three goods trucks. When we got to Allenstein my first impression was one of

[1] Committee of Public Safety.

intense dislike. The station, and all the immediate neighbourhood, was swarming with Russian and Polish troops and the usual nondescript individuals among their hangers-on who had something to sell, or were merely loafing about. I felt again as if transported deep into Asia, and I saw that Doktourka herself was anxious to get away from the place as quickly as possible. Only a part of the town had been destroyed, the greater half appeared to be quite intact and densely occupied by Poles.

We went to St. Mary's Hospital and saw a doctor and several cigarette-smoking nurses. The Doktourka carried on an animated conversation with these, while I paid a visit to the seven German nurses who were leading a shadowy existence at the top of the house and were not being called upon to do any nursing.

Three days later the Doktourka took me with her to Osterode, to fetch the bottles of petrol, ether and other liquids from the medical stores allotted to our dispensary. I didn't feel altogether happy about this expedition, as I had no desire to become better known among the Poles. On the other hand, I naturally welcomed an opportunity of seeing Osterode under feminine protection.

The town had been sadly devastated and was much less lively than Allenstein. I saw a good many people hanging about the sub-prefecture, and a few bicycles and horse-drawn vehicles. We called on the district doctor—the only doctor available at the time —did some bartering at the chemist's, and made various little purchases for our out-patients' department and for the Doktourka's housekeeping, which was beginning to flourish. We also went together to visit the five German Catholic Sisters who had remained behind in the parsonage, and to whom I was able to give greetings from St. Elisabeth's Hospital, their Königsberg training school. I was again given a great deal to carry, including a bag of bones for our kitchen.

The train service between Osterode and Allenstein was a somewhat laborious affair, as the Russians had removed the second line over the whole stretch. There were only two passenger trains a day in either direction, one of which consisted of cattle trucks, and even these had some difficulty in getting through, as the line was constantly blocked by goods trains. These came fully laden from Berlin and travelled back empty. The Russians were using them to transport to the east everything they had taken to pieces in Germany, either packed in big crates or loose. Ten to fifteen of these trains were said to pass through every day, worked by German railwaymen as a rule, under Russian guard. I sometimes had a talk with these men when the trains stopped at Biessellen, and gave them letters to various addresses in Germany, in the hope that one or other of them might reach its destination. Getting away by one of these trains would prove almost impossible, since they were constantly searched on the journey, but I hoped none the less to seize some such opportunity one day, for of course I was longing to be with my own people again, and I didn't want to let myself be tied to this place.

The Russian railwaymen often took advantage of the stops at the stations to do a little private looting. I once saw one of them panting towards the line with a sofa on his back. As the engine had meanwhile run a long way out of the station with the railwaymen's staff wagon, he was forced to tramp some 400 yards along the embankment in deep snow; but he had hardly reached the wagon when the train slowly receded, and he had to carry his burden all the way back again. Even this was to no purpose, however, for just as he reached it, dripping with sweat, the train started off so suddenly that there was nothing for it but to throw the sofa away and jump on in a hurry. A tinge of malicious pleasure on our part when we witnessed such incidents was perhaps excusable in the circumstances.

The Polish signalmen have anything but an easy time with the Russians. When disasters occur, their only hope of salvation lies in total disappearance. One morning the regular train from Osterode ran into a Russian military transport in the dark, and there were many serious casualties. The furious Russians wanted to arrest the guilty pointsman, but he had bolted betimes, though not without dropping a hint to his brother in the village, who thereupon decided to decamp himself, since he had good reason to fear that the Russians would take it out of him instead. Escape didn't really present any very serious problem, for hardly anybody had anything left but what he stood up in, and the risk of being pursued in such unknown country was relatively small.

As Christmas drew near we had to solve the difficulty of procuring a little fat—a bottle of oil or something of the kind. I ended by seizing my old brief-case and stuffing a green satin dress into it, which had belonged to one of my cousins and had been found by us in a rubbish heap, buying a ticket in Biessellen and taking the train to Allenstein.

When I got there, I first wormed my way as inconspicuously as possible through the rabble at the station, and reached the Sisters in St. Mary's Hospital unharmed. They gave me a few tips, and I made my way to the market to try my luck with the dress. The market was being held in two narrow streets, not originally intended for the purpose. In spite of the wintry cold, the hubbub, the shouts of the vendors, the loitering, bargaining and importuning reminded me of a summer visit to Serajevo, so far removed did I feel from all that had once been Allenstein.

There was really nothing there worth trading for. The most I could see was matches, onions, remnants of material, clogs and old garden tools. All the same, the minute I allowed the tiniest corner of my satin frock to peep out of my case I had a crowd of interested parties round me, all trying to pull the stuff further out and finger it. I retreated slowly to the stall belonging to a woman selling matches, who looked fairly promising. I shoved the case stealthily towards her, and she disappeared with it under the counter to examine the frock in peace. It wasn't much to boast of by now, and I only wanted enough for it to buy a bottle of oil, 600 zloty, that is. But the woman wouldn't give that much for it, and handed me back the frock and the brief-case. I was at once surrounded again by the mob. Suddenly a very determined-looking woman, who must have been watching us out of a window, came out of a house nearby, pushed the people aside and drew me into the entrance hall. We went upstairs to her flat and she vanished with the case, to try on the dress. It was a really nice flat, which had obviously belonged to a doctor at some time, and I was astonished to see how comfortably the woman had managed to establish herself there under prevailing conditions. She soon reappeared, clad in the green frock, which was far too tight and short for her, besides being threadbare in several places. I couldn't help laughing. She joined in the joke very nicely, and began telling me in tolerable German how she had come to be in Allenstein. She was the wife of a doctor, who was busy somewhere else at the moment, and she was trying to keep his post open for him here. As a matter of fact she didn't seem too sure whether he would return, or even come back to her at all. She was standing, so to speak, at the edge of existence, like everybody else here.

I packed up my frock again and went back to the street. As I passed the matchseller she beckoned to me and bought the garment quickly for 500 zloty. As I still had a little Polish money left, I was now able to buy the longed-for bottle of oil. It dated from the

German period, of course, like every pleasant trifle these countless little shops have to sell.

Christmas drew near. On my walks through the wood I gathered beech-nuts, some of which I scattered again at my aunt's request. 'Whenever you have any beech-nuts about you,' she said, 'throw a handful here and there on the Fünflindenberg; we always meant to plant it.' We kept the rest for roasting. Now we had oil as well, and a lot of wheat flour, so we were well supplied.

During Christmas week I held services in several places; on Christmas Day itself in a private house where the family's biggest room had been put at my disposal. Reading the Christmas story to all the pathetic people before me, I found it difficult not to break down. Afterwards my aunt and I paid some visits in the village, and let people talk to us about themselves. They had all gone through the same things, but it seemed to do each of them good to be able to speak of their personal experience. They had all had their husbands and sons, in many cases even their daughters, carried off. And although there was really nothing left to loot, they were still exposed to raids by the militia or by Russians marching through. The Russians came searching for buried treasure with long, pointed iron stakes, and the villagers were trying to discourage them by burying empty tins near their houses. As the robbers usually made for any spot that looked tidy, they carefully smoothed the earth over collections of useless objects.

The winter was fairly mild. There was a lot of snow on the ground at times, and the tracks of game in the forest made us dream of a day's shooting, especially as not a soul ever entered the wood except ourselves. 'You'll have to go and shoot something,' said my aunt, 'or you'll get bored to death.' I asked her how she imagined I could, as we hadn't any guns. But we had, she said, one of the old men had muttered something about a carbine being hidden near the ice-house. He must have meant, under the reed thatch of the ice-house itself. When it was dark we went there, and actually found two guns, with the ammunition belonging to them. With the utmost precaution we took one with us into the house to clean it. Then we hid it again.

Next day the weather was very dull and foggy, and I was able to go stalking. It wasn't far to the wood, and the risk of meeting anybody on the way was very slight. I had decided that if I shot anything at all, it should be a red deer or a boar, and then only if I was sure not to miss. But darkness fell before I had a chance.

Next morning I stationed myself at a predetermined spot in the wood, and my aunt walked towards me through the plantation facing me, known as the rose-garden, with the object of driving any game there might be in it towards me. There were some wild sows in the plantation, but they broke out sideways, and I had no luck that time either. All the same we enjoyed the feeling of having gone shooting together at least once in these hard times.

Even without a gun, those walks through the forest held an endless attraction for me at that time. With all the beech trees bare of leaves, and the snow bringing out the full splendour of their smooth round stems, I was always tempted to leave the path and run leaping down the hillside to the clear mirrors of the lakes, in whose dark depths the fish were swimming around. We both knew, all the time, that this was a period of grace we were being granted.

When I arrived in Biessellen on the 11th January, I was told that the UB had been there to fetch me, apparently for some serious reason. I felt I had no choice but to go at once to the guard room, but the people there seemed somewhat surprised by my voluntary appearance. I asked if anybody was ill, or what else they wanted of me. Surrounded as I was by at least fifteen armed men more or less under the influence of alcohol, and some of them only half-dressed, I didn't feel very comfortable. They eyed me contemptuously for a time, and then announced that I was not allowed to hold any more meetings. They wouldn't give me any reason for this prohibition, but let me go again.

Saturday, 12th January

It rained in torrents. I found a note from the Doktourka in Biessellen telling me to go at once to the district doctor in Osterode, to assist him in an operation. This struck me as hardly credible, since as far as I knew there was neither an operating theatre nor any surgical instruments in Osterode at that time. Drenched to the skin, I mounted the engine footplate of the train to Osterode, and made my way to the doctor's house by secret paths. My colleague received me with heart-warming friendliness, and asked me to hold the fort for him for the next four days, to start with. He had to attend a course of lectures at Allenstein. Just as I thought, there was no question of any operation. But as it happened, a young Polish tractor driver had just been brought to him, whose right upper arm had been shot through by a comrade. They had been sitting side by side on the tractor, when the passenger's machine pistol went off. We found the bone shattered, and had to think of some way in which the man could be transported to Allenstein, to have his serious injury given proper surgical treatment. As there were no more trains that day, the penitent gunman was despatched to find the only available car in Osterode, belonging to the militia. Meanwhile the patient was given a temporary dressing. He clung to me and begged me to go with him to Allenstein, and I discovered to my no small astonishment that he came from Finckenstein. He couldn't say whether or not the castle was still standing, from which I concluded that it had been burnt down. This was all the more likely as it was the finest of all the manorhouses in East and West Prussia.

We had a very good supper at my Osterode colleague's, after which we had to wait an hour or two because the militia had gone out. Late in the night the car drove up at last, a sort of short American lorry with a flat nose. We put the injured man aboard and started off at a tearing speed to Allenstein, by the road going through Jablonken and Dietrichswalde. When we came to the wood at Grasnitz I tried to jump out, as I had nothing to do in Allenstein, but the Pole held me back. He had already been sick more than once, involving me considerably in his plight. At about one in the morning we drew up, not at the St. Mary's Hospital, but the Allenstein. Cigarette-smoking nurses received us, and we laid the patient to bed in a smoke-filled room. We were to have driven straight back, but the petrol appeared to have given out, so we had to spend the rest of the night where we were. The drivers knew of a warm place; we drove to the metering room and settled down comfortably on three tables beside red-hot radiators.

Under the light of a glaring lamp my two companions were soon fast asleep, but it took me longer. My clothes had been in a soaking condition for nearly twenty-four hours, and I didn't dare creep out of my wet pack because it was always safer to be ready to start at a moment's notice.

Sunday, 13th January

There was a slight frost, with slippery ice on the roads. One of the drivers set out in search of petrol. He found some about ten o'clock and came back to fetch us. We drove through the whole town and stopped at a house from which three milk cans full of petrol, with lids that wouldn't shut, were fetched out and loaded on to the lorry. The tank was filled up, and then six people got in, who wanted to be taken to Osterode. This time we went through Hohenstein; it was a longer way round, but a much better road, and of course we had to drive at top speed. What else is a car for?

We raced through bare country. After a time Hohenstein came in sight, totally ruined again, as it had been in the First World War. The Tannenberg monument, the front and rear towers of which had been blown up, passed by us like a bad dream. Then came the forest. The road was even smoother here than outside. I could only see out of the back of the hood, but I suddenly noticed with horror that our course was becoming more and more irregular. We skidded, first to the right, then to the left, then to the right again. There was a loud crash, the lorry reared up at the back, we shot forward, then found ourselves, drenched in petrol, back in the hood of the overturned vehicle. Astonishingly enough, the roof had stood the strain. As I had been prepared for something of the kind to happen, I was the first to crawl out; the others followed one by one. None of them had been hurt. Our lorry lay helpless in the ditch with its wheels in the air, and beside us on the road stood a passenger car, obviously the cause of the accident, because we had had to come off the crown of the road to avoid it. One of our passengers got into it, to be driven back to Allenstein for assistance. He had a stiff leg, and there was no knowing how long we should have to wait here until help came, for we couldn't possibly set our lorry on its legs again unaided. After we had drowsed there for half an hour, a lorry exactly like ours appeared from the direction of Osterode, as usual at a tearing speed. We signalled to it from a distance, it braked, skidded; we leapt off the roadside into the plantation. The lorry made a turn of 180 degrees, hit a tree with its stern and stopped dead. After the first moment of fright we came in for a thundering cannonade of curses from the crew, who were also members of the Polish militia. Gears were shifted to and fro, the lorry turned about and off they went.

Not long after this a peasant came driving from the opposite direction. When he caught sight of us there in the ditch he tried to pull up, but his miserable horse slipped, lost its footing, and lay helpless on the road. The peasant's attempts to help it up were useless, but eventually the horse was set on its legs again by our united efforts. The man drove on, very cautiously.

I had gradually got cold in my rain- and petrol-soaked clothes, and decided to break away. I walked slowly along the road as though I merely wanted to see round the next bend; then, as soon as I was out of sight I quickened my pace. I wanted to reach Grasnitz that evening if possible. A sentry was standing at the crossroads in Hohenstein, but as I was going east I didn't arouse his suspicions. I turned north, came through Manchengut and paid a short visit to old Skibba, whose daughter had come back from Cheliabinsk in such a terrible condition, and was treated to another recital of the frightful things their own countrymen had done to one another up there in Russia. In February, eighty girls had travelled across Russia for weeks in a cattle truck, without food or water, and without the truck having been opened once in all that time. Many were dead when they were taken out; the survivors' sufferings went on—the same that we had been through in Königsberg. Skibba's daughter died four weeks later.

As I was leaving I heard to my joy that the old Minister of the Prayer Association had held a service there that day, Sunday. Thank goodness, the militia does at least allow him to do this. But later, when I had nearly reached Biessellen, I became suspicious. A one-horse vehicle overtook me, driven by the Commandant of the Biessellen militia. He hesitated when he saw me, but then drove on without taking any further notice of me. I had the feeling that something was brewing, but got safely to Biessellen and was given coffee in our out-patients' department. I went on in bright moonlight, made a little detour across the field to inspect our potato clamp, found it undamaged, and reached my aunt's house about ten in the evening.

Monday, 14th January

I set out for Osterode early in the morning, in dry clothes; I didn't want to leave the district doctor in the lurch. Except for this my days in these parts were now definitely numbered, since I had attracted attention in wider circles. I wanted to try and get through to the West before they involved me in Osterode in some commitment of indefinite duration.

My aunt went with me through the wood. The time we had lately spent together seemed to us like a chapter out of some favourite nursery tale. Now we must say goodbye. Fresh snow had fallen in the night; there were fresh tracks of deer and wild sows everywhere in the forest. The sense of home was so strong and immediate. A parting word; then I ran off and reached Biessellen just in time to jump into the train to Osterode from the wrong side.

I began by visiting the five Catholic Sisters, who received me very kindly. The youngest of them was ill, and the priest had just come to give her Holy Communion. When he heard I was a doctor he pulled up one trouser leg and showed me a wound that wouldn't heal. I put a dressing on it and gave him directions for further treatment. Then he donned his priestly robes to visit the patient, and the other Sisters followed him reverentially.

I left my rucksack with the Sisters, and observing the usual precautions went to the hospital, where I was to deputise for the doctor. Being outside the town, the Osterode Hospital was outwardly fairly well preserved. The interior was being cleaned, and a German deaconess, who was sharing in the work, showed me rapidly over the building. To my astonishment I found parts of our Insterburg equipment lying about everywhere, which we had sent there a year earlier, to save it from the Russians. To no purpose whatever, of course: the Russians had arrived here a day earlier than in Insterburg. There were a few bedsteads about, and in a carefully locked room there were tablets and ointments sent by UNRRA. I had been allotted a little room with a very comfortable bed.

There followed three fairly uneventful days at the hospital. As everywhere else, most of the people that came were women and girls wanting to know if there was any remedy yet for their disease. It's dreadful, how thick-skinned one has become where they are concerned.

At the doctor's request I drew up a list of everything needed in an ordinary operating theatre. He's going to try and get some of it in Warsaw.

Thursday, 17th January

As the district doctor was expected back that day, I decided to push off to the West. As soon as it was dark I fetched my rucksack from the Grey Sisters, made my way stealthily to the station and jumped on to the first goods train I came across. It was going east; so I should have to change into one going the other way at the first opportunity.

At the first halt in the open I went forward, found the German staff under the guard of two kindly Russians, and was allowed to travel with them on the footplate. They were taking parts of a factory to Russia, and reckoned to be back in Germany again in two or three months. I offered my services as a stoker, but they were against it, as they themselves had papers with Russian and Polish entries on them, and were always having to show them.

I had to get out at Allenstein. It was so dark on the platform that I ran no risk of being discovered. There were a lot of goods trains standing in and near the station; the empty ones were going west. I approached several German drivers, but none of them wanted to take me along. They were obviously under great pressure. When at last it began to grow light again there was nothing for it but to crawl into an empty truck at the rear of a train, which moved off soon afterwards.

Friday, 18th January

Towards midday we were back in Osterode again. The temperature had fallen to twenty degrees below zero, and I was so frozen that I simply couldn't travel any further. I got out, and decided to go straight back to the hospital; it was just possible that nobody was aware of my nocturnal excursion.

As I was crossing the line I saw the Commandant of the UB coming towards me, to my no small alarm. He too seemed startled to see me. 'Doktour, come with!' What was he after? Did he want to take me to a patient? It wouldn't be the first time; he had even been my patient himself once. Or was he going to arrest me? Anyhow, I had no choice but to follow him. We walked side by side a little way in silence, and then entered a house before which stood a sentry. There I was surrounded by at least twenty uniformed Russians and Poles. I had fallen into the trap.

Half grinning, half bored, the Russians looked on while I was disassembled. My beautiful, carefully selected escape luggage was taken to bits, and the separate pieces handed round: a new pair of trousers of earlier date, stockings, a pair of shoes—what hadn't I suffered to bring this ballast all this way! 'Ah, Doktour go home!' They laughed maliciously. Well, of course it was plain that I had meant to decamp. After the rucksack it was the turn of my pockets, and all the places where something might have been sewn in. Two watches came to light. Looks grew grim, and I felt a bit ashamed to be still in possession of such things, although they were mementoes of the dead. Far more dangerous, however, was the little notebook that was next laid aside—my diary. There was nothing in it but brief notes on daily happenings, but that would be enough. Fortunately the writing was very small, and in German script, which they might not be able to read. They left me the fur waistcoat I had on, and a loaf of bread. My little Bible would have to be examined. I asked why they had arrested me. 'You talked political, and shot with people in Gusenofen.' Two reports had been heard, they said, while I was there. The first charge related of course to the services I had held with their permission, the second was pure bluff. There was nobody in Gusenofen but a few poor, miserable women and children, anyhow. 'Who said that about political talk?' I asked. 'German man say.' I couldn't counter that, for unfortunately it was only too possible. Then down with me to the cellar.

A low-ceilinged room, about eighteen feet square, little windows high up. Thirty men on two-tiered beds, an iron stove in the middle of the room. Except for four or five Poles all the inmates were German. One of them drew me down on his bed and explained the situation. They had all been in Russian camps from which they were released at the end of a few months, had come home very ill, found Poles living in any of their houses left standing, and been taken to prison by them under the pretext that they had belonged to the Nazi Party. Until lately they had had the place to themselves, and had been able to keep more or less clean; but now there were Poles there, who were not co-operative, and lice had begun to spread again. Some of the men were led out to work by day, usually to clean the streets. Several had died, none had been released. There was saltpetre in the food, which burnt one's tongue badly. I was strongly advised to forgo my belongings and escape at the first opportunity.

The sentry fetched me at midday, thrust a coal-shovel into my hand, and ordered me to light the fire in a stove on the second floor. Perhaps they thought I shouldn't know how. I fetched some live coals out of the stove in the guard room, where they were still all lounging about on tables. Above all, no hesitation! I felt like a tamer in the lion's cage. On the stairs leading to the second floor I was alone for a moment with the red-hot coals. If only I could have set the whole house on fire there would have been a fine confusion, and a lot of people could have made their escape. But the next moment the door of a big room opened, and I beheld a very bulky Russian officer enthroned on the sofa against the opposite wall. Under the table, at his feet, lay a terror-inspiring white mastiff. He took no notice of me, evidently I was only meant to light the fire. This accomplished, I was taken down to the cellar again.

In the evening we were driven out to the yard at the back and given soup in a stable, distributed by a woman doctor. She was a prisoner too. After the collapse she had been able to go on practising in Osterode for a time, then she was fetched away by a militiaman to attend his child, and had not been released again. Without the slightest change of expression, and as though we were carrying on the most ordinary conversation, she told me how to get out of the yard. I must try and get into the next stable, and out of that through the window. While I was attempting to slip away at the back, she tried to divert the sentry's attention. He looked like a Red Indian squaw, but he was on the look-out and pushed me back with the butt of his rifle.

That night my thoughts went to and fro. I didn't feel sure this time whether I ought to escape or not. I had an inkling that I had been imprisoned because I was supposed either to have organised the religious service in Manchengut in spite of the interdict, or even to have held it myself, so that in a sense I was here in the cellar as a defender of the Gospel. What ought I to do? Life was so lovely, and it was such a pleasure to snap one's fingers at all these people here pretending to be the representatives of order. God help me to do the right! And lying there on my guard bed I was on my way, in spirit, across the yard, into the stable, through the window, up the slope, through the block of houses, along the streets and in a wide arc round the town towards the lake, though I didn't know whether it was frozen over yet.

An endless night. Our Polish fellow-prisoners played boisterous tricks on one another. A German militiaman, who had escaped from Russia and been arrested here three months earlier, bemoaned his fate piteously; all the others lay silent. Now and then somebody got up and shovelled more coals on the stove. A thundering noise broke out overhead at short intervals.

Saturday, 19th January

Towards seven in the morning the sentry unlocked the door above us, came down the cellar stairs and opened our door. An old man went up with him to brew coffee. I stole along behind him and stopped on the top step. The door was ajar, with the sentry standing behind it. A long time went by; it was freezing hard, and I began to grow stiff. It was getting light outside. All at once the sentry was called from somewhere or other; he answered, and moved away a few paces—as if in a dream my hand pushed the door open, I was out in the yard, reaching the stable, crawling through the window, running up the slope—suppose someone looked out of a window!—reaching the block of houses, out on the street, running towards the west, turning off to the left, then more and more to the east in a wide loop. I must lure my pursuers on to a wrong track on account of that dog. He was the only one I was afraid of. I picked up a handy piece of iron from a ruined house to defend myself with, ran past the hospital, over the Hohenstein road, through gardens—nobody about yet, so far—and then across open country. Further on, I crossed the railway line, then the road to Jablonken, and made for Lake Schilling, so as to by-pass all the villages. Nothing but snow and flat land. Then little bushy pines, humpy ground, sandy subsoil. I ran across the drill-ground. Solitary trees, bristling with hoar-frost, were beginning to glow with the pink shimmer of dawn. Blue shadows still on the ground. I ran and ran, till in front of me, sudden and steep, a slope falling away towards the lake. Beyond it, the forest! The sun was just rising behind it. I slid down the bank to the lake, knocked a hole in the ice with the iron, then went slithering, throwing myself on my stomach now and again, over the cracking, crackling ice, and reached the forest. O life and freedom! On the slope above, among the glorious boles of the Taberbrück Forest, I sat down and watched the shore from which I had come. Nothing stirred on my tracks.

I went on in a beeline towards the east, across the main forest. Nobody could have been there for a year. In the middle of the maturing plantation a herd of red deer got up in surprise, but made no attempt to move till I was almost in the midst of it. I felt sure nobody would follow me here. But all at once I heard a great dog baying behind me. I felt suddenly very tired; I leaned against a tree and clutched the iron tighter. The baying came nearer, there was a crackling in the underwood...my God, a stag at a quick trot, and behind it a great shaggy dog! Life flowed back through my veins. I waved my hand, the stag turned aside and trotted away, and the dog retreated guiltily and disappeared. My heart swelled with thankfulness. That morning the whole forest belonged to me.

An hour later I was in Grasnitz. Nobody there could yet have heard of my latest escapade, but for safety's sake I kept out of sight. I found my aunt at home. She hadn't gone to work, on account of a strained muscle, and wasn't in the least surprised by my sudden appearance; we had lived through too many unexpected things together. Nobody had been there to look for me, but they might do so at any moment. I lay down on the bed while my aunt boiled some dumplings for me and kept a look-out for callers. We considered what we should do next. I must leave again at once, in any case; but what would happen to her? Wouldn't the Poles make her suffer for this? Yet I couldn't take her with me, with her lame leg, and in such cold weather, nor did we know where to go. So, far more confident than I, she stayed behind, waving to me when I left, an hour later, unseen, this time with far scantier luggage.

I thought it safest to go first to Ponarien, where I had found Preuss three months earlier; I was not likely to be pursued that far. Taking advantage of patches of woodland, uneven ground and other cover, I got as far as Brückendorf. There I saw a carriage coming towards me along the road. I recognised the Langgut steward by his horses in time to slip into an empty house. Dazzled by the midday sun, he drove past without having noticed me.

Beyond Gallinden I took a short cut through the Tomlack Forest to Reichenau. There, in the barn of a deserted farm, sitting in the straw, I waited for the dusk. It was miserably cold. I was fairly exhausted, and anxiety about my aunt weakened the urge to go on; but when it grew dark I got up, and reached Ponarien by a roundabout way through the forest. There wasn't a soul to be seen. I knocked at Preuss's door : it was locked. But the coachman's cottage alongside was open, and Frau Klein came out, greatly alarmed. Preuss and his wife, and several other families, had been turned out in November. Her husband had been absent for a year; but Böhnke the smith was still there, and she took me to see him.

Sunday, 20th January

I stayed that night and the whole of next day with the Böhnkes. Fräulein Görke, who was still there, cooking for the Polish steward, was told of my arrival and came to bring me a piece of bacon. Frau Lemke, whose husband had disappeared, came too, and brought two pairs of socks with her. There were more Poles here than in the autumn. Preuss was turned out of his house because they wanted his chattels. (We heard later that he and his wife had died on the transport.)

Towards ten that evening I started off again, under a full moon, by a country road as far as Hermenau, and thence along the highway to Mohrungen. Not a soul on the road. But just outside the town some men appeared suddenly round a bend, coming quickly towards me. It was too late to avoid them, so I went to meet them on the crown of the road. They were soldiers, regulars, and it's always easier to get on with their kind. The first one stopped me as I was passing, murmured something about 'starosta', saluted, and allowed me to proceed. Perhaps he had taken me for the Polish sub-prefect. The others took no further notice of me. I turned to the right on coming to the town, went behind the barracks, through exercise grounds with barbed wire fences and frozen trenches, crossed the railway line and reached the road leading west again. Judging by the wheel-tracks, it was in far greater use than the roads I had come along earlier, so I should have to be on my guard.

I soon reached Bestendorf woods and the village of Bestendorf itself. The manor house was still standing. Wild shouts and yells came from the village. Towards midnight I allowed myself a moment's rest in a barn on the left of the road, and set fire to some straw to warm my hands, but put it out again at once, not wanting the barn to burn down on my account.

At the cross-roads near Maldeuten the problem became acute. Should I go to Marienburg and thence further west, or to the place where my parents and my brother were still living only a year ago? Take the risk of having to cross the Weichsel on ice floes, or go home once more to the graves, and then let come what might? I knew the Russians were in Januschau, yet I longed to go there. Perhaps there were a few Germans left in the neighbourhood. I yielded to the powerful temptation.

The milestone said: Eleven kilometres to Saalfeld. The old place-names in Russian script again. Saalfeld looked badly damaged from a distance; I left it on my right and crossed the line to Liebemühl; here too the rails had been removed. The next place, Weinsdorf, had suffered considerable damage. I was walking through it when I suddenly heard footsteps and took cover behind the church. Two men hurried past, shivering, and went into a house. After another hour of walking, Gerswalde loomed up before me through the moonlit mist. I debated whether to go through the village, but ended by turning off to the left. I came to the lake, walked past a long row of fishermen's wooden houses without attracting any attention, crossed the wide frozen surface of Lake Geserich and came ashore again near the ranger's lodge at Eichen-laube. A sounder of wild sows broke through the young oak trees, quite fearlessly, in the moonlight. One more look at the lake, then I crossed the road to Schwalgendorf, went through the main forest and reached the provincial boundary by the main road.

West Prussia! Finckenstein Forest! How homelike it felt! The
Heide Mill was still standing and appeared to be in use; the roads
in that direction had been broadened by wheel-tracks as never
before. Now came the Januschau Woods. Here too the main drive
through had been cut up to the width of a big traffic artery. What
could the Russians be doing? In the plantations on either side,
however, all was as it used to be : the view of the lake between the
beech trees, and every bend of the road full of a thousand
memories of days and nights in a former existence. One man alone
could hardly grasp it all. But at the end of a forty-mile walk I was
again in a mental state that included the notion of another walking
beside me.

Outside in the fields the road had been widened even further
by traffic; the ground on either side looked as if a roller had been
driven over it. Day was just breaking when I made for the park,
across the fields. The lodge had been burnt down. Another minute,
and I should see the graves. And then I was really standing where so
many of the dearest people had found their last rest; I looked across
the field in the morning twilight, and laughed in spite of myself
to see that the graves had been ransacked, with broken tools left
standing in them that were not intended for digging. What were
you looking for here, you foolish creatures? You evidently gave
yourselves a lot of trouble.

I went a little further, to get the view across the park. The dear
old house was still standing there. A glaring lamp on the verandah,
all the windows lighted up, doors slamming, cursing, noise of wheels
. . . that was the Russians.

It was growing gradually lighter; I must find a lodging somewhere. I could still manage the two miles to the manor farm at
Brausen; there might be some Germans left there. Just short of
Brausen, where the road crosses the big canal, a Russian on horseback overtook me at the usual high-stepping trot, but took no
interest in me. Soon afterwards I met a wagon with four muffled
figures in it; it stopped, I stood still. We looked at one another
searchingly for a moment : it was old Tiedtke and three Januschau
girls on their way to work. They gave me a brief account of the
main facts. Anybody from Januschau that was still alive was now
in Brausen. Last winter's trek had only got as far as Stuhm, about
twenty-five miles away. My mother and brother had been shot
there by the Russians, and sixteen other people from Januschau
had died with them.

I asked who could put me up in Brausen, and they suggested Lasner; he could probably manage it. They pointed to the house in the distance where he was now living. But I must be cautious, the village was guarded. Soon afterwards, singing loudly, I strode past the sentry, who was leaning against the turnpike, in a fur cap and slippers, with a machine pistol under his arm. Ten minutes later I was lying safe and sound in Lasner's bed.

7

JANUSCHAU

21st January to 2nd August 1946

Monday, 21st January

A FEW slices of bread with some delicious beet syrup soon set me
up again; besides the pain in my travel-worn feet I had felt very
short of breath towards the end. To my astonishment I was told
that the Commandant's thermometer stood at 30° below zero; in
spite of my relatively thin clothing I hadn't suspected it.

I learnt that the land and all the surrounding estates were being
retained by the Russians.[1] All the livestock, all the stores in the
granaries and all movables of every kind had been amassed here.
The paddocks were piled high with thrashing-machines, ploughs,
wagons and other machinery from the whole neighbourhood. The
Poles had only been allowed the ruined town of Rosenberg and
the evacuated peasant villages. There were some hundreds of
Germans in Brausen, women, children and old men, besides a lot
of Russians whose numbers were constantly changing. The Commandant was said to be quite an affable person. No work was being
done in the fields, only the livestock was being tended—some 140
cows, the remainder of the herds that had been lost in the winter,
besides a few pigs. They were being fed on sugar-beet peelings,
fetched from the sugar factory in Rosenberg. The whole village was
living on these peelings as well. Work in the cow-house was much
sought after because of the skim milk that was left over. Nobody
had died of starvation here, only a few people, at the beginning,
from cold and disease. There were still plenty of potatoes to be
had, because several hundred acres had been planted in the spring.
The corn had been harvested, and some of it was still lying in sacks
in the granary. The Russians were evidently less feared here than

[1] The Red Army had converted most of the big agricultural estates into
kolkhoses for the supply of the troops, and many of them remained in
Russian hands after the Polish Administration had taken over everywhere
else.

in any of the other places I had known them in up to now. With those that had been here for some time considerable intimacy had grown up.

In the evening I was taken across to the house over the way, where the old ranger, H., and his wife were living with two married daughters and their three children. His ranger's lodge at Zollnick, in the forest, had been burnt down. He was now employed by the Russians as a trapper and woodcutter, and had to accompany them when they went shooting. The daughters were working on the farm, one in the dairy and the other in the Commandant's fowl-house. Their home, consisting of one large room and a small kitchen that could be divided by a curtain, they now had to themselves. Until a few weeks ago they had had to share it with another family and several single persons; but after the Russians had taken a number of people with them to the West, those left behind had been able to spread themselves a little more, and the H.s were in a position to take me in. The bed behind the curtain in the kitchen was given up to me, and with unutterable content I stretched my tired legs in it.

Tuesday, 22nd January

We discussed what was now to become of me. It was too cold to continue my journey, and I couldn't remain concealed here much longer, for my presence had probably been talked about all over the place already. H. thought the best plan would be to take me to the Commandant and tell him I was the doctor; I belonged here and had at last come back.

The courtyard was closed by a big wooden gate, above which a portrait of Stalin had been fixed. Some of the Russians were occupying the manor house, which was entirely undamaged. The Commandant, a fat, elderly man with the rank of lieutenant, was just re-entering the house from the garden; he had nothing on but a fur coat and a pair of top boots. I was presented to him. He agreed, without asking for further information, that I should remain there and attend the sick. I was to live with H. We took our leave, and made our way through the crowd of Russians camping in the hall with their usual informality, a great deal more assured than we had come.

In the evening I was given details of the flight. The fugitives had left Januschau a year ago on their trek, the children and old people in the wagons, the rest on foot. When they reached the outskirts of Stuhm they sent a cyclist ahead to Marienburg, to see if there was any hope of getting across the Nogat bridge. He came back, and said it was doubtful, as there were innumerable other treks making for the bridge. This confirmed my brother and the Inspector-in-Chief in their opinion that flight was useless anyway. So they stayed at a little manor farm near Altmark, waiting for the Russians. They came on the 25th January, towards evening. In the ensuing chaos, which needs no description since it was the same everywhere, my brother was severely wounded with a knife. My mother was just able to bandage him up for the time being; then the Russians came, asked who he was, and shot him and my mother together. I was deeply thankful to know that it was all over so quickly, for ever since I had heard that they hadn't escaped from West Prussia, the thought of their possible fate had haunted me at every step.

During the encounter with the Russians another sixteen persons had been shot or burnt alive. The women suffered as they did everywhere else. Any young men left were carried off. In spite of his gamekeeper's uniform, H., most surprisingly, lost only his boots, and was afterwards able to remain concealed for a week, with his family, in an out-of-the-way farm. They then went home through deep snow, half dead with hunger, and reached Januschau just as their strength was giving out. There they, and many others, were quartered in the school, where the women were maltreated. Then they were sent to Brausen, to which most of the former inhabitants eventually returned. A German who could speak Polish, and understood the Russians, became the confidant of the latter, and although up to then he had been quite a harmless fellow, he did his fellow-sufferers a lot of harm in their distress until he died, in the summer, to the general relief.

Wednesday, 23rd January

My feet had recovered sufficiently for me to accompany the daughters of the house, Frau S. and Frau L., on an expedition they had planned for some time. They wanted to see the district town of Rosenberg for once from the inside, and try at the same time to exchange one of their tablecloths, which they had succeeded in burying, with the Poles for some fat. We left the village unobtrusively and reached our destination without incident.

The town was a pitiable sight, the market-place a heap of ruins. We saw a few Poles in the streets, but to all appearance there were none of the former inhabitants left. After some hesitation we entered a small shop. The heavily made-up saleswoman—'Warsawianka', according to the sign over her door—looked us up and down, a cigarette in the corner of her mouth. We showed her the tablecloth, and a lively bargaining ensued. She spoke broken German. But when we espied two Russians sitting at the back of the shop we retreated slowly, before an agreement had been reached. In the next shop, a bakery beside the post office, we had better luck. The owner, a friendly woman, gave us rolls and money for the cloth. These were the first rolls I had seen for a year. The bakeress warned us against the militia. We slunk through the ruins of the town. On the way back I took a look at the empty hospital, which had not been destroyed and even had a lot of glass still in the windows.

Thursday, 24th January

Today I held my first consultation in one of the new houses for two families, in which Nadja, a Russian hospital nurse, had been practising alone up to then. The front door stood open because it didn't fit the door-frame. There was a considerable snowdrift in the hall, with a bench beside it for waiting patients. The door to the consulting room had no handle, because all door-handles had been wrenched off and carried away at once. Nadja gave me one for my personal use. Our services were chiefly needed for festering legs. By way of medicaments we have some loose tablets, the remains of some ointments from army stores and some unidentifiable mixtures in beer-bottles with labels written in Russian. Nadja is quiet and easy-going, speaks passable German, and doesn't set much store by cleanliness.

Saturday, 26th January

The Russians went shooting today, taking their ammunition with them in two potato-sacks. They came back in the evening with one red deer and one wild sow; several animals had been wounded. As the beaters took part in the shooting as well, some two thousand cartridges had been fired. Although shoots of this kind take place twice a week, there are said to be a great many red deer left. (Last time we shot here, thirty-five cartridges were fired and twenty-six head of game were killed.)

In the evening H.'s daughter-in-law came through the wood from Schwalgendorf, bringing us some fish. She hadn't seen her in-laws for a long while. Her father used to rent the Geserich and several other lakes. She had come back alone from the flight, and was now cooking for the Russians who were living in her house and carrying on with the fishing. Before that she had worked for a few months as a mechanic, with the Russians, somewhere near Marienwerter. The presence of this young, strong, fearless creature had something liberating about it.

Sunday, 27th January

My anxiety about my aunt, left behind in Grasnitz, increased daily. What had happened to her? Had the Poles carried her off, or had nothing further happened? I could find no rest till I was sure of her fate; I must try and go back there once more.

In the afternoon, therefore, I accompanied young Frau H. on her return to Schwalgendorf. We avoided Januschau on account of the Russians; they were said to have a depôt of about a thousand horses there. The forest was untouched, the old felled timber was lying about everywhere. A year ago we had gone shooting here, well aware that it would be for the last time. It seemed almost incredible that I should be walking here again. We went past the lakes, crossed the East-West Prussian border, which was also the boundary of the Januschau estate, and saw the 'white man' standing beside the road. This was a whitewashed man of wood that somebody had once set up at a fork in the road, to frighten one of his guests who would have to drive past it. Now there was only half of him left, the Russians had shot away the back of his head.

Half an hour later we reached Schwalgendorf, the big fishing village by the Geserich. There are still a number of Germans living there, as usual women, children and old men. The younger men, if still alive, are either in prison or in the West. Nobody has had any news of them. We called on the old fisherman, Kuczmarski, in his cottage. The people there live mostly on fish purloined from the Russians' catches. All the men are roped in to fish.

I stayed there a little while, and then went down the steps to the shore of the lake and made my way over the ice to the village of Weepers, where I had been told there was a fisherman who was thought to have a map of the country. I found him at home, and succeeded after some persuasion in getting him to show me his map. He wouldn't let me take it with me, so I studied it very carefully and made a little sketch of the main roads and villages lying in the right direction. The old man shook his head dubiously and warned me against the Poles.

At dusk I went through Gablauken, where there were still some Germans living, with whom I exchanged a few words. By the time it was dark I had reached the last outflow of the Geserich at a spot known as the Kragger Corner, which I had always known by name but never seen. From there I started walking along the canal, thinking to make a short cut, but I found it was taking me too far in the wrong direction, and had to turn back and follow the route I had marked. This led me through a village, then back to the canal and along it for some distance through meadow land to Liegen. From there I went straight across the fields to the little town of Liebemühl, which had been so badly damaged that I took it to be uninhabited. Ruins stood up starkly in the dawning moonlight to right and left of the road. Not a sign of life anywhere, although it couldn't be more than six o'clock. Luckily the bridge over the canal was still standing.

I crossed the market-place—suddenly the church clock struck, clear and sharp, sending a tremor through all my limbs. I had reached the town exit, where the road forks right to Osterode, left to Mohrungen, when I saw a light on my left and was held up by a Polish militiaman. He asked where I was going, and gripped my arm with a mocking laugh when he realised I was not a Pole. I got my hammer out and he let go. I gave him a shove, and ran, before he could recover his balance, some way down the road to Osterode, turned left, and made for the wood across the fields. As I ran over the frozen ploughland I wondered what would happen if I just stupidly broke my ankle. Another mile or so and I was safely in the wood. The sentry would scarcely have risked following me in the dark.

Groping my way along the edge of the wood I reached the road to Mohringen and followed it a little way, looking out anxiously for the next bend in it, where a wood path branched off; if I missed this I should have to go a long way round. I soon recognised the critical spot, but started back at the sight of a huge black object that appeared to be barring the path I was looking for. I stared at it for a long while before realising it was yet another of the many shot-battered tanks.

The path through the wood had a human track on it that soon turned off to the right, after which there were only signs of game about. I couldn't miss my direction now, for the sky was clear and the Pole Star showed me the way. I soon found myself surrounded by a sounder of wild sows, which broke up quietly to either side. Later, in a clearing, a herd of red deer let me approach quite near; then I found myself unexpectedly on a road again. I looked round me : on the right, at a little distance, another road branched off in an eastward direction. Eckschilling! I sat down on a stone to rest for a few minutes, profoundly thankful to have reached this unmistakable spot in the middle of the forest. Somewhere about here I should find the tip of Lake Schilling, which I had crossed a mile or so further south only a few days ago. Another hour's walk eastwards along the woodland road, and I came on a striking land-mark, a very stout pine leaning to the right over the road like an arch, a sure sign, I felt, that I must be nearing some inhabited place. I proceeded more cautiously, found the wood thinning, and discerned a house on the left, a tall railing on the right with a paddock and some more houses behind it. This must be Taber-brück, the most coveted area forestry office in the whole province. It was from here that Napoleon's 'bois de Tabres' was exported to Paris.

I now had to turn to the right, crawl through the railing and jump over a few superficially frozen ditches, then, passing quite close to the rangers' lodges, which appeared to be untenanted, I found the road to Dungen and came out of the wood. I gave the village a wide berth. When I broke through the ice in a big ditch some dogs started barking, but a moment later I had reached familiar ground : the forestry office at Pupken, where we used to visit the Polish ranger, Wönicker road, Graznitz forest—as beauti-ful as a dream. At the edge of the wood in the chestnut avenue a sounder of sows made way for me unwillingly, I reached my aunt's house and tapped at her window, breathless with suspense. A figure appeared—it was she. I stepped out of the darkness. Nothing much had happened since I left. The militia had called once and asked after me, without giving any special reason. The villagers thought I must be in prison in Osterode. It was not yet midnight, so I still had plenty of time to sleep.

Monday, 28th January

My aunt stayed away from work on account of her lame leg, and we spent the whole day together, talking of the dead and thinking of all those of whose survival we were not sure. Towards ten at night I started off again. My old shoes were no more use, and I shoved them in my rucksack. I pulled on a pair of felt boots that I had repaired myself a short time before, and took with me a New Testament and the book of watchwords for 1935 which agreed with the current year as to Sundays and feast-days and had belonged to my youngest brother. I went back to Liebemühl the way I had come, and then bore right and went along the canal, looking for the railway bridge, a long way outside the town. Fortunately it was still standing. As I crossed it, holding my breath, the church clock struck again. Two strokes.

After this I had a long stretch across country: there was no danger of losing my way on such a starlit night. By the time I reached the Kragger Corner the soles of my boots had worn through, so although it meant going a little out of my way I went on over the lake on the ice. When I reached Weepers it was beginning to get light. I called on the old fisherman again, and asked him to direct me across the lake. Half an hour later Schwalgendorf loomed up before me through the fog. I rested a bit at Kuczmarski's, where I was given fish for breakfast and a whole rucksack packed full of fish to take home with me.

When I came to the Zollnicker Berg, over the border in West Prussia again, I discovered too late that the Russians were out shooting. They drove past me, and one of them took aim at me; there might have been a disaster, but H. was with them on the sleigh and saved the situation. I was allowed to go on.

There was a dead fox lying at the edge of the wood, which I had found on my way out and hidden there. The skin was still in good condition and might bring in a little money if the Poles took a fancy to it. I slung the animal over my shoulder and landed up in Brausen again about midday with my tongue hanging out.

I held a consultation in the afternoon. A little twenty-two-year-old Armenian with the rank of lieutenant, and listed as the 'medical lieutenant', has come here to serve as a doctor. He has been quartered alongside the consulting room. He knows a little German, and has confided to me that he doesn't know a thing about medicine. 'Sick people come; Hans, you look, I talk,' this is how he plans our collaboration. He never stops singing and whistling German song hits ('Marianka' and so on). He has been to Berlin already, and has a lady friend there, whose attractions he described to me in the most intimate detail. He appears to like me, and is arranging for me to live alongside of him in the kitchen, which two Russian women have just vacated.

We skinned the fox in the evening, and in the meantime H.'s two daughters set to work to make my kitchen habitable. They scrubbed the walls, and brought the floor to light again with the help of a garden hoe. Before we went to bed I read the Bible aloud.

1st February

The weather has suddenly changed; it's thawing and raining. I went into the forest, and close to Zollnick I found the blood-trail of a stag from yesterday's hunt. It ended in a death-harbour close to the road to Peterkau. The dead stag had evidently been picked up by a Polish timber wagon. On the way back I passed the spot where, on New Year's Eve 1933, I had brought down a very heavy wild boar, and then I crossed the Klavier bridge, where more than twenty years ago I shot my first woodcock. The little fir tree under which I flushed it is now a respectable tree.

H. went to Schwalgendorf today, to see the new Polish ranger, who is afraid of coming here himself on account of the Russians, and got H.'s daughter-in-law to ask H. to pay him a visit one day. All the woods in the neighbourhood are in his charge, more than 50,000 acres, that is. But he needs more assistants. He seems to be an ardent gamekeeper, with great understanding and love of the forest and the countryside. He takes an interest in the people of Schwalgendorf, too, and gives them work in the forest by which they can earn a trifle. H. hopes very much that some day a chance may occur to move over there.

3rd February

The Commandant has allowed me a cart to fetch wood in for my living-room. I drive to the spot known as the Milking Place, near the edge of the wood, and load two cubic metres of alder wood. All the other carts are out for wood, because the traction-engine employed for generating electric light uses up twelve cubic metres a day. Thousands of cubic metres are still lying in the forest, everything that was felled in 1943 and 1944 and could no longer be carted away, including the hundred-and-eighty-year-old stand of pines, just behind the border, which we always used to show our guests when they wanted to see really valuable timber. Now the magnificent trunks are lying in all directions, slowly rotting. The annual rings are still just visible.

A number of women and the twelve- to fourteen-year-old boys

are employed as drivers by the Russians. The boys are well on top
of things, and hard to beat for insolence. It sometimes makes one
gasp to hear their remarks in the presence of the Russians, since
the latter have learnt quite a lot of German by now. But they don't
seem to mind; for one thing, no doubt, because they are opposed to
any form of discipline for children, and for another because they
themselves do nothing but swear all day, even if it's merely a matter
of telling one another the simplest and most unimportant things.
'Damned women' has to appear at least once in every sentence, even
if they merely want a light for a cigarette. As a result of the war,
some German swear-words have crept into their language—if their
gibberish can be so called.

A bath tub has been installed in the dairy, which I have permission to use, and there is an Armenian at the school who cuts
people's hair. That is a special treat, gratefully appreciated by all
as a proof of Russian culture.

4th February

Temperature 5°C today, with a gale of wind, but shooting went
on just the same. Result : one buck, one fox, one squirrel. The
number of shots fired is again reckoned at 2,000.

I went with Frau L. to trade in Rosenberg. We got a kilo of
bacon worth 400 zloty for a tablecloth. The H.s had hidden a lot
of things besides this, but they were very soon discovered. Even
here the Russians still go searching now and then for hidden
treasure with long, pointed iron rods, which they get the black-
smith to make for them. We hear that some of our local Russians
are soon to be transferred to Liegnitz in Silesia—their next headquarters! Michael, my Armenian colleague, invited me and three
of his compatriots to a schnaps party. The schnaps had been made
by the former cowman—now responsible for all the livestock as
well as the cattle—out of the beet-parings, and was very cloudy.
One could only drink it with bread stuffed up one's nostrils, so a
Russian warned me. My head buzzed all night, and in the room
alongside, instead of 'Marianka', Michael sang a very Oriental,
warbling sort of song that gave me visions of a sun-drenched karst
landscape with herds of goats.

6th February

Temperature 3°C. The ground has been thawed out for some
days now. All the drains are stopped up. From one house door to

another, and over to the pump, we either walk on duck-boards or jump from one brick to another. The cowman has made me a pair of clogs.

I visited patients in the nearby villages of Faulen and Albrechtau. Russians, Poles and Germans live there together. The dung from the cow-stalls is carted out to the park and piled up yards high. There too there are ploughs, mowers, harrows and thrashing-machines lying about in the paddocks. The manor house in Faulen has been burnt down. Most of the houses are still standing in Albrechtau; the road to it has been enlarged by traffic to a width of a hundred yards. My practice is increasing. A lot of people come to have their teeth out, because it has been reported that I possess a dentist's forceps. I've been given a stove in my room, made by a 'specialist'; it gets red-hot in a second and cold again just as quickly. I've been sawing and chopping up wood. In the evening I tried to make some shoes out of binder twine. We ended with a reading from the Bible.

9th February

The afternoon was free, because the Russians have to go to the poll tomorrow. A little Lithuanian painter, who lives above me, has already produced forty-five portraits of Stalin for the occasion. We spent the time making syrup. Owing to the lack of space, each of us had to keep strictly to his allotted station. The sacks of beet-parings had been 'semi-officially' fetched from the granary. A little fruit-press, saved by the H.s, wanders through the village from hand to hand; when people knock at the door, it's usually to ask for 'de press'.

10th February

All the local Russians, and the Lithuanians that work for them, went to Bellschwitz today to the 'elections'. There was obviously a lot of schnaps to be had there.

We separated binder twine for knitting. Frau L., as the expert, throned it on a stool on top of the linen-chest, and divided the stuff with upraised arms. Two of us sat at her feet and made it into skeins, which were then wound into balls, to be knitted or crocheted into all kinds of necessary garments. Special praise is due to the firm that invented this binder-twine for the corn; they probably never dreamed of the help it would be one day to hundreds and thousands of people.

11th February

Michael had a visit from a first lieutenant and a second lieutenant, both of them ladies. First lieutenant took precedence, and had been exhaustively described to me beforehand. Second lieutenant set about the washing in the meantime, and tried unsuccessfully to hang it out on a wire during a driving snowstorm.

13th February

Some of the Russians came to have bloody heads treated. So long as there's nothing serious the matter, big head bandages are specially appreciated. The Lithuanian painter told me about the elections. He had gone to the major's house a few days earlier to help with the preparations in Bellschwitz, and had been to see Graf Brünneck's library, which is slowly but surely going up in smoke as cigarette paper.

B., the cowman, is the only fairly young man here among four hundred natives. He happened not to be with the trek when the Russians came, and found his way back here from Pomerania later by a circuitous route. He knows how to deal with the Russians, and has been allowed to take charge of the livestock again as a result. The butter is intended for Liegnitz, but as a cart only goes there once in four weeks, it is stored up in tin pails in the granary meanwhile. They have recently started making skim milk into curds in a bath tub, with a fire lighted underneath to accelerate the process. The burnt curds are then distributed as part of the five-day food ration to the workers, to whom I belong.

17th February, Sunday

Clear weather and gales. With three little milk-cans full of syrup, which we wanted to exchange for fish, Frau L. and I went to Schwalgendorf. We by-passed Januschau, as usual, and did the return journey as a non-stop forced march. Kuczmarki gave us a surprise in the shape of bread and butter; he still has a goat. His daughter, Frau Bucholz, had collected some patients on the quiet, who had begged to come if I ever happened to visit them. The dentist's forceps was in great demand. Some Polish families have arrived in Schwalgendorf recently. Laden with fish, we reached home by moonlight, with a gale blowing.

18th February

A north-easterly gale and driving snow. Tiles fell off all the roofs.

All the hay wagons that were to have come from Peterkau today were blown over. In the forest, H. was swept off a cartload of timber by a leaning tree and brought home badly bruised and half frozen. Michael left today for good, and I moved into his room.

19th February

In yesterday's gale some thirty old pines at the edge of the wood near here were torn up by the roots and fell, all in the same direction, into the main stand. A lot of trees have been brought down in the forest itself as well.

I went to Rosenberg with Frau L. The bakeress bought the fox for 500 zloty. A pound of sugar costs 90 zloty. Sunshine and fresh snow on the way back.

Nadja fetched me at night to attend the Commandant's present wife, who was doubled up with stomach pains. She had eaten something or other. Nadja seemed familiar with the case, and made her drink two quarts of milk three times running and bring it up again. All that good milk! We could have done with it.

20th February

I tried to give some lessons to Alice and Peter L., aged eight and seven respectively. All beginnings are difficult—for both parties. In the evening, after dark, a cart came to take me to Faulen; Nadja was sitting at the back and two Russians in front. We drove off from the front door at full gallop. Ten yards further on we were caught on a heap of stones, the cart split in two, leaving Nadja and me sitting in the stern, while the forepart of the cart raced on. I started off on foot, but halfway there a second cart overtook me, escorted by men on horseback. I got in reluctantly; the coachman drove standing, flogging the horses with the ends of the reins, determined not to let the riders get by. The cart ran through some snowdrifts, but came to no harm.

In Faulen I found thirty or forty people standing smoking round the bed of a young Russian with a deep knife wound under his right collar-bone. He called out to me, to know if he'd got to die. I said, yes, if they didn't all leave the room immediately. A shower of curses from the patient produced a prompt clearance; he was able to breathe again, and soon calmed down enough for me to take the necessary measures. He seemed to have had a lucky escape.

21st February

Frau Petschat has made me a new pair of trousers out of two sacks, bright yellow, with patch pockets, and tied round the ankles. This is the latest wear for both men and women. In the evening I fetched a sack of beet parings from the farm, which Frau L. had put aside beforehand. At the present time twenty carts, driven by women and girls, go daily to Riesenburg and return in the evening with beet parings. Riesenburg is Polish, but the sugar factory is guarded by Russians.

23rd February

Twenty degrees of frost again today, with hoar-frost. It grew warmer later and gales sprang up again. The Russians celebrated Red Army Day; all I saw of it was bloody heads. I always ask them, by way of a joke, what is the matter with them. 'Head kapoot' is the automatic answer. In the evening a regular blizzard set in. I whittled crochet-hooks out of a tough bit of beechwood, for crocheting shoes with. In addition to binder twine we need tyre rubber and telephone wire, both of which are available in plenty, for there are broken wheels lying about everywhere, and the telephone wires hang down from the poles.

26th February

Not a day goes by without gales, sometimes with snow, sometimes without. The scantily clad girls are on the road for nine hours a day, carting beet parings. Max, a militiaman from Saxony, who is employed as a fitter by the Russians, has told us of a drive he got with them to Danzig. I'm wondering whether I won't try and get them to take me with them next time.

3rd March

Moderate cold, gales from the south-east. I went to Schwalgendorf and held a consultation at Frau Bucholz's house. The Polish ranger passed by and was very friendly; he speaks German well. After eyeing me for a time he asked if I wasn't very cold, and if he mightn't give me something to put on. I was almost offended by this disparagement of my costume, of which I am very proud. Our patients gave us fish again, and cotton yarn, of which a whole quantity has been found in Weepers.

5th March

It's thawing and raining. All able-bodied people spent the day in Rosenberg loading potatoes, and didn't get back till nine in the evening. An hour later the men were called up again, and I joined them. We drove off in a number of wagons; it was so dark that we could hardly see our way. Russians and Germans from the whole neighbourhood were assembled near the station. Nipkau, near Rosenberg, appears to be the Russian headquarters. As we could see nothing, we began by setting fire to the wooden potato barrows standing about everywhere. We found ourselves among a number of potato clamps alongside the railway line, on which stood a goods train. Our people began hacking open a clamp. We trod on potatoes everywhere in the darkness. No control was possible; it was left to each of us to decide whether and how to get the potatoes into the train. We carried them over in sacks. At times nobody did anything. When it began to grow light there were some two hundred men squatting, tired and stiff, in the open clamps. We were supposed to be getting some soup soon, but as nothing had happened by midday I took my leave and went home to my consultation. The safest way to go through Rosenberg today is in clogs, with a pitchfork over one's shoulder. The Poles call the town Susz.

Russian soldiers and civilians are hard to tell apart; they wear the same clothes, and all use firearms. Our Russians were mostly prisoners in Germany and are afraid of Russia now.

7th March

Several women came from Schwalgendorf to have their teeth out. In the afternoon I went to Rosenberg to bargain for sugar, bacon, onions and yeast. With the yeast we make a sort of beer out of the syrup, in the milk can. When it's three days old it's quite good to drink. Three thousand Russian soldiers are expected in Rosenberg; the Poles are only allowed to live there provisionally. The Russians are uneasy, and talk of war; some Americans and English are said to have marched towards the Elbe and to have armed the Germans as well. Today is the Russians' Mothers' Day.

10th March

Today is Sunday; the Russians don't keep it. I baptised the youngest grandchild at Lasner's, the last pure German in the place. The mother's birthday was celebrated in the evening, and the Russians were invited too. Three of the old men that came, who have worked here for a year, had made themselves musical instruments out of boxes and wires. The melody to their din was supplied by an asthmatical concertina. As a finale the Russians danced their national dances like madmen.

11th March

Wassili, known as Waschko, the brigadier, went shooting yesterday and wounded a red deer near Klein-Brausen. He followed the blood trail through the lake swamp and Heidemühler wood as far as a 'river' he couldn't cross. The 'river' is the stream connecting two forest lakes. I went there today and picked up the trail on the other side of the water; three hundreds yards further on lay the dead game; an oldish hind in calf. I disembowelled it and hung the liver on a tree, to save it from poaching dogs, two of which I had seen nearby. I found it heavy going in the soft snow, and didn't reach home till late in the afternoon. Waschko, to whom I reported, was very surprised, and had the horses put to at once, to go and fetch the deer. I begged him to distribute the meat in the village. He agreed, and went with me in the cart. When we reached the place where the deer lay it was quite dark, and he asked me with some hesitation how I had found the way. 'I know every tree here,' I said, but this was obviously beyond his comprehension. When we got back he told me I might distribute the venison myself.

12th March

The cowman helped me to skin the deer. We used to think an animal like that hadn't much on it; now this one will provide a feast for some two hundred people, who have had no meat for months.

The Russians here seem to be preparing for war. Stalin is said to have made a speech against England. A lot of horses are being drafted away; in Januschau they are slaughtering them for canning.

15th March

I went to Nipkau early yesterday to fetch medicaments, chiefly for the itch, from a Russian chemist. On the way back I was held up in Rosenberg by the UB, the Polish secret police, and locked in a prison cell. My companion there was a young Pole who had killed somebody in a scuffle. He prayed most of the night. As we had only one mattress between us we took it in turn to lie down.

In the morning we were let out for five minutes in the yard, and invited to take receptacles with us from the rubbish heap for our food. I found half a preserving jar and had coffee poured into it, which I used to wash it out. In the afternoon I was brought before the Commandant, who was interested in a tablecloth found in my rucksack in addition to the medicines. He was in mufti, and spoke good German—might be a Russian. After some discussion, and on my telling him the Russians in Brausen were waiting for me, he gave me, to my surprise, 500 zloty for the cloth and sent me back to Nipkau under escort by a sentry. The sentry had a long pow-wow with the chemist, and then left me there. I asked to be given a pass, so that I shouldn't be arrested again the next minute, but he wouldn't agree. Instead, I was first given something to eat, and then told to wait for the next Russian cart going to Brausen. 'When will that be?' I asked. 'Oh, perhaps tomorrow, perhaps in three days' time. You stay here, sleep, not worry.' So I lay down till it was dark, and then walked back to Brausen, giving Rosenberg a wide berth. In the evening we sat around at Lasner's discussing what to do if it really came to war and the Russians suddenly left, taking everything with them that could still be of use. Oughtn't we to try and conceal at least a few cows in some remote forest farm before it was too late?

17th March, Remembrance Sunday (2nd Sunday in Lent)

Ten degrees of frost and a great deal of fresh snow. The Russians have gone shooting again. Result: three deer, two hares, one full-grown boar and one stag wounded. The latter were not followed up, and unfortunately I couldn't do it this time because I was in bed with a temperature.

20th March

Yesterday, in addition to fish we brought a live cock from Schwalgendorf. A few hens have come to light here and there; we ourselves have no less than five, but we had lost our cock, killed by a little Russian lad with a Tesching rifle. We brought the new one back with us as a surprise. By way of thanks for a tooth extraction, Schlichting drove us back from Schwalgendorf as far as the border in his sleigh. He still has an old horse.

In the evening the Lithuanian painter came to supper. We were celebrating my Oldenburg grandfather's birthday. There was fish in various forms, hot and cold, dished up with all the frills. Frau

S. learnt cooking in a big household and Frau L. ran a bakery for three years. The lamp hung low over the table, so one couldn't see the beds. The Lithuanian shook his head at the sight of all that our women had managed to produce in spite of the general poverty. He said this urge to resist chaos was one of the things that made us Germans seem so uncanny to the Russians.

22nd March

Heavy spring gale. Starlings, peewits and cranes have arrived. The village pond throws up great waves; along the village street the water is eighteen inches deep, and we have to go a long way round to the pump with our cans. The Russians have suddenly had the idea of storing ice in the ice-house, which they had neglected doing up to now. The women are standing in the manure pond in the farmyard with sticks, trying to secure the middle piece still floating there. The Russian tailor came in the evening, bringing me a pair of grey trousers, to the bottom of which he has sewn something like eighteen inches of black lining material.

24th March

Going through the little wood full of bird-calls, I came upon the tanner. He goes to work with a plane on the small and medium-sized oaks, because the bark is needed for tanning. This means that they are stripped of a complete girdle, three feet wide, which they are hardly likely to survive. I tried to convince him that it would be better and easier to fell a couple of oaks and peel off all the bark; but he couldn't see my point. They don't care a damn what becomes of things, anyway. What is the source of this disregard, this lack of relationship to anything existing in its own right? It's not met with in any animal, except perhaps in a domestic one that has been robbed of the basis of its existence, and then it is only due to fear. I find myself continually wondering how humanity originated. Can man still be a purely natural phenomenon once he has been spoken to by God? Is not Christ's saying, 'Man shall not live by bread alone, but by every word that proceedeth out of the mouth of God', a very clear confirmation of this, and a reference to an obligation that we cannot escape?

26th March

Spring is arriving in force. I went to Januschau·and put the graves in order. Five swans were swimming on the flooded meadow beside the Heidemühler road. In the little cottage in the park that was built for my mother's fifth birthday the Russians have established a schnaps factory. On the way back I walked along by the Dead Lake looking for fish. A couple of ducks were swimming about on it; there was still some ice in the middle.

27th March

We did some shopping in Rosenberg in the afternoon, after making some money out of another tablecloth. We have made friends with some of the shopkeepers by now; even 'Warsawianka' smiles a little, so far as her puffy, besmeared face allows. The snowdrops are in bloom at the hospital; I took one of the last remaining window-panes from there for my room. Three rats were caught at night in our trap in the space of ten minutes; they will keep eating our shoes and shoelaces, and are particularly keen on the fish, which we have to hang up on wires in consequence.

31st March

I went to Schwalgendorf with Frau L., for the first time in the shoes I've made myself. The island in Lake Tromnitz is already peopled with herons and cormorants; the latter are increasing to a serious extent, and have already driven some of the herons over to the other island. The way they throw their weight about reminds me of the Russians. There was still some ice on the Geserich, which melted during the day; when we left, the sun was glittering on innumerable little ripples. When it was nearly dark we were attacked by two Russians on horseback just outside Brausen; they hit me over the head and carried Frau L. off with them. Frightful things followed. I lay awake all night afterwards, wondering whether it would have made any difference if I'd had my hammer with me. Frau L. soon came home.

1st April

With my four pupils and four-year-old Helga S. I went to Albrechtau to look at the church. It has been half gutted, but the altar is still there, and so is the angel above the font, except for one of his feet. The children asked some fundamental questions, and inevitably came up against the crucial problem: Why did God let the serpent into Paradise? The people in Albrechtau are keeping some sheep and young cattle. A few Russians are living there on good terms with some German families.

3rd April

Some Russians came here with lorries to fetch potatoes, said to be for Königsberg. I succeeded in speaking to one of the drivers, who declared he knew 'the Sisters with the big caps', and took a note from me for Sister Raphael, begging her to advise everybody who could do so to make their way into the country, preferably as far as this. Unfortunately there's little probability that she will get my scrawl.

We are having the most lovely spring weather, with a temperature of 20 degrees centigrade. H. and I went to Merinos, where the Finckenstein sheep used to be dipped. The village is deserted. The shore of the lake was more dappled with frogs than I had ever seen it, and pike were stirring among the reeds.

5th April

The woods are full of anemones, hepaticas and daphne. I bathed in the lake at Januschau and watched the fish for some time. A ring-snake came swimming past. On my way through the pine plantation I came unexpectedly upon a strange Russian at the edge of the field, who was going shooting. Fortunately he was as much taken aback as I was, and asked if I had seen any 'kossas', by which he appeared to mean deer. I tried to think where he would do the least harm, and sent him to Annhof, the old fishing hut by the lake.

7th April

I went to the lake with some fish-traps, but couldn't set them because there was a skiff lying there, and shots were falling near me. I felt afraid for the swans, which could hardly be missed on account of their size and tameness, especially when sitting abroad on their nests. The amount of blossom throughout the wood is overwhelming.

Some of our Russians are moving to Bellschwitz today, and our people are afraid of being taken with them. The Russians can't understand this. 'Have lodging there too,' they say. Living at home doesn't exist for them. When they move out of a place they take everything with them, even the windows. We sent eight-year-old Alice to see if a certain party of Russians had gone. 'No,' she reported, 'the windows are still in.'

Anatolj, whom I operated on recently by candle-light, opening an enormous abscess in his leg with a razor-blade, came to celebrate with me, with some schnaps he had brewed himself. Fortunately I saw him coming just in time to escape through the window.

Frau Aust, the old ranger's wife from Faulen, is living in Klein-Albrechtau with her still older sister in a little room below the Poles. They did once escape as far as Pomerania, but were forced to return. Frau Aust's husband died last summer. The two women are knitting stockings and gloves for us out of binder twine.

11th April

A crowd of Russians have come to take possession of the potato clamps beside the Rosenberg road, our last reserve. I'd seen that coming for a long while, but had unfortunately not taken precautions in time. We could easily have dug into one of the clamps long ago, and made a depôt somewhere in the field. I crept up to the opened clamps at night, to see how many potatoes were left, dug a hole three feet deep, and began filling it from the clamp. By the second sackful I was challenged from the road. I tore across country, the patrol fired three shots in my direction. Once out of reach I described a big half-circle that took me through the little wood. Such a lovely spring night! The wood-owl called enticingly. Two badgers chased each other, snarling, along the path; one of them turned a somersault from fright as it brushed against my trouser leg. I fought my way through the long-standing weeds to my house door and crept back unobserved into bed.

14th April

Young Frau H. came from Schwalgendorf yesterday with some fish for my birthday, and we had a grand celebration. Today, Sunday, three of us took her home again. We had left Januschau Park behind us and were going across the fields towards Zollnick Woods, when a herd of red deer came trotting towards us from the left. A couple of shots fell suddenly behind us, and we looked round. Up there before the door of the manor house stood some Russians, firing on the deer from a distance of at least 800 yards—or perhaps on us. But their machine pistols wouldn't carry that far; the bullets hit the ground a long way behind us.

When we were near the wood a second herd came swiftly over the field, still further to our left, a glorious sight. They are keeping exactly to their old runs. Following my usual habit I ran to the edge of the wood and let one head of game after another trot past me into the wood, as I did in the old days.

A walk of this sort through the wood, past the lakes where the waterfowl are getting busier and busier, is always an entrancing experience. At one time even a drive to Schwalgendorf was looked upon as quite an undertaking. Now we repeatedly walk the whole distance without counting the miles. Life consists altogether much more of movement, and feet are now beginning to serve their real purpose. Schwalgendorf was being visited by the militia from Saalfeld, and as we entered the village I was promptly arrested. But as we are working for the Russians I was set free again out of prudence. We are gradually learning to play off Russians and Poles against each other. On the way home we avoided Januschau altogether by going along the chain of lakes past the Annhof fishery, and thence along the edge of the wood. As we were walking in the twilight across the Milking-place—a grazing-place among birches and alders at the edge of the wood—a flight of woodcock streaked past us in such numbers as I had always longed to see but never had.

16th April

Another day of sunshine and warmth. In the old days we should have worried about the drought and have longed for rain, but as nothing has been sown in the fields we can enjoy the weather with no qualms of conscience. The land is a matter of supreme indifference to the Russians, because presumably they will soon be leaving it, and the few Poles cultivate only just enough for their own needs.

The birches are showing green. Late in the evening I took the Lithuanian painter for a walk through the little wood, by the light of a full moon. At first he was rather scared, but then we sat down on a fallen tree and he told me about his wife and two small children, whom he had had to leave behind when the Russians carried him off. He has heard nothing of them for nearly two years. I tried to console him, with the only consolation to be had on earth, and begged him not to give himself up so much to despair and schnaps, the effects of which have already left their mark on him.

17th April

Four Schwalgendorf women paid us a visit on their way to the militia in Rosenberg; two of them are going there to look for their husbands, whom the militia carried off by way of playing a trick on the Russians. In the evening two of the women looked in again on their way home. The other two have gone on to Charlotten-werder, because they have gathered from various hints that their husbands have been taken there.

Late in the evening, after two heavy thunderstorms that broke out to the north and south of us, I was invited over to the Lithuanians'. Eleven of them are living in one big room. Out of one large and one small glass, which went the round, we all drank beet beer and beet schnaps, while student songs were sung to German tunes.

18th April

The Russians really appear to be leaving; there's a new password every day. H. wanted to have a talk with the Polish ranger and try to find accommodation in Schwalgendorf, where several houses are still standing empty, and I went with him for the sake of visiting patients in Schwalgendorf, this time at the house of some newly arrived Poles. We returned with a lot of fish. The two old men from Schwalgendorf, one of whom is Schwarz the joiner, are actually held by the militia in Charlottenwerder. If the Russians haven't come and clawed them out by then, they intend trying to make their escape during the Easter festival.

Our official food supply is becoming very meagre, and is anyway only distributed now to twenty 'workers', including myself. But there is still a great deal of musty flour lying about in sacks in the granary, and the two girls working at night at the mill have resolved to get some of it over to the people of the village. We too were to be given a sack. So, as arranged, I presented myself at the yard gate at one in the morning and was escorted into the mill; then the Russian was made to switch off the light at the engine until I was safely across the yard again carrying a hundredweight sack.

19th April, Good Friday

I visited patients in Little and Great Albrechtau. In one house I found two women and six children sitting round a table, knitting, both boys and girls. The binder twine is inexhaustible. In the evening I read the story of the Passion according to St. Luke.

21st April, Easter Sunday

I held a service in my surgery, which we had arranged very festively. There was some very good singing, in spite of the lack of hymnbooks. Even the Russian tailor, who appears to belong to some sect or other, joined the congregation. I took my text from the story of the Resurrection in the Gospel of St. John. As my hearers were nearly all women it seemed the most suitable.

In the afternoon we hid little Easter eggs the size of peas, which I had procured in Rosenberg, for the children to find in the gravel-pit in the little wood. They were in raptures. On our way back from there we suddenly saw a fountain rising above the wood, followed by a detonation. The Commandant was fishing the Dead Lake with explosives, and some time later I found the surface of the lake covered with little fishes. There was another bang at Annhof. They had tied the skiff to the back of the cart and driven a mile and a quarter across country with it to the next lake. The rest of the Russians celebrated the day with schnaps and a grand free-for-all in the village. The women stood in the doorways, looking on in a great state of excitement.

22nd April

Five Russians came for treatment, with gaping head wounds from yesterday's affray. They had wanted to rob the Lithuanians of their schnaps, and broke into their house, but had been knocked down with a fence post by the biggest of the Lithuanians and thrown out of a window on the other side. The whole village had watched them running in at the front and flying out again at the back. Today the tall Lithuanian is in jug.

Seeing a thick cloud of smoke in that direction, I went to the Dead Lake and found a considerable forest fire raging. From the lake shore, where the Russians had lighted a fire, the dry under-wood was burning in a semi-circle over a stretch of some 300 yards. I took off my shirt, and succeeded in beating a few breaches with some fir-branches; then, standing on a footpath, which the fire was approaching on a diagonal front, I succeeded to my surprise in smothering it altogether. Fortunately it hadn't yet caught the tops of the trees; the old stumps went on smouldering. It's so dry and hot that we must be prepared for further outbreaks, especially now that the Russians are lighting fires everywhere, to roast the exploded fish on the spot.

I took a pail with me to the Dead Lake in the morning, and extinguished the stumps. A long walk with H. in the afternoon. There was another great cloud of smoke hanging over the forest, a long way off this time. We have started receiving 'pay'. I rank

next after the cowman and the smith, and get 77 Polish zloty a
month. (A pound of sugar costs 90 zloty.) For the others it drops
gradually to 18 zloty. Three Russians are busy in the 'Office'
working out the different amounts on calculating machines.

28th April
Rain at last during the night, finest summer weather again all
day. I went to Schwalgendorf with Frau S., viâ Annhof and Zollnick. The latter, which consisted only of the ranger's house standing
in the middle of the forest on a little clearing between two lakes,
has been burnt down. In the yard, under the maple tree, we found
a grave with a cross of birch-wood and a steel helmet. Frau S.
showed me a buried chest in the barn, which the Poles had found
and opened. Beside the chest, which lay empty in the ground, some
sporting rifles are still buried. We took some chives with us from
the garden. We crossed the border at the Weisse Bruch, which
used to be my favourite stand on our shooting parties, because
owing to the lack of undergrowth one could see a long way through
the wood, and there was nearly always some game in sight. On
stalking expeditions, too, I often got a shot there.

In the middle of the forest we found a mowing-machine, with a
dead man lying near it. In the four-year-old pine plantation in the
State forest we both stopped short at the same moment with a
shout of delight, 'Morels!'. Morels already! And what beauties!
We soon had both our rucksacks full, and left them lying there
till we came back, so as not to excite the envy of the Schwalgen-
dorfers. From the garden of the deserted ranger's house in Alt-
Schwalge we took the first rhubarb, and from a crow's nest within
easy climbing reach, two eggs for H's birthday. Two young plantations have been burnt to the ground in Schwalgendorf, and so
has a farmhouse on the outskirts; the Pole occupying it only intended burning off the old grass in his meadow. On the way home
we passed by the lakes again; a swan lay dead on its nest near
the shore. The reeds are growing thick, rollers and hoopoes have
arrived. We have been going barefoot for weeks.

This walking barefoot has led me to read the Gospel story of
the washing of feet differently than in other years. For when one
comes home barefoot in the evening, the need to wash one's feet,
or to have them washed for one, is actually very great, and one
begins to understand why the Saviour employed this particular
means to throw light on the most important relationship between

Christians—the need to become clean, to maintain our union with Christ and with one another. I believe we Protestants make things too difficult for ourselves in this connection. Like Peter, we imagine that the forgiveness of sins means the cleansing of the whole man. But Jesus said to Peter, 'He that is clean needeth not save to wash his feet, but is washed every whit; and ye are clean ... through the word which I have spoken unto you.... If I, then, your Lord and Master, have washed your feet, ye also ought to wash one another's feet.' Has not Jesus spoken to us too? I feel that we don't lay sufficient claim to this fundamental cleanliness of ours, and go on dragging with us all the burdens on our conscience far longer than we need. If we were to keep the image of the washing of feet before our eyes, we should probably soon learn to feel our offences, the daily occurring, almost unavoidable ones, only as disturbing as the dirt of the road on bare feet. And we should make far greater use of the power of our fellow-travellers to cleanse us from it.

30th April

Yesterday and today were the birthdays of the H.s, husband and wife. We had cakes. Work has almost come to an end here; the pigs have gone and only the cattle are left. The cows have been lowing in their stalls for days, because they could smell the fresh grass, but the Russians were afraid to let them out into the paddock. They have at last been persuaded to do so today, and the creatures have been capering about out there all the morning, drunk with joy. In the evening Frau S. and I worked in the burial place and planted flowers on the graves. At sundown we went home shouldering rakes and spades.

Tending the graves of my loved ones is one of the happiest tasks it has been granted me to carry out these days. How great is God, to allow me this satisfaction, and to let me love life in spite of all we have endured! My youngest brother was the first. He fell at Maubeuge, at eighteen, ten days after the beginning of the French campaign. After taking part in twelve reconnaissance patrols, some of which he had been allowed to lead himself, his life was cut short in an encounter with French tanks, when he was shot in the head. His death shattered me; I hadn't seen him for nearly a year. We had met for the last time here in Januschau, a few months after his school-leaving exam, while he was doing his labour service. War was in the air at the time. We went shooting for the sake of being together. When I was leaving, at four the next morning, I went to his room as he had begged me to do. He was awake. We eyed each other a little uncertainly, but before the anxious question of the future had had room to intervene, his indestructible sense of fun flashed out and saved the happiness of the moment. His image is always present to me, not as a stable, motionless picture, but always astir, coming and going, giving and receiving. I see him coming downstairs to greet people waiting for him—a trifle more slowly than usual, a little more awkwardly than he need, a little wrinkle of annoyance on his forehead because of all the eyes upon him, but powerless to prevent a wave of his own joy in life communicating itself to those waiting below. He had brought something new into our family circle. Even before he was born my mother had been different from her usual self; she seemed somehow to be floating over the ground, and the child himself always produced this impression on other people. In his presence the world grew wider, the sky more lofty; objects of dispute lost their importance, and bad impulses were checked by a feeling of shame. His personality lent a quite new, much clearer aspect to our rather muddled, commonplace view of our fraternal relationships. We looked upon him as belonging to us, intrinsically ours, and yet we treated him with a certain diffidence, because we felt that he didn't belong to us alone, he would go his own way and we shouldn't be able to prevent him. I shall always remember how someone who had been watching him intently said to my mother, 'You'll have to let that one travel early—a great deal, I mean.' He was five years old at that time. Very soon all the children in the neighbourhood collected round him without his calling them, grown-up people liked to have him make fun of them, it was so comforting; and I never knew anybody to be jealous of him for any reason. 'I stride over bridges although I could fly.' These words from a poem by Hermann Kükelhaus always recur to me when I think of him.

When he fell, he was buried by a brother ten years older than himself, who was serving in the same regiment, with the help of eight comrades, by the roadside, wrapped in a piece of tent-cloth. And when the French campaign was ended, his brother did what was forbidden : he dug him up again and brought him secretly to Januschau, thinking his mother wished this to be done. The grave has been here ever since.

Beside him lies the next youngest brother, who died six weeks later. At the age of eighteen he had had a heavy fall from his horse on the racecourse at Karlshorst, and had never really recovered from it. The death of his dearly loved brother dealt him the last blow. He hardly spoke at all during those last few weeks, and then a sudden cerebral hæmorrhage put an end to his life. When I think of him I am seized with a deep sense of guilt. He was smaller than his brothers from birth, and developed more slowly to begin with; then, by sheer force of will, he made up for lost time, became a splendid horseman, learned more easily than his brothers, showed a more stable character and resembled the youngest in the sense that he thought nothing of himself, and was always standing up for the under dog. But he had no compensating balance, no real self-reliance. Too much was demanded of him all his life, even a year after his skull had been fractured. When he was still no more than a shadow of his former self, we let him go into the army. He carried on with the remains of his strength till his final collapse. We were blind at that time. Now it all comes back to me, and I can guess what he suffered.

A few steps further on there is a stone bearing the name of the brother nearest to me in age, with whom I was in a constant state of feud during the whole of our childhood. He was harsh, passionate, full of sharp corners, and it was not till he had become a soldier that he succeeded in governing his temperament and making the best use of his human qualities. After the French campaign, in which our youngest brother had fallen at his side, he served in Russia, first before Moscow and then in command of a reconnaissance squadron before Leningrad. It was when he was transferred there, in November 1942, that we saw him for the last time. He had spent three days in Berlin, and realised something of the abyss above which our leadership was playing; he had the courage to draw the unavoidable conclusions. 'I know it's all wrong for me to go to the front now, to my squadron,' he said to me. 'Once you're out there with your men, you think everything's all right so long as you do your duty. And yet everything is lost, and you're merely driving your men to their ruin. I ought to be doing something else. But three days is simply not long enough to make up one's mind, so I must choose the easier way once more.' In the night of the 14th to the 15th of January he appeared to me in a dream in a gigantic form. I knew he had fallen, before the news reached us by telephone. He had waited with his division on the shore of Lake Ladoga for the attack by the Russians who were advancing over the ice in successive waves, and had succeeded in holding it up to begin with. Then he had rushed to drag a wounded man out of the danger zone and been mortally wounded. Somebody told me that only the day before he had assured his men that one could die no better death than in saving a comrade.

My oldest and last surviving brother and my mother belong to this place too, but although they were killed not far from here, their bodies can never be brought here, because, as I said earlier, many weeks after their death they were shovelled into a common grave elsewhere. My brother, who was too old to share in our childish rivalries, and often chided us for our somewhat thoughtless behaviour, was nevertheless devoted to us, and felt responsible for us. He had spent the whole of the war in Poland, the Danube Provinces and southern Russia, only coming home once or twice to see to his Januschau estate. He had obtained leave for this a few days before the collapse of East Prussia, and we had talked to each other over the telephone on the 19th January. It is a relief to me to know that he and my mother were together at the time of their death.

I find it difficult to talk of my mother. She is still so near, will always be just as near, even if I still have many years to live. Our existence was shaped by her; we lived her life far more than that of our father, in whose clearly defined occupation of horse-breeding we took a passionate interest, but whom we naturally felt to belong to an older generation. We never felt this with my mother. We couldn't help shaping our lives by hers, and this led sometimes to a breaking-test; but I don't know what sort of man I should be if it hadn't been for my mother. She was the measure of all things for us, and we were always anxious to live in harmony with her. Not that we always shared her views in detail or did what she expected us to—on the contrary, it sometimes enhanced our zest in life to swim against the current of her ideas, though only within her reach, so that if things grew serious we could always let ourselves be hauled aboard again. She was a woman of action, standing in the midst of events, or rather, the stream of events went through her. Her spontaneous reactions sometimes had a painful effect, but they always resulted in the straightening out of a false situation, the exposure of a latent untruth. She could act wrongly and yet intrinsically rightly; in any case, right and wrong meant far less to her as alternatives than great and little. She could wound, but she healed even more easily, and when it came to the most difficult decisions, she could rescue one from the dilemma with the assurance of a sleep-walker. When my youngest brother fell, she went through a serious crisis. It began with that suggestion of floating that we had noticed before his birth. His friends and comrades came to her, and their orphaned state upheld her. But then they fell too, one after another. She left off eating. Although the tie with the rest of us remained as strong as ever, she seemed so far away at times, when she thought herself unobserved, that I felt the decline could hardly be arrested much longer. But the fresh demands upon her, her contacts with persecuted Jews in Berlin, where my parents were then living, the increasing gravity of the war, the air raids, all combined to set her up again. When my brother was killed in Russia she was staying with me in Insterburg, and I had to break the news to her in the morning. Hard as it was, I'm thankful now that it was given to me to do it. When I took her to the station that evening she said, 'Don't imagine I have ever wished myself dead. I know that I'm the most fortunate of mothers.'

1st May

The first of May is really honouring its name. In recent years we have nearly always had snow at this time. This year the birches have been in full leaf for a long while, the oaks are growing green, lilies of the valley are out, may-bugs are on the wing and the cuckoo is calling. We went on a big outing, entirely in honour of the day. We even took four-year-old Helga with us, sometimes on foot, sometimes carried pickaback. She slept the whole way home, peacefully buttoned up in an overcoat hung on a pole, which two of us carried on our shoulders. Our objective was the Uroviec, a beautiful lake near Schwalgendorf, which we had so far only gone past. It's said to be 240 feet deep, and the water is the clearest imaginable. When we got there, we first filled the rucksacks with morels again, and then bathed in radiant sunshine in the lake below the Alt-Schwalge ranger's house, where a little stage runs out into the water. There young Frau H., who had come to the birthday party, left us again, and we went another big round through the woods. We took some more rhubarb from the garden at Annhof, and came home late in the evening.

4th May

We are making a garden for ourselves. We have dug up the

ground immediately behind the house and cleared away a thick tangle of burdocks, nettles, thistles and horse-radish, and we are spreading pressed beet parings, in the process of fermenting, over it by way of manure. The garden measures twenty-one feet by twenty-one. We are fetching poles and wire netting from the wood to make a fence. People laugh us to scorn, first because the Russians will tear everything up, they say, and second, because we shan't be here long enough to see things growing. But we're not letting ourselves be deterred; the work amuses us, and somebody will get the benefit of it anyway. We put some plants in in the evening. In Faulen, where there is a sort of little nursery garden, Frau H. has even picked up some tomatoes, ten small plants, which are being set along the wall. We hope to get seeds in Rosenberg.

Two German soldiers came to see me today; they are working under the Russians in Januschau, but I hadn't seen them before. One of them has his wife with him, diseased like so many through the fault of the Russians. The Commandant in Schönberg kept her prisoner for a long while, and there is still a danger that he may fetch her back again. It must be frightful in Schönberg, the Commandant is a sadist. It's a blessing we have nothing to do with him.

Our fat Commandant left here today; the cattle are to go too very soon.

8th May

It was still hot and rather dull during the day, but in the evening it turned clear and very cold. We are afraid for the enormous amount of hard and soft fruit blossom of this unusual spring. I went to Schwalgendorf with the two young women to fetch potatoes in a child's go-cart. There are none left here, and we want some to plant. We had a hard time coming back with our load, sometimes along sandy paths, sometimes through the middle of the main forest. One of us had always to act as advanced guard, while the other two pulled and pushed the cart, the axles of which were no longer parallel to each other. It overturned more than once, and we had to collect the entire contents over again. On the last part of the journey the wheels had become so completely locked that we had to drag the cart over the fields like a sledge, and we didn't get home till nearly midnight.

9th May

The Russians celebrated the anniversary of our capitulation today. Many of them can no longer stand the smell of schnaps, and stuff bread up their noses. What they consider most worth the effort of drinking it is the after-effect, not the taste. I visited some patients in Rasenfeld. There are some typhus cases again among the Germans. After that we went to Merinos and fetched some rhubarb, our chief food at present, boiled in syrup.

Schwalgendorf has had some mail from the Reich! Two women came to tell us about it. People are affected by it in most contrary ways, for not all the news is pleasant. Many husbands who were thought to be lost have shown up again, but they don't seem inclined to resume contact with their wives and families, having formed new connections elsewhere. Some of the letters are regular scandalmongering affairs, which threaten to disrupt the settled harmony of the heterogeneous community of the village.

12th May

Slight frost again this morning, within the period of the ice saints. We've covered our tomato plants with paper bags. It grew warmer during the day. A German militiaman, who works for the Russians in Rasenfeld, came with a serious injury to his hand. The Russians who brought him drove us to Nipkau, where we were able to give him an anti-tetanus injection. Coming back we drove at a gallop almost the whole time, with the result that the backboard of the luggage cart fell off, and was left lying in the road, because the driver didn't consider it worth his while to stop for such a trifle.

In the evening I went fishing in the lake at Januschau, opposite the bathing-place, where the osprey has built an eyrie on a Scotch fir. The lake, about a mile and a quarter long, entirely surrounded by woods and connected to the neighbouring lakes by little brooks, is one of the greatest centres of attraction for me here, because it has completely recovered its quietude, and the life upon it is just as it used to be. The only thing I miss, among the cries of the smaller and larger ducks, the divers, marsh harriers and ospreys, is the occasional bark of a dog from the Annhof fishery across the water, which always broke out as soon as anyone approached. There is even a pair of swans still here, although as a result of the disturbances in the spring they have not succeeded in hatching out any young. On the way home I walked for miles through fields that were a wilderness of weeds, stirring up clouds of midges and other noxious insects.

14th May

Sun and wind, increasing to gale, very hot in the evening. A most unusual year. I went to Gross-Albrechtau to baptise two children of Russian origin. The attitude of the mothers to these children, of which only a minority are the result of rape, differs very much, and it is hard to foresee what their future will be like. Some of them seem to be loved in a perfectly simple, natural way; others are put up with because they are there, many are looked upon merely as a nuisance. But the existence of these children presents no problem here for the moment. Later on, if people ever return to more orderly relationships, there may be difficulties here and there. At the present time, owing to the excessive supply of men, many of the women are so much under the spell of their passions that there is little likelihood of their coming to their senses.

On the way back from Albrechtau I looked up old Frau Aust, who is working in the gardens of various Poles, and is paid in food for herself and her invalid sister.

To my intense surprise, when I reached home towards evening I found a letter waiting for me, which had come from the West and been forwarded by my aunt. It was from my sister, dated the 21st January; so one of my own letters must have got through after all. My sister tells me of a lot of people who are still alive and well. Half dazed with surprise I left the house again and roamed about the fields. The fact that there are still people waiting for me is something I can only gradually absorb. With this letter a new period has begun. Lost in thought, I went as far as Grünhof, a little place on the other side of the wood, which is still standing empty. There, in one of the deserted gardens, a single blue iris shone its rays towards me, like a symbol of a former existence preparing to bear flowers again.

15th May

I took a letter to Rosenberg. In the post office, which I entered somewhat cautiously, a friendly Polish woman asked me—in spite of my peculiar clothes—whether I was a 'studierter'. She offered me the books in her house. Very grateful, less for the books than for her general attitude, I nodded, and made her show me her house, in the distance, on the Riesenburg road. Frau S. has lately made some contacts in Rosenberg too, and goes there daily to work for a family with two children.

Three days ago all our cattle were driven to Rosenberg to be sent away by train. Today the whole herd has come back again for some unknown reason. Late in the evening the new Commandant consulted me about a very painful pleurisy. He is considerably thinner than his predecessor, and appears to dislike schnaps. He has shot to pieces some of the schnaps distilleries in the village, but there are still some left.

17th May

The neighbouring manor of Falkenau is quite deserted and partially destroyed. I went there to forage in the gardens. In the manor garden itself I found a forest of rhubarb that no one had discovered. As I was walking through the empty stables, something slipped out of the doorway in front of me and vanished round the corner. I was just able to see that it was a human being, and I ran after it a little way, but could find no trace of it. In a corner sheltered from the wind, however, I came across six glorious yellow tulips.

The cattle went to Rosenberg today for the second time. A hundred head were entrained, for slaughtering in Liegnitz—all beautiful milch cows. The remaining forty came back.

19th May, Cantate Sunday (4th Sunday after Easter)

I feel like singing too. I've decided to visit my aunt. We simply must talk over all the exciting news the letter from the West has brought me. I pulled a child's go-cart behind me as far as Schwalgendorf, which I mean to pick up on the way back, filled with potatoes, and after giving medical advice to some families there I went on eastwards with a full rucksack. Young Frau H. rowed me across the lake to Weepers. Beyond Gablauken I overtook four German women carrying cans of water. They were going to the grave of their husbands and sons, who had been carried off a year ago and were later found dead in the immediate neighbourhood. They had buried them, and set up a little cross made of two boards, which had since been shot to pieces again. I sat down beside it. The women tended the grave, and then we sang, and I read a psalm.

Afterwards I followed the canal through the meadows, exchanged a few words with some German women living in Liegen, and then struck across country again through some paddocks beyond Liebemühl, and crossed the canal by the railway bridge. I nodded to two Polish anglers standing there as I passed; they looked at me in some bewilderment.

I was soon within the Taberbrück Forest again. The beech foliage has been caught by the frost in many places. Eckschilling appeared in the distance. This time I walked along a dead straight path on which stood a number of 'pulpits' for shooting deer, and which ended in a swing gate like the door of a barn. Woodcock rose here in greater numbers than I had ever seen; it must have been the second flight, that one usually pays no attention to. I waited by the swing gate till it was dark. Bugle-calls came over from Taberbrück, obviously sounded by an expert. How familiar it sounded! It seemed so stupid to have to by-pass the next villages again. But I was soon in Grasnitz woods once more, and the ground was dotted with glow-worms. I heard the snuffling of a lot of sows near the burial ground. Then I was standing before the house door. It was locked on the outside, and I started back at the sight of a sheet of stamped paper stuck on it.

I tapped cautiously on the window of the next house and stepped back into the darkness. Frau Langanke opened the door, let me in, and fetched Gross and Fräulein Jokuteit down from their attics. They burst into tears. A few days earlier my aunt had been fetched away at night by at least twelve armed men and presumably taken to Allenstein. No reason had been given. We spent the whole night together, discussing the incident and the possibility of finding out anything more. They fed me on the best they had, and wouldn't accept what I had brought with me. Lorchen the fowl had refused to eat after my aunt left, and had suddenly fallen down dead.

I remained in hiding throughout the day and started home again about nine o'clock in the loveliest summer weather. The woodcock were madly active again. I came upon three lots of red deer. The nightjars churred incessantly and accompanied me with the peculiar trilling and clapping of their mating flight. There was always a spice of danger in walking below the 'pulpits', but the risk of any one of them being occupied was never so small as at present.

After I had crossed the bridge at Liebemühl a fox barked at me. I took cover in a wayside ditch from a group of men coming towards me in the morning twilight. The dew was shrinking my

home-made shoes to such an extent that I had to take them off
and go on barefoot. I reached Weepers by about five o'clock.
Frau P., the former innkeeper's wife, made me some coffee and
engineered my passage across the lake. Nobody has a boat on that
side, so we walked along the shore and over the dyke built out
across the water, as far as the first island. From there she shouted
across the water between her cupped hands, until a dog began
barking on the other island, upon which a woman appeared on
the shore. We waved to her; she unmoored the boat, came over,
and took me to Schwalgendorf.

24th May

There's a rumour afloat again that the Januschau Russians have
left and the manor house is standing empty. I went up to it from
the park side, feeling fairly unconcerned, and stopped in surprise
at the sight of a fiery bush, twice a man's height—our *azalea
ponticum,* covered all over with blossom in four different shades
of red. Then, going on for the sake of seeing the front of the house,
I fell slap into a heap of at least twenty Russians. I turned quickly
to the nearest, and enquired zealously if there were any sick people
about. They directed me to the village, where one of the two
German militiamen was actually lying ill; I was lucky to have got
out of it so easily. All round the manor house there are rubbish
heaps, as everywhere else. The big stone balls have been thrown
down from their pedestals; in front of the verandah on the garden
side there is a Russian grave surrounded by a red fence, on which
washing was drying. Decaying horses lie about everywhere. Out of
one of the rubbish heaps stuck one of the two curious antlers
that always used to lie on the table in the hall. I took it with me
as a memento. Besides the manor, I took a look at a little forest
property called Gräberberg, with a house standing in a small
clearing. Nobody appeared to have been there for months; all the
rooms were knee-deep in paper and rubbish, nothing left of any
use. But in the garden stood a forest of rhubarb, some of which
found its way into my rucksack.

26th May, Rogation Sunday.

I held a service in my two rooms. A lot of people came; Waschko
sent them home from work on purpose. Although I hardly ever
exchange a word with him, I have the feeling that we understand
each other in a way. Our people like him. In the afternoon I held

consultations again in Schwalgendorf. On the way back we found the Alt-Schwalge ranger's lodge, hitherto empty, freshly occupied. The new ranger called me in to see his sick wife, and we were given a pound of bacon to take with us in return for the consultation. We then bathed in the Uroviec. The Russians are said to have taken eighty hundredweight of carp in it lately, at a single draught.

7th June

There were some extraordinary incidents again in Schwalgendorf today. The place was occupied by Polish partisans when we arrived; forty of them had come in two motor lorries, and the Russians belonging to the place had been locked up in their own cellars, in their underpants. Other Russians, who had apparently arranged to meet there and had driven in during the day, were disarmed in the village street, *coram publico,* stripped and led away to the cellars. Their horses were unharnessed and ridden round about. I myself was applied to by the partisans in a medical capacity, and afterwards invited to the meal that Frau H. junior had just cooked for the Russians. Nobody was allowed to leave the place during the day. Late in the evening they buzzed off again. We stayed the night in Schwalgendorf and left at four in the morning, laden with potatoes, fish and honey, which the other Polish ranger had given us. He was particularly nice to us, and so was his wife. He used to work in the Corridor district and his wife was a teacher in Lodz.

There are a few colonies of bees here again. Old Jepp the miller has himself contrived to bring on a few swarms, but he's keeping them concealed for the moment. In the winter the Russians opened all the hives and took away the honey; now they can only find some occasionally in hollow trees along the roads, and they have set people to search for such trees and fell them. These fall mostly across the road and are not removed, from sheer indolence, so that all traffic has henceforth to go over the ditches into the fields, with the result that the roads have become more than fifty yards wide in some places. This is of no importance, however, because the fields are not cultivated anyway.

We reached home about eight o'clock. The partisans came here at night, stopped at the farm and fired on the traction engine at work. One Russian happened to have a hand-grenade in his trouser pocket and flung it over the garden fence. A lorry tyre was hit, and burst, whereupon the partisans left the lorry standing, with the booty, and took to their heels. The Russians went on shooting for another hour.

9th June, Whit-Sunday.

I held a service in the surgery and read the story of Pentecost. Shooting was going on all the time. Two motor vehicles full of Russians came to await the partisans, and in the evening some thirty unknown Russians went into the houses. There seems no hope of the women ever coming to their senses again.

Most of the Germans in Schwalgendorf now call themselves 'Masuren'. This is a new invention, and is probably intended to stress their membership of the Polish race and deny their German extraction. I can't very well dissuade them from 'becoming' Masuren, since it is less important at the moment to champion the German way of life than to remain alive. A few of them still have things hidden away, which they can gradually sell to the Poles, or exchange for food. I am sometimes called on for advice on these occasions, and have to act as a go-between, because the people are too easily robbed once it's known that they still have any possessions. Frau Tiedtke has some suits still buried which had belonged to her husband. Her house has been burnt down; she's living with a crippled sister and an epileptic one. The epileptic one has fits whenever she sees any Russians; she had had to jump out of their burning house from the balcony.

Our Russians are very excited about the partisans, and shoot at anything moving. The old H.s were fired upon when they were gathering herbs in the Grosser Graben.

We spent the morning digging, and planted potatoes in the afternoon. Sudden alarm signal : a lorry with heavily armed men drove through the village. The Russians lay hidden in the weeds and didn't stir. An hour later the same lorry returned and was again allowed to pass through in silence.

Two Poles who used to work at Zollnick at one time came to see H., and brought schnaps with them. They want to settle in the neighbourhood, and behaved in a very friendly fashion, despite the fact that H. had once thrashed one of them pretty soundly. After lessons I retired to the little wood, met two black storks in the drive, and picked bilberries. Our Russians talk of war, but so they often do. The partisans went to Finckenstein and slaughtered some pigs.

16th June

Yesterday all the Russian troops suddenly departed; only the Commandant and the civilians are left behind. Again, nobody knows what this may portend. We picked bilberries, chopped wood and made shoes. On my way to some typhus patients I met some Poles on bicycles who were looking for an empty house to live in. They were leading a cow behind them, and asked if I knew where there was a *billy*-cow.

Faulen has been handed over to the Poles; Januschau and Schönberg are soon to be evacuated too, so we hear. The Poles are still to be seen ploughing and planting potatoes everywhere.

We have set a hen on eighteen eggs under my writing-table. A Russian came a great distance to have one tooth out, and paid me 100 zloty for the job.

23rd June

After the Sunday service we picked several pails full of bilberries and strawberries at Annhof and Zollnick. We had no competitors, for nobody dare go so far into the forest, not even the Russians or the Poles, for fear of the partisans.

The grave in the yard at Zollnick has been broken open again, and the empty chest in the barn has gone, together with the rifles that were buried alongside. The pump in the yard, which was still giving water, has been dismounted.

Today an enormous amount of effort has been expended on bringing back the agricultural machines of every kind, which had been hauled away five days ago by motor vehicles and tractors, and overturning them in the field behind the school. The Poles are not to have them.

2nd July

The heat has been brooding over our village for days. I was fetched for work and made to go with some Russians to Albrechtau, where another thrashing-machine has been found hidden in a barn belonging to the Poles. With indescribable difficulty it was hauled as far as here, and left standing in the middle of the village street; eight other thrashing-machines are lying in the paddock as it is. Apart from this we spend the whole day in the hayfield. The three- and four-year-old clover is being cut and carried. It stands as tall and thick as rushes, and winds itself round our legs like wire. What is to eat it we don't know. At any rate it will keep

9—EPD

us busy for a long time, for the whole district is full of it. It's extraordinary how the hares have increased inside it; both boys and girls are very clever at catching the leverets.

I'm not well. I haven't any spit, and have to carry a can of water about with me and take a mouthful every ten minutes. In the evening we go home singing. The limes are in flower. Marushka, the dreaded Commanderess—a Pole, so they say—always used to come riding into the field on a fat white horse, to be greeted at once with a torrent of curses by the women and girls. Now she has to work with us, as a punishment for attacking a supposed rival out of jealousy and beating her up in bed with a log of wood. In the breaks between work we pick raspberries in the thickets round the fields.

Ten days ago we had a piece of bad luck. In the morning, as we were trying to slip away, barefoot, to Schwalgendorf with four tins of syrup, Frau L. and I ran into the Commandant, and were forthwith locked up in the school cellar. We spent a night there, then Frau L. was set free again. For the next few days I had good food given me by the watch, out of the Russian kitchen, besides having all sorts of berries handed to me through the window-bars of the cellar. My lodgings had been turned out, in the course of which, it seems, some very dangerous poison was found, probably in one of the beer-bottles with Russian labels belonging to the days of my predecessor Nadja. There was great excitement over this, and I was to be punished. Besides which, a woman of our own village had told the Russians I was a spy and in league with the partisans. Things looked pretty critical, therefore, and on top of all this I was taken with shivering fits and a high temperature; all my midge- and flea-bites began to fester and I got cramp in my calves. On the third day I was fetched out and taken before the Commanderess. She shouted at me, and took my temperature herself, because she didn't believe I was really ill. I replied in much the same tone, because that always serves one best. To my great surprise I was then allowed to move into the attic above my former quarters. I'm living there now. I think Waschko must have said a word for me.

7th July

Work has been stopped today because of the rain. The women have got to mend sacks, as usual. More than a hundred little Russian cars came through the village from Januschau. We retreated as usual into the little wood to pick berries. We're not really allowed to leave the village, but our movements can't be detected among the tall weeds growing everywhere. Burdocks and thistles have grown so high that one can almost stand upright in them without being seen. Fresh schnaps distilleries have been set up among them too.

13th July

After days of sunshine and gales it's raining again. I've been sitting all day in the smithy sharpening cutters for the harvesting machine. Yesterday I worked with three Lithuanians in the granary, where the flour is gradually rotting in the sacks. A motor lorry came and knocked down the little outbuilding beside the kitchen of the manor house, having made too sharp a turn. The barn is full of ruined cars and furniture of all kinds piled up in a jumble. The other day the Commandant was grabbed by the tall Lithuanian, whom he was about to arrest, and kicked so heavily to the ground that he found himself lying on the doorstep. The Lithuanian went into jug, but has come out again. In the afternoon we shovelled rotting beet parings from the granary into the yard.

The Russians are in a state of excitement again on account of changes in official plans. Cattle are to be sent here again from Silesia. The pigs, which have grown enormously fat on the beet parings, are not to be killed but given some sort of laxative to make them thinner again. Now and then a horse disappears, probably sold in secret by the Russians themselves; one was found lately, after a wide search, at a Pole's house some eighteen miles away. The Pole had bought it from a Russian who turns up here only occasionally nowadays. Nobody knows where he lives. The Commandant has outlawed him; anybody that sees him is to shoot him dead.

2nd August

I was ill for a fortnight with a high fever and a severe headache, sometimes not quite in my right mind. Now I'm thoroughly pulled down, lying in bed in H.'s kitchen again this last week, because nursing me in my broiling hot attic had become too difficult. The mice ran to and fro along the beam above my head, and when I called out nobody could hear. It began on a Sunday. We were working in the hayfield near Gross-Albrechtau in scorching heat, and had a short midday break in the church. I'd been feeling ill all the morning; I saw the fat Marushka, now lording it again on her white horse, as through a veil. In the afternoon some Russian soldiers came in a lorry to fetch the Lithuanians away from the field, probably to Russia. One of them escaped and disappeared in the forest; the tall one had taken to his heels some days earlier. We didn't get home till sundown, and next morning I couldn't get up. Now I'm slowly beginning to recover.

The partisans have been to Januschau; they've taken all the horses, and robbed the six Russians still left there of their boots and guns. One of the Russians came running past us here, on his way to Nipkau to fetch reinforcements. He was arrested in Rosenberg by the UB, and locked in the cellar for a night. We never know here who is against whom. The Polish police are definitely mortal enemies of the partisans, but they never miss an opportunity of snapping their fingers at the Russians.

In our little garden behind the house everything is growing enormous in the tropical heat: cucumbers, tomatoes and onions. The Rosenberg Poles have sent me word that I must move over to them as soon as I can, because their doctor has been put in prison. They have turned the old Health Office into a hospital. Frau S. has put my name down there as a patient in any case.

8

ROSENBERG

6th August 1946 to May 1947

I'VE been in Rosenberg Hospital these two days. The Polish doctor received me very kindly, and so did the German woman who works here as a nurse. The house lies close to the shore of the lake. Frau S. came to fetch me, and we left the village and reached the high road unnoticed. There we parted company. My escort went through the town with my rucksack, because she is well known there now. I chose the way through the fields, round the lake. But there were some workmen on the road, who saw us leaving each other, and one of them cycled into the town to alert the militia. As a result, my escort reached the hospital many hours later than I did, after being thoroughly searched and questioned.

I have a room on the first floor with a view over the lake, and a lovely bed with white sheets. For the moment I rank as a patient, and only hope the Russians won't fetch me away again at once. We have good food out of American tins.

There are thirty beds in the hospital, nearly all of them occupied. I'm allowed to go the rounds with the doctor. I'm a bit sceptical with regard to the diagnoses. Half the patients are supposed to have typhus and the others pneumonia, but the majority look remarkably fit. The typhus cases, both men and women, are recognisable by their shaven heads. This measure seems to me not only very draconian but quite unnecessary, since it is only resorted to in cases of spotted fever, of which there can be no question here. No temperature charts are kept. There are enormous quantities of drugs available, but little choice among them; they have all been sent by America and are only labelled in English and French, so that their use has been somewhat problematical up to now. There are 180,000 sleeping tablets among them, besides bottles of concentrated hydrochloric and sulphuric acid. But the most coveted item, and therefore most liable to be pilfered, is a ten-litre container of pure, unmethylated alcohol. Sister Erna has the key to it, to the regret of the other nurses.

Here too the most loathsome of all diseases is rife, which has haunted us at every turn. Fortunately we now have drugs in plenty at our command. About forty cases are under treatment at the moment, all of them with one and the same hypodermic syringe. Sister Erna, who had had no sort of medical or even nursing training, but just got stranded here by chance, has already acquired an astonishing expertise in intravenous injection. Ten to fifteen patients visit her every day, healthy young men, and women too. Many new cases have come to swell the number lately—one dare not think of the future consequences all this is going to have.

Rosenberg, which the Poles call Susz, used to be a peaceful country town of some 6,000 inhabitants, the focus of a circle in which the large landed estate was the rule. Now the little town lies in ruins, the land, far and wide, has been devastated and the fine manor houses mostly reduced to rubble and ashes. Round the ruined core of the town the Poles have moved into any houses left standing, but only a minority appear to be really settled. The majority are in a state of perpetual unrest, and the train that runs once or twice daily over this section of the line is crammed with adventurers who come and go because they haven't yet found anywhere to stay, or are on the lookout for better openings. They come from every part of Poland, and represent the most diverse types, eastern and western, who have hardly anything in common with one another as regards their disposition and mentality. There is obviously a very sharply drawn dividing line between east and west running through the middle of Poland. All they have in common is the fact that they have lost their roots, otherwise they wouldn't come here of their own free will, to a country lying waste, and with which they have no connection, except perhaps the few that worked here on the land during the war, and are now trying to build up a new existence for themselves on the deserted farms. The others first arrived here a year and a half ago, immediately behind the Russian army. They are relatively the best off, because they were able to secure a lot of things that had been overlooked in the original looting. They go more or less clothed, and already represent a sort of social stratum, if a somewhat loose one.

Every newcomer tries to take up some sort of trade, or to assume an office. We already possess a burgomaster, a priest, a doctor, a lady dentist, a solicitor, a forester, a postmaster, a station-master, a chimney-sweep, a hairdresser, a shoemaker, a tailor and so forth, although none of them appears to be particularly well versed in his profession. Tradesmen, too, of all kinds, from baker, butcher and innkeeper to simple matchseller. They make a living, and their activities are limited only by the general poverty and by the presence of the militia and the UB, which discharge their dreaded offices according to the most primitive and temperamental points of view.

There are only a very few Germans still living in the town, they can be counted on the fingers of both hands : two old men and a few women and children, who clean the streets, remove the rubbish and do domestic work in Polish households. Any other Germans left in the district live on the estates, mostly under Russian surveillance and in closed communities. Separately, they would hardly find the means to live, and would be at the mercy of every despot's caprice.

The little hospital in which I am working gives me a chance to observe all this from a fairly comprehensive standpoint. I have been civilly treated on the whole, having had the good luck to make a favourable impression early on by some successful surgical interventions.

My first patient was an eighty-year-old peasant with an enormous carbuncle on his neck, who was brought here by his anxious relatives in a cart. Doubting very much if the old man could still be saved, I pointed out the seriousness of the situation and made preparations for the operation. The two Polish nurses, who assured me they had often seen interventions of this kind, wanted to assist me, but rushed out of the room with every sign of horror as soon as I had made the first of four long incisions. They thought I was going to cut off his head. The old man felt the relief at once, recovered, and intends sending me a goose as soon as his neck is quite healed again. His sons have moved into the farm on the other side of the lake, and have taken him and his likewise eighty-year-old wife to live with them. I go over there every three days to renew his dressing. The second dramatic case was an arrested birth. The midwife came to me wringing her hands, and after the requisite examination we went into the kitchen and boiled the forceps, which were fortunately available, in a saucepan. The child then came fairly quickly into the world, with the midwife continually crossing herself because she was sure the child was still too high up for me to reach. After the successful outcome of these and some other rather tricky cases, I'm beginning to feel safe to some extent. Moreover, I'm told that signatures are being collected to a letter to the militia, asking that I should be given as much freedom as possible. Anyhow, if things should become serious, I have a stout rope in readiness in my room, by which I can let myself down from the window, for I don't mean to let myself be put under lock and key any more.

Thanks to the daily injections, in which I assist Sister Erna, I've come to know quite a number of the younger police officers, and I have a feeling that they will leave me in peace so long as nothing special happens. All the same, things became critical one Sunday morning, when two rather older men in uniform, whom I hadn't seen before, entered the hospital and asked for me. Contrary to their usual behaviour on the arrival of men, the two nurses retreated into the furthest corner. We stood for a while facing one another in silence. They looked me up and down. To my question as to whether they were ill they first made no reply; then one of them pointed to his teeth, while the other walked slowly round behind me. I stared at the immaculate set of teeth of the man opposite, thinking, 'Yes, that would just suit you, my friend behind there! But if you move a finger I shall be on the stairs at one bound, out of the window and lost in the wood before you've had time to think.' But the inspection of my reverse side apparently gave no occasion for intervention either, and the two visitors left without a word. The two nurses came out of their hiding-place at once, and congratulated me on this unexpected outcome of the encounter. Those were the two most dangerous people in the whole district, they said, the Commandants of the UB and the militia.

My first drive to see a patient took me almost the whole day. A peasant came to fetch me with a horse about the size of a fairly good goat, and we proceeded at a snail's pace, much more slowly than on foot, along sandy roads to Heinrichau, about nine miles distant. The very sick man was lifted into the cart—it would have been much simpler if the peasant had brought him along in the first instance—and we went back a different way, through Neudeck and Langenau, the two Hindenburg estates. We found the Reich President's manor house burnt down as well as the one in Langenau, and Neudeck village also badly damaged. The fields as usual, of course, hidden deep under weeds.

I'm often sent for to see sick people in the town itself and in the immediate neighbourhood, which helps me to form some idea of living conditions. In many cases my patients are not legally married people but young couples who have found each other by chance, and probably only for a time. Even so the birth-rate is surprisingly high, and Cecylia the midwife is glad to have found a help in me, even for uncomplicated cases, because she can't cope with them all alone. I often stay for hours, sometimes whole nights, with a family of this kind, until the arrival of the child, which is mostly greeted with joy in spite of everything; sleeping at intervals on some chair or other, or on the floor, made to drink a schnaps now and then, and getting to hear a lot of things that these people wouldn't normally relate. The war threw them all into the most lamentable confusion, in which it is hard to tell from which side, west or east, they suffered most injury and injustice. I'm often deeply shamed by the readiness with which, in return for a word of kindness, they will repress all their justifiable feelings of revenge, and look upon all that was done to them in Hitler's name as an aberration foreign to the German nature. And it is the very ones that have lost and suffered most, with whom one can talk most easily of these things. But that doesn't surprise me, for it's the same the world over, especially when people understand something of forgiveness.

Except for the few that have their hands in the American almonry, and know how to feather their nest, they are a needy lot, and will have no chance for a long time to come of obtaining more than the barest necessaries of life. There is too much disorder and despotism for that, too little mutual trust; clothes and provisions are too dear, and schnaps is too cheap in comparison. There's hardly a man among them that doesn't resort to it immoderately as a source of consolation. Czysta Vodka tastes quite nice to me, compared with the abominable beet schnaps, but drinking it of a morning on an empty stomach is a bit of a strain, and hinders me considerably in the exercise of my medical duties. All the same, it's often the only way in which I can avoid offending people. The women like drinking vodka as well as the men, and many of them are clearly affected by the results.

The food in the hospital is excellent, thanks to American gifts and the eatables occasionally handed to us in secret by our patients. Many of them actually pay cash up to 100 zloty for a tooth-extraction, and between 500 and 700 zloty for a delivery—unimaginable sums in our circumstances. One can buy a pound of sugar for 80 zloty and potatoes from 600 to 700 zloty a hundredweight, bacon from 800 to 900 zloty a kilo. Rye costs 1,500 zloty, wheat 2,000 zloty a hundredweight. Nothing else interests us for the moment, for provisions are scarce everywhere, and as I personally have everything I need at the hospital, I can pass on to our people anything I earn on the side. Our own people have been coming to see me for some time now, from a distance, and I'm glad to say that my Polish fellow-workers put no hindrance in my way in this connection. When necessary, we are even allowed to take them into the hospital gratis, and treat them exactly the same as the Polish patients. They even wink at it if we take a person in who isn't really ill but only in need of protection and care.

Fortunately the American drugs include an assortment of narcotics, which have now become popular, though at first I had to overcome a great deal of resistance to their use. Now all at once everybody wants to have something injected into their veins when an incision has to be made or a tooth extracted, and every day we have one or two people lying about in the refectory, sleeping off their intoxication.

There is usually a certain amount of trouble with the young men of the militia and the UB, very well-nourished individuals and particularly inured to alcohol, who are not easy to narcotise. The scenes I go through with them ought to be filmed for transmission to posterity; I can hardly describe them. As a first move, I invite them to take the hand-grenades out of their trouser pockets, to which they usually fail to react, merely eyeing me with contempt, as though this was none of my business. In the end I lend a helping hand, and deposit the hand-grenades in a safe place. Then the subject is strapped to a field operating table and given the injection, which mostly only lasts until the intervention is begun. Then, as likely as not, the patient stands up by force, bending the table, crashes down with it, gets up again and dances round the room with the table on his back, while I hang on to one of his grinders with the forceps, solely concerned to prevent him from crashing into one of the windows, or the glass cupboard. With Sister Erna's help I usually succeed in obtaining the desired result, while the other two nurses regularly take to their heels.

Apart from the above-mentioned forceps for drawing teeth and for obstetrics, my instrument equipment is very primitive. Major incisions are made with razor-blades; the only available scalpel I keep in my bed, so that it shan't be used for sharpening pencils, cutting string and even grosser purposes. A red pencil, which I had procured at some pains for the temperature charts, disappeared for a long while, till the colour of the housemaid's lips put me on the right track, and I found it again on the window-sill in the kitchen. The scraping operation so often called for in the case of women brought to us unconscious from loss of blood, I perform with a sharp spoon, because we have no curette, nor any prospect of procuring one. No major operation can be performed here anyhow; all such cases have to be sent to Marienwerder, now called Kwidzyn. The ambulance presented by America was intended for this purpose, but it is mostly employed on business journeys to Danzig, Allenstein or Warsaw, so that as a rule we have to look about us for other means of transport. This wastes a lot of time, because the UB, which has the only other car, a little Volkswagen, at its disposal, usually has other uses for it. So it ends in our having to procure a horse-drawn vehicle of some sort, which always takes hours to get there.

People often come with shot wounds, which is not surprising, considering the enormous number of machine-pistols they go about with here. The militia brought me a case in the middle of the night. I woke up to find at least twelve men with dark lanterns bursting into my room, covered with dust. Down below, on the table, lay one of their comrades with a bullet in the region of the groin. As the missile might be lodged in the abdomen, which would entail a major intervention, I advised them to get the man to Marienwerder with all possible speed. Whereupon they all vanished as quickly as they had come, ostensibly to look for a car, and left me alone with the casualty. Not till six hours later did a few of them reappear and relieve me of the man, after quenching their fright at the inn. According to their account, they had come upon some partisans in the night, had fired at random and hit one of their own men.

A few days later they brought me a young man with a flesh wound in the upper part of the thigh, whom they declared to be a partisan. He was put to bed, and guarded by a sentry who was relieved every twelve hours. We were threatened with all kinds of things if we allowed him to escape. One bright morning, however, when the sentry, who had not been relieved at the proper time, had fallen asleep, the man did succeed in getting away—quite simply by the front door. The fury was great, and we were within an ace of being imprisoned for it.

On the language side it's no longer very difficult to come to an understanding with the Poles. Most of them know a little German, especially when they're ill, and of course I've picked up the most necessary words in between whiles, so that in the matter of food and illness I can hold a fairly fluent conversation with them, though their very difficult grammar has to be ignored. My Polish is much like their German, a language consisting of nominatives, infinitives and missing articles. 'Doktour, come to my wife, child come,' a kind of Esperanto that every German is familiar with, who has had to do with Poles and Russians. Of course one must be well up in Polish swear-words if one wants to get away with it. I've been practising them for a long while, and have sometimes made use of them. My greatest success in that way was in a ward with four young men, who had all been admitted for observation in respect of venereal disease. The little Polish nurse Jadja couldn't manage them, and came to fetch me. 'Herr Doktor, you must come, the men are so cheeky.' 'Well, what am I to do? They won't listen to me.' 'Oh, just curse them; that's what the cheeky fellows need.' I ran upstairs, flung the door open, shouted all my swear-words one after another, and then went on in German : 'You lads just wait till I know enough Polish, and then I'll teach you something !' They were speechless, then burst into a roar of laughter and were thenceforth quite easy to manage.

Even my knowledge of English and French has proved useful here. The postmaster and various other people have come to have letters received from France and America translated and answered for them, besides which, as I said before, all the medicaments we possess are labelled in those languages.

Russian patients are not much liked in the hospital. Jadja usually announces them in this way : 'Herr Doktor, there's a Russian here, and what a one! Come quickly, or he'll smash everything up.' It's not often as bad as all that; but they feel they are the masters and can take whatever they want. There was the case of the Russian woman unable to give birth to a dead child, when I was called upon to lend a helping hand with the forceps. This was an anxious business, because three Russians were standing in the doorway all the time, and were only prevented with difficulty from rushing in. Of course there was a major laceration, which had to be stitched, but I came out of the affair fairly well. A week later the three Russians turned up again and took the woman away, without giving us any notice or showing any gratitude to the hospital.

Outside in the street people treated me with great reserve at first.

Nobody greeted me, and I sometimes felt a little neglected. Now the situation seems to be easing up, especially since the hairdresser drew me into his shop and cut my hair for nothing, in full view of all the people waiting there. It's really a very pleasant feeling, being officially regarded as a human being again.

Of the two churches here, the Catholic one has been repaired, and mass is now said regularly there. The priest has a difficult office, because in the absence of any sufficient judicial authority he is called on by the population to settle their disputes. Specially drastic decisions are announced in the sermon, which is attended by many among even the less religious.

The summer is going by, and I've not been able to renew my old walks or visit the accustomed places and people. But the people come to me, and I'm kept posted up as to what is happening over there. The wife of the new forester in Schwalgendorf came here for her confinement. Her husband was in prison in Allenstein at the time, and came to see me later. The Head Ranger came as a patient. Frau Tiedtke has sent me things to barter; she wants me to procure a goat for her. On the 13th September the H.s will be moving to Schwalgendorf, where he has found work under the Head Ranger. Frau L. is to act as the Head Ranger's housekeeper. The Russians are going to hand Brausen over entirely to the Poles, and evacuate the district generally very soon. They are taking everything with them that can still be used; even the houses are being hastily looted once again. There is said to be only one Russian left, temporarily on guard, in Januschau, otherwise the village is empty. In Schönberg the Russians turned all the Germans out into the street in the space of two hours.

On the 30th September H. came on his bicycle to fetch me to his sick daughter. I took the bicycle, to get there more quickly, found Frau L. better already, was shown over their new house, and paid some visits. I spent the evening with the Head Ranger; he had shot a stag in very poor condition. We inspected the antlers in the cellar, where the head was being boiled down. We had stag's liver for supper, and I was given a piece of it to take with me.

On the 13th October, a Sunday, Sister Erna went for a walk with me through the Januschau Forest. We had had some fairly sharp night frosts, but under the crystal-clear sky the land still quivered in its autumn glory, and the golden beech foliage lay reflected in the deep-blue water of the lake. We came to the Januschau manor house, where a single, glowing-red trail of wild vine had clambered two storeys up the bare white wall to the roof. Through the front door, which still made the old, familiar sound, we stepped into the hall and took a look at the garden room—one huge wilderness. From a bed of straw a man arose—the Russian guarding the house. He looked at us enquiringly, uncertain how to behave, and was obviously relieved when we decided not to inspect any more of the house. In the forest the timber felled earlier is still lying about. We heard a couple of shots in the distance. As we approached Zollnick Hill three cyclists suddenly took cover in the undergrowth ahead of us. I was inclined to retreat, but my companion was determined to go on. When we reached the spot, the Head Ranger and two forest officials came out of the bushes and we greeted one another with relief. They had taken us for Russians, a large company of whom had been disturbing the forest again for some days.

The season of the ceps—the edible boletus—the abundance of which surpassed all records this year, is over. In the Zollnick clearing the cranberries were ripening. Cormorants, herons, hoopooes and rollers have left, and so have most of the waterfowl; but where the beech hanger drops down to the lake a pair of swans were swimming in slow circles round each other on the still water.

It was such a joy to be showing somebody all these things and telling them what it was like here in the old days. About my Olden-burg grandfather,[1] with whose name this bit of the country will always be connected, as long as the concept of Prussia and Germany exists. Of his humanity, which endeared him to everybody, and to which so many anecdotes bore witness; of the support that his very existence afforded to those who, in the changing years, were threatened with the loss of their worldly position, and feared they would no longer be able to fulfil their responsibility before God for their family, their tenants, their estates and their country. And of my personal relationship with him, of which I am immeasurably proud, and which has meant that he is always present to me when I am faced with some problem of human behaviour.

I told her of all the exciting events we had been allowed to take part in from early childhood, not least among them the visits of the old Field-marshal—later Reichs-president—Hindenburg. How the whole village joined in, lining the way on his arrival and flattening their noses against the dining-room windows in the evening.

---

[1] Elard von Oldenburg-Januschau (1855–1937), a well-known agriculturist and politician, and a Member of Parliament of the German National People's Party.

Ever since September I've been getting letters from the West, from all sorts of people, one almost every day. How the post contrives this I can't imagine. The letters take four weeks to come, apparently viâ Warsaw, but so far as I can see they are not censored. My replies reach their destination too, almost regularly. I'm unspeakably envied for these letters, in the hospital. Jadja hands them to me half admiringly, half reproachfully. 'Herr Doktor, another letter already!' She takes it for granted that they are all of feminine origin. The address has of course to be written entirely in Polish. I've had two letters from my father, written in French. One day I was sent for to go to the post, because a most seditious-looking letter had come for me. The address was written in gigantic letters diagonally across the envelope. I recognised the handwriting from a distance, and couldn't help laughing at the fuss the Poles were making about it. It did mean something special to me, however, for it was from Count Brünneck, one of the best-known and most highly esteemed men of our province. The Russians have made his manor house at Bellschwitz their headquarters, and are using up his famous library as cigarette-paper.

These letters have brought the West still more palpably near, and the longing to see these people again, to whom I am bound, grows daily stronger. Besides which, I keep thinking that once over there I should be able to do something for the Königsbergers. On the other hand I feel bound to this place too, and shouldn't like to give up my post without some definite 'leading'. I must first find out, too, what is to become of my aunt. I've had a letter from her, from Osterode, through an intermediary, and have been able to send her some money by the same channel. She is a prisoner there.

In the middle of October the frost became more severe, and towards the end of the month it began to snow. This early onset of winter makes conditions in the hospital more difficult than ever; the heating still functions, but nobody sees to getting in the coke, although it's perfectly easy to do so. The only place to get warm in is the kitchen, which we avoid as a rule because it's the focus of all the gossip and slander that goes on. A violent war of words is carried on there, occasionally leading to blows, and originating for the most part in jealousy or superstition.

One morning horror reigned; two white lines of human footprints were seen on the coal-black, soot-covered ceiling, one larger and one smaller. The evening before I had been the last there, and had tried very hard to make friends with the two-year-old daughter of the caretaker. She always ran away from me, screaming, whereas her five-year-old brother was very trusting, and always wanted to ride on my shoulders. I suddenly had the idea of lifting him up by his legs and letting him walk along the ceiling, head downwards, with his bare feet. The effect, a surprising one to me too, made the children shout for joy. The little girl immediately jumped up to me, and I had to trace a ghostly trail with her feet too. I should have liked to put mine alongside, but even so it was enough to set the people in a wild commotion.

Superstition in its most primitive forms celebrates orgies here as it is. The cards are laid three times a day, and faces are cheerful or depressed according to what comes out. It doesn't matter in the least whether what is foretold lies within the limits of time and space. The prospect of having two children plus a husband before the year is out is enough to put one in a good humour for the whole morning.

Light and water supplies are also getting lower and lower. The wires are still there, and the electric light still burns at times, but one bulb after another disappears and can't be replaced. I'm anxiously guarding a big, 500-volter, which we screw in and out as required in the operating theatre and the labour ward. Another bulb, which wouldn't burn any longer, I managed to 'repair'; that is to say I turned it round so that the ends of the wires were reconnected. As a result I now find the most impossible things laid on my table for repair.

Up to now the water could be pumped; but one pipe after another freezes up, and only two pumps are now in working order for the whole town, one of them at the railway station. Washing-up water is drawn from the lake, hardly twenty paces away, where we have broken a hole in the ice.

Among the German female patients that come to see us there are some with whom we have to be on our guard, because they are obviously acting as spies for the Russians. One of them, of whose pure German origin I became very doubtful in the course of conversation, declared herself to be a distant relation of my grandfather's. When I pointed out that this was hardly possible, she switched to another subject. Letters had come from the West lately, she said, intimating that *D.S.* would soon be back in East Prussia; this could only mean *German soldiers*, of course, and what did I think of it? I advised her, quite innocently, to be more cautious about repeating such things; she shouldn't let herself be upset by such stupid letters; if she was ever really in trouble I would try to help her. Upon which she decamped rather hurriedly, and I only realised afterwards that the conversation had been intended as a provocation.

During this period I have christened two more Russian children and held little celebrations on the occasion. The mothers' desire to have the children baptised seems to me to warrant this, although if I'm not mistaken the real motive is a very superficial one. It amuses them to have me coming to see them, and they have no other way of attracting me, so long as they're not really ill. But I once refused to celebrate the baptism straight away, saying I would like to have a preliminary talk with the mother. I had known the person concerned in the past, and her manner of living with the Russians seemed to me no longer admissible, even allowing for all unleashed passions. The discussion took place, and now I'm waiting for the woman to call again.

On the 24th November Jadja came in great excitement and announced, 'Herr Doktor, there's a woman here who looks like you . . .' I sprang up—my aunt was standing behind her. She had escaped from Osterode, travelled in a transport train as far as Deutsch Eylau, and come from there on foot. We had made preparations for this : she was first to be admitted as a patient, and then live with a Polish family as a domestic help. The whole household was as delighted as myself, and did all they could to make her stay a pleasant one, after the renewed hardships she had been through. We spent three happy days together. Just at the right moment a Polish patient put a live duck in my wardrobe, while I was out, and this formed the *pièce de résistance* of a banquet to which Frau S. was also invited. But it was a farewell party at the same time, for my aunt didn't want to remain here, but to try and get through to the West, where her family is awaiting her. A Polish woman friend of ours procured her a ticket to Stettin, and with this she started off on the 27th November—a pretty risky undertaking with no papers. After a week of anxiety we had a letter from Stettin. She had used the bribe-money she had taken with her to smuggle herself into the emigrants' camp, and was staying there until the next transport left. As this might not be for some time, she had taken a job in the camp kitchen, and was very sorry she had left her clogs with us on my advice. She had to stand about all day in ankle-deep mud.

Just about that time I was taken on some motor drives by the militia. The first was at night, in the American 'Sanitarka', to Deutsch Eylau, now Ilawa, to see a man of the UB who had been shot. The beautiful town is unutterably ruined, and really only recognisable by its lake. Fortunately I didn't have to endure the extraordinarily menacing atmosphere of the UB for long; the affair was soon settled, and we were allowed to bring the man back with us. The tempo on the way home was terrific as usual, thanks to the alcohol that had been consumed; we only braked once, very sharply, to pick up a hare that had been run over near Schönberg.

The next was a drive in the militia's Volkswagen, westwards to Bischofswerder. A man had come from there, seeking a doctor for a friend who was in great pain. He had been three days on the road without finding one. This was a good enough excuse for the militia to tear through the district with me as if we were out to save a drowning man. The north-west wind, which was heading us, was so strong that every time we went through a built-up area we were nearly flung against the walls of the houses. Four miles from our destination we drove on to a kerbstone and tore off the near front tyre and mudguard. This didn't matter much, as that side of the road was slightly convex and we could get along without a tyre. It merely meant that we now got a continual stream of gravel in our faces (there had been no glass in the windscreen to start with). I pulled my coat over my head, and kept a watch on the edge of the road through a buttonhole. It was all right for a time, then we crashed into one of the wrecks lying in the ditch (actually, I had jumped out a few yards further back). The drive was at an end. We had another half-hour to walk to the sick man's house. As we opened the door he drew a deep breath, lay back, and declared that everything was now O.K. Because of a sharp pain in his left side, he had been afraid to breathe normally for the last three days; he had waited for the doctor to come. I stayed with him while the car was being repaired, and then we went home again at the same speed.

On the 10th December I was fetched again in a snowstorm, without being told at first what it was for. In Riesenburg—now Prabuty—two trains had collided, practically the only ones running on this section anyhow. Several coaches had been telescoped, and the wounded had already been removed to a hospital train that was to take them to Marienburg. Thirty-five people had come to grief, some killed outright, others with crushed legs. I was taken along to Marienburg, where we landed up with our casualties to-

wards eight in the evening at the hospital. Forewarned, I was prepared to speak no word of German, but I was immediately greeted
in German by my colleague and his assistants, and given a very
kind reception. We attended to the wounded together in the
operating theatre until the morning; then I was given a bed, and
after a few hours' sleep, a breakfast with real coffee. Refreshed by
this, I went for a little tour of the town. Unlike the modern part,
the old town with its characteristic arcades has been completely
destroyed. The castle, only recognisable now by its outlines, stares
to heaven like the skeleton of a gigantic goose. Not a soul to be
seen anywhere. I was the only mourner present.

Shortly before Christmas I went to Deutsch Eylau again in the
car. Two patients were to be fetched from Raudnitz. I got out in
Deutsch Eylau and went to see Frau F., the former owner of the
hairdressing establishment, who is going to make me a thick jacket.
I'm making her a pair of shoes in return, and paying her something
as well. She lives in one of the little wooden huts on the shore of
the lake, built on piles over the water. All the remaining Germans
are living there together in a sort of ghetto. The interior of the
town has been destroyed; the Poles live in the outskirts. Now that
I've received a shirt from UNRRA and a patient has made me a
pair of leather shoes, my dress has gradually become considerably
normalised; besides which, we have secured a quantity of material
for Christmas presents.

I've done a lot of bartering for the Schwalgendorf people. For an
ultra-violet lamp, which she brought me in secret, Frau Tiedtke
got another goat. As I couldn't test the lamp in the hospital owing
to the failure of the electric current, I handed it in good faith,
though rather imprudently, to a patient who is an electrician by
trade. I heard nothing for three days; then the fact that the lamp
was functioning became self-evident, for the man was going about
the town with a face as red as fire.

I managed to acquire a young pig weighing fifty pounds in the
market, without attracting attention, and got the vendor to bring
it to me at a prearranged spot. It was fetched from there by
Frau L. who had come in the night with a hand-cart. Five hours'
return journey through the forest, and she had it safe at home as a
surprise for her parents.

I got to know the lady dentist who works here by attending her
one-year-old child. She speaks German fluently, and treats me in a
very friendly way. Her drilling apparatus, worked by foot, is in

great demand by the Russians; but she doesn't let herself be easily intimidated. If an extraction is needed she often sends the people to me. Her husband is working in Bromberg. There are two ways of getting there, either through Thorn, which is a long way round, or through Marienwerder, which takes some courage, because the new railway bridge, built over the Weichsel by German prisoners under Russian supervision, is said to be very rickety, and to be showing serious cracks in its joints already.

We spent Christmas peacefully in every sense. I was invited to supper by the lady dentist and her husband, attended Christmas mass afterwards, and was then sent for to the town to a confinement. Next day I started off with a heavy rucksack, sat for a while with old Frau Aust and her still older sister, who are still living in Albrechtau as the last Germans there, stayed a few hours in Brausen, paid a short visit to the graves at Januschau and reached Schwalgendorf before dark. There I paid a lot of visits, spent the night with H., and was driven back next morning to Rosenberg by one of the Polish foresters in his one-horse carriage.

For some days now we've had hard frost without snow. To my great astonishment I can see Venus standing in the leaden-grey winter sky at midday. One sees so many things nowadays that escaped one's notice before; one has come to attach great significance to apparently simple and self-evident things. One's spiritual ear has become sharper too, making one readier to follow spontaneous impulses. I've never found it so easy to come to a decision as I do now. I suddenly have the feeling that I must go to Schwalgendorf at once, and when I arrive there a few hours later, I'm sure to be greeted with the words: 'Ah, there you are already! We were just wondering how to fetch you over.'

I began the New Year by dropping a brick. Not wanting to appear a spoil-sport, I did as I was asked by the assembled staff, and lifted up one of the six flower-pots arrayed before me on the window-sill. Underneath it appeared a little grave. They were all aghast, and declared it didn't count, I'd raised it too quickly. I must try again. Again the grave appeared. 'You see?' I said. It was like a rap on the knuckles; nobody dare say anything more. But it served as a good cure all round; since then, laying cards has gone somewhat out of fashion.

I was called to the dying several times just then; once to Schwalgendorf, where I spent the night, and then to Gollnau to the father of nine children. On the other hand, a man I had believed to be long since underground turned up quite hale and hearty and thanked me for my visit.

In Brausen the Russians are preparing for their definite departure. I went there to say goodbye to Waschko and thank him for having intervened for me in a difficult situation. He looked at me half suspiciously, half surprised, and called me in. We seated ourselves at a table with two other Russians; tobacco was handed round, we smoked in silence; it was an ordeal. At last I got up, saying something polite. They responded briefly, and I was outside, taking three deep breaths. We hadn't understood each other; the thanks were out of place and therefore disagreeable; he hadn't done it for that reason. A pity! I shall stick in his memory simply as some sort of oddity.

In the first half of January we had thirty degrees Centigrade of frost. There was no coke for three days, and we were forced to send most of the patients home. Those that remained behind were given all the blankets, in spite of which their cheeks and noses got frozen. Six of us slept in the room belonging to our stoker-cum-medical orderly, on the floor beside the little iron stove. I was always out during the day, and didn't feel the cold so much. There was hardly any place within a radius of five miles that I didn't visit during that period, many of them for the first time. From many of these outings I only got back at night; twice from Charlottenwerder along the railway line, once from Gross-Albrechtau, where another Russian child was due. Great-grandmother, grandmother, the sixteen-year-old mother and the expected infant were all assembled in the room. The dim lamplight just enabled us to ascertain with regret that the friendly little Mongol must be accounted the father of the coming Russian. 'Look! Another of Slit-eye's!' said the grandmother, holding the newborn baby for the mother to see.

On the 16th January the thaw suddenly set in. My Polish colleague came to fetch me with the ambulance for a drive to Stradem, near Deutsch Eylau, to examine one of his patients. On the way there I told him about my first motor drive with the Poles and its premature end in a plunge into the ditch. It was exactly a year ago, to the day. He listened at first with only half an ear; then he suddenly asked, 'I say, where did it happen?' I described the place; whereupon he stopped the ambulance and told me about the accident himself; he had seen it more clearly than I could, having been a passenger in the car that stopped beside us on the road when we clambered out of the ditch. He had expected to find us all reduced to pulp.

On the 20th January we brought Frau Aust and her invalid sister here from Albrechtau, because the fresh onset of the cold had proved too much for them. Frau Aust was now housed with the bakeress as a nurse to the children, and her sister admitted as a patient. Unfortunately this arrangement was of short duration, for the sister died, and Frau Aust herself had to be taken in as a patient. She had fainted from the cold in her room, which had no heating.

People here are coming to the conclusion that I'm more or less fit for society, which is very kindly meant, but is liable to put my situation in a false light. I was twice invited to a party where, believe it or not, they were playing bridge. When the third time came round I was fortunately prevented by an operation. On the fourth occasion I was obliged to make my refusal rather more pointed, at the risk of being misunderstood. But my birdlike freedom, my virtual outlawry, stands me in better stead than the fictitious membership of a stylish milieu. Not long ago I was on the point of escaping from this entanglement by flight, and looking upon the calls to the West in the letters from my people in the light of a command. I approached the Russians who were leaving for Liegnitz, but felt so inwardly divided as a result, that I was glad when Sister Erna discovered my plan and convinced me that I ought to stay on.

I now had the first direct news from Königsberg, in a letter from Else Peto, which had reached an address in the West and been sent on to me from there. The news she gave me was no surprise, but it moved me profoundly. She wrote that Erika had died on the 22nd December 1945; she had spent her last weeks praying for me.

At the beginning of February there was deep snow on the ground. A covey of twenty partridges appeared near the hospital. We drew our water supply now entirely from the lake, because the last pump had frozen. The ice was more than thirty inches thick, and every pail we drew up through it was full of tiny fishes. The Committee was taken aback when I offered them one to wash their hands in.

The cold was still intense; but the white blanket of snow and the gradually higher sun stirred us to action. We drove to Schwalgendorf on two occasions with the sleigh and a borrowed horse, at a walking pace, and mostly on foot alongside, to spare the horse, but we all enjoyed it immensely. We were able to plan the route so as to be within the forest for almost the whole twelve miles.

The 19th February was the coldest of all the many cold days, with forty degrees Centigrade below zero. The snow was so deep that the trains couldn't run, and the weather remained cold until well into March. I was laid up with influenza for a week, confined to bed, part of the time without any heating, and reading *Quo Vadis*, for the sake of acquainting myself with a Polish author. In such primitive times as these, one reads quite differently and much more intensively than usual. At any rate the book, which I had read in my teens, and had always regarded as a sort of popular best-seller, moved me profoundly this time. And I was even more impressed by Bergruen's *Grand Tyrant*. I shed real tears of pleasure over the last two chapters.

By the middle of March I was on my legs again and well enough to go on a forced march to Schwalgendorf. Frau L. came to fetch me, and we tramped in single file, through snow and wind, along the track she had made in coming, exchanging positions from time to time. I arrived in a bath of sweat, and weak at the knees. Frau Aust, who had been there for some weeks—we had brought her over in the sleigh—had erysipelas and a high temperature. I thought of all the people in Königsberg who had died of it; but thank God she seemed to be getting better again. While I was there it began to thaw. I stayed a day in Schwalgendorf, rested, paid a lot of visits, drew some teeth, and spent an evening in pleasant conversation. Next day I went back past the Heide Mill. A white-tailed eagle flew over the still frozen Geserich. The Heide miller drove me as far as Albrechtau in his sleigh.

I often go to Finckenstein, where there are still a number of Germans working under Polish stewards. In the old days one's mouth went dry, so to speak, as one entered the castle yard through the iron gates. Now in the burnt-out castle there is not a suspicion of the atmosphere it diffused through two centuries. The only reminder of culture was the dachshund belonging to the keeper of the granary, the first thoroughbred dog among thousands of mongrels I had seen for the last two years. Its owner, who used to live on the Polish side, by Lake Karrasch, got it from Schönberg. He told me a tablecloth had been found in Januschau, with coats of arms embroidered all over it, which was now lying on the bed of one of his colleagues, not far from there. This was known as the marriage cloth of my family, and of course I began thinking out how to get possession of it again without attracting attention.

And now the spring is coming in again in full force. The night of 23rd-24th March was full of the whistling and whirring of innumerable wings; in the morning the starlings were singing on the roofs, ducks and pigeons were sweeping over the lake, and on the opposite shore we could see the peewits turning over in their tumbling flight. The ice was melting apace. In the midday sun the first butterflies ventured out; the temperature had risen forty degrees all at once.

Two days later I went for a walk through the forest. Cranes were calling, the herons were standing on their nests on the island. On the shore of the lake, where the ice had melted away, ducks and divers were playing about. It's a divine grace to be allowed to witness the awakening of Nature once again.

The 30th March was Palm Sunday. I asked Frau S. to go by train with me to Heinrode, and walk from there to the place where my mother and brother had met their death more than two years ago. She was present at the time and could show me everything in detail. In Altmark we called on the Catholic priest, with whom they had spent the night, with the trek, before the Russians came. We stayed there to dinner, and then went by a very muddy road to the little village of Kuntgen, close to the railway line, where the trek came to an end. Children were playing beside the wall of the house against which the dead were finally left lying. Further on, in the allotments, stood a home-made wooden cross without inscription. A man living nearby came up and told us he had arrived here three weeks later as the first of the Poles, and had buried the dead. Except for one in the allotments, they were all lying beside the very house wall where the children were now playing.

As we were walking back to the station, skeins of wild geese swept low over the flat land. We sat down in the ditch, waiting for the train and reading the Palm Sunday Gospel of Christ's entry into Jerusalem.

We went to Schwalgendorf again at Easter. Frau S. has given up her job in Rosenberg and is remaining in Schwalgendorf to help her parents. On Easter Monday I was fetched from one house to another, by both Germans and Poles, and made to eat something everywhere, especially by the Forester's secretary and her mother, who always addresses me as 'Herr Professor'.

Since the Russians left, things have grown daily worse for the Germans in Faulen and many other places. They can really only live now by begging and stealing. The wife of Schmolla the shepherd is in particular distress. She has managed to bring up five small children, and now goes about clothed in nothing but a frayed-out blanket, in which she has cut holes for her two arms. She is no longer quite right in the head, and has several times been on the point of throwing herself in the lake. Up to the present, however, I have been able to save her from the worst. For months past people have been given to believe that the next transport to Germany will soon be starting, and that they will be taken by it. They are squatting, fifteen to twenty in a single room, with their chattels in bundles, awaiting the start. For the people in Brausen life becomes more miserable every day.

Two women are living all by themselves in Januschau. They seem rather better off, and have evidently found our buried silver, as I gathered from a Polish shopkeeper to whom they had lately sold three silver goblets fitting into one another. He showed them to me, and is prepared to sell them to me for the price he gave for them, a mere song. There are many other things in his shop that used to belong to us. But it's not worth while telling him this, for he's always been very nice to me, especially since I pulled out a lot of his teeth without hurting him. To myself, the women have prudently offered only a lot of hymnbooks and our family Bible, which they have found. I accepted them gratefully for distribution in Schwalgendorf.

It's astonishing how the poultry has increased in such a short time. The peasants live on it almost entirely, and like to bring me eggs in payment for medical treatment. They are relatively cheaper than anything else : fifteen to twenty for drawing teeth and so forth is nothing out of the way. With these I can alleviate many a case of want. There are a lot of fowls in the town too; the dressmaker is surrounded in her room by six sitting hens. People keep their livestock, even the larger kinds, as near themselves as possible, because they have become so used to having it stolen, or being turned out of their quarters and having to leave everything behind that they haven't got close at hand.

On the 10th April a young Polish woman I know came to the hospital and whispered to me that the UB in Deutsch Eylau wanted to speak to me as soon as possible; it would be best for me to go there by the next train. I asked her what this meant, and whether

I hadn't better take to my heels straight away. She assured me there was no need for that, it had nothing to do with my person. So with very mixed feelings I betook myself to the lion's den. Whatever the occasion, visits of this kind are always paid against the grain. The mere *mise en scène* is terror-inspiring, and the noises one hears suggest something horrible behind every door. Even if one is addressed in German, in a relatively friendly fashion, the impression remains; this might be a trick too. This time, however, it really had nothing to do with me, but with conditions in our hospital. The information I supplied was very scanty, for I had no reason to expose anybody. They enquired most particularly into the whereabouts of the alcohol presented by America. I didn't conceal from them that we took a sip of it now and then. This amused them royally; then, hardly believing my ears, I received something like thanks for my hitherto unpaid services, and found myself safe and sound again in the street.

After some cold days the weather turned warm again in the middle of April; on the 19th we began going barefoot in the forest, and I took a dip in the Uroviec. The first swallows had arrived. As I came out of the water I saw two deer getting up from the morass on the opposite side of the lake. A few days later the forestry student from Schwalgendorf came to fetch me with two bicycles. For the sake of showing him more of this lovely district we rode back through the forest instead of by road through Grünhof. His chain broke soon after the start, and we had to push our bicycles. He began to feel rather frightened as it grew slowly dark and we got deeper and deeper into the woods. But I was able to show him the cormorants on the Tromnitz lake, which he had heard about, and finally, to his great relief, we came out of the wood in the pitch-dark night, right in front of the Forestry Office.

On Sunday, 17th April, I went to Januschau to look for peewits' eggs. The woods were full of anemones, hepaticas and daphne in flower. By the carp pond in the big forest glade that ranked so highly in our hunting days, I met with four stags. With a bunch of flowers for the graves I went through the deserted fields by the footpath that we have trodden out ourselves this last year on our way to Schwalgendorf. Near the Crown Prince's Canal I found four peewits' eggs, but left them lying because we were not in any real need. The peewit thanked me with cries of jubilation, and I responded with an indescribable cry of joy. How a shout that nobody hears can liberate the soul! I've lately learnt a number of tunes and songs out of the hymnbook that I didn't know before, and sing them at the top of my voice on my walks.

I often go to Finckenstein and the villages around it, mostly on foot, but sometimes in the most impossible vehicles. Something always happens on these drives; either we run into a tree or the ditch, or the horse stops dead, a wheel comes off, the pole breaks—if there is one—or the harness comes undone. And of course, even without any mishap, it takes much longer than on foot; but I dare not offend the good people, because they are very proud of being able to drive.

On the 29th April I ran over to Schwalgendorf to fetch Frau Aust. I had been told of a little transport that was to start next morning for Germany viâ Stettin, and she was so anxious to go to her son, who has a ranger's lodge in the West. A peasant in Schwalgendorf lent us his horse, and we were back in Rosenberg just in time to shove Frau Aust into a party of women assembled at the station. But we had no luck, unfortunately. The women were driven away; no transport was leaving, and they were not allowed to travel by the ordinary train. I have now lodged Frau Aust in Brausen, so as to have her nearer in case of need.

On the 4th May I was sent for from Brausen for a confinement. It was freezing hard at sunrise. Just as I was leaving again the news came that motor vehicles would be coming about ten o'clock to take everybody there to the camp at Deutsch Eylau, whence they would be sent on to Germany, and I decided to wait for this. The cars actually came, and everything had to be done at top speed. One small package was the allowance per head. Frau Aust was smuggled in, although she was not officially included.

Once they had really started I went back to Rosenberg. I saw that the Germans in Faulen were being taken too, and I was much relieved, because they really had nothing left to live on. In the afternoon I was lying on my bed, wondering whether I ought to make myself another pair of shoes, when suddenly three militiamen came into my room saying, 'Doktour, want to go home?' 'Yes, very much,' I said, 'When?'—'Come with, at once!' 'How much may I take with me?' 'Forty pound.' 'I haven't got so much.'

I quickly packed my things in the rucksack and took a hasty farewell of my somewhat bewildered feminine staff. Then I was taken along to the guard-house, where people kept coming to bid me goodbye. They won't be left without a doctor, because a few weeks ago a pleasant colleague arrived to take the place of Dr. B., who has joined the Navy, and he has been shown all over the hospital. It's for this reason only, no doubt, that they are letting me go.

I had to spend the night in the guard-house. The Commandant sent for me to have supper at his house, and wanted me to sleep there in spite of the cramped quarters, but his new colleague wouldn't agree, so I was bowed back to the guard-house. I found an almost naked Russian there, who had been arrested for kicking up a row, being interrogated—and thoroughly pummelled and pinched into the bargain.

In the morning I was taken to the station, along with a German militiaman who has been working here as a smith, followed by people waving to us in a friendly way. We went to Deutsch Eylau and were taken to the camp, where the people fetched the day before were already assembled.

We waited three days for the transport; we were to be coupled to a train coming from Allenstein. We were not really supposed to leave the camp, but the militia kept taking me to see their families, and as a result I succeeded in exchanging all my Polish money, which I must otherwise have given up, for articles of food. The militiamen are very sceptical about our destination, and above all they think it unlikely that as a doctor I shall be allowed to leave Poland; I must be prepared, they say, to be hauled out somewhere on the way, and appointed somewhere else.

To our surprise we were given soup twice a day in the camp, and the farewell rifling was not too drastic either. Fortunately the sub-prefect was present; I had come to know him on his friendly side. He prevented our clothes from being ripped up, though a few things that had been sewn in had to be given up all the same. I would have liked to save my three silver goblets, and asked the sub-prefect about them. State property must be given up, he replied, but as my name was on the goblets the affair seemed doubtful. He thought it over. In the end he gave the man in charge a hint, and the case was settled.

Before we were finally conducted to the station, a curious scene was enacted. We were drawn up more or less in battle array— some four hundred of us—and then the sub-prefect asked me to say a few words to the assembly on his behalf. Somewhat startled, I asked what he had in mind. He said he was anxious to emphasise that the way we were being treated here, as Germans, was not mere chicanery, but according to orders. The Germans had done the same to the Poles. We must therefore share in the atonement, even if as individuals we hadn't shared in the guilt. So I stepped in front of the company and spoke more or less to this effect: 'Dear fellow-countrymen, listen all of you! The Herr Sub-prefect here is sorry that we have to leave our home country under these conditions, but he can't help it, because our people did the same to the Poles earlier on, and unfortunately that is true. But we will thank him for the good soup we were given in the camp, and beg him to see to it that the next transport is as well treated. And now let us hope that we really do get to Germany.'

By that evening we were trundling along in a goods train through the country, thirty people to a wagon, through Thorn, Bromberg and Posen. The fields everywhere were as neglected as with us, but the towns seemed to be in much better condition. We were allowed to open the doors during the journey and hang our legs out.

At the end of two days we reached Kohlfurt; there we joined other transports and were detained for two days, dusted with louse-powder and checked over once more. The two German doctors working there let me spend the night in their quarters; they would have liked to go with us if they had been able to, but in spite of the nearness to the frontier escape was as difficult here as with us. Wading by night through the closely guarded Neisse was the only chance.

Then we went on, as in a dream, very slowly over a little river; and at the next stop we were allowed to get out without being immediately shooed back again. We were in Germany.

We reached Wehrkirch towards evening. There we were greeted by a banner bearing a portrait of Thälmann. The sick were taken from us and kindly treated. At night the train rolled slowly on, and arrived in Hoyerswerda in the morning. The Elsterhorst camp, our last checking-up station, was close by. It consisted of a rectangular enclosure, surrounded by a great deal of barbed-wire fencing, and divided in two by a road with hutments on either side of it. We were led in. A few hundred yards away a similar complex had been fenced round for the sick. Doctors and nurses were at work there in sufficient number; they admitted me to their company, gave me a room and let me take part in their examinations. They even allotted me a ward.

At the sight of my patients I felt I was back in the Königsberg days. They were almost without exception dystrophics, so called—

victims of famine, barely alive, skeletons with mask-like faces and swollen legs. How had I deserved to go about among them again, in the pink of health and in full command of my senses? They were recruited from a section of our camp, separated from it and surrounded by an extra thickness of barbed wire, in which the so-called 'roughs' were housed—young men carried off to Russia from the Danube Provinces on the score of their German nationality. They were said to have become quite brutalised and were therefore shut away from the outside world with particular severity. Their graveyard lay not far off, a small rectangle in the white sand, adorned with little crosses made of twigs. One had to be very cautious when speaking to them; one felt instinctively, Here you must do no more than is absolutely necessary. Above all no questioning, no stirring of any emotion. One little flicker of the soul might be the last of the vital spark.

We spent Whitsuntide in the camp, and then our ways were sundered; that is, we evaded the imminent typhus quarantine by flight. After I had worked Frau Aust through the barbed wire, at dusk, into the arms of her nephew waiting outside, I couldn't hold out any longer. I flung my baggage over the fence, clambered after it and took the next train to Berlin.

And then the reunion! I was like a drunken man for days and weeks on end. So few people really knew what we had gone through in the East, and what a lot there was to tell! But one day someone to whom I was describing things took a piece of bread from her pocket while I was talking, broke it and handed me half of it—an accustomed gesture in the days of famine. Then I knew it was time to take the first steps along the road offering me a new existence. And I was faced with the question: What will this new existence be like, and who is to determine it? Will it be an indifferent one, one of the thousands that needn't have been lived at all? Or will God in his mercy ordain that I and all those that have gone through the same experience may be given grace to bear witness by our lives to the great things we have heard and seen?